GEORGE ̄

PARTHIA

Elibron Classics
www.elibron.com

PARTHIA.

THE STORY OF THE NATIONS.

Large Crown 8vo, Cloth, Illustrated, **5s.**
The Volumes are also kept in the following Special Bindings:
Half Persian, cloth sides, gilt top ; Full calf, half extra,
marbled edges ; Tree calf, gilt edges, gold roll
inside, full gilt back.

LONDON: T. FISHER UNWIN, PATERNOSTER SQUARE, E.C.

ROCK SCULPTURE OF GOTARZES AT BEHISTUN.

PARTHIA

BY

GEORGE RAWLINSON, M.A., F.R.G.S.

LATE CAMDEN PROFESSOR OF ANCIENT HISTORY IN THE UNIVERSITY OF OXFORD;
CORRESPONDING MEMBER OF THE ROYAL ACADEMY OF TURIN; AUTHOR
OF "THE FIVE GREAT MONARCHIES OF THE ANCIENT
EASTERN WORLD," ETC., ETC.

London

T. FISHER UNWIN

PATERNOSTER SQUARE

NEW YORK: G. P. PUTNAM'S SONS

MDCCCXCIII

CONTENTS.

V.

VI.

VII.

XVI.

XVII.

XX.

XXI.

XXII.

XXIII.

ERRATA.

Page	10, line 29,	*for* " Turiun "	*read*	"Turiua."
,,	113, heading,	,, " Scythes "	,,	" Scyths."
,,	168, line 18,	,, " Iehnæ "	,,	" Ichnæ."
,,	346, heading,	,, " Artabanus IV."	,,	" Artabanus V."
,,	346, line 3,	,, the same	,,	the same.
,,	346, title of coin,	,, "Vologases VI."	,,	" Vologases V."
,,	348, heading,	,, " Artabanus IV."	,,	" Artabanus V."
,,	350, heading,	,, the same	,,	the same.
,,	352, heading,	,, the same	,,	the same.

LIST OF ILLUSTRATIONS.

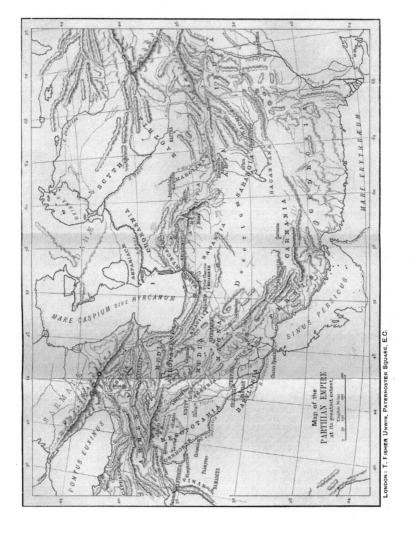

Map of the
PARTHIAN EMPIRE
at its greatest extent.

English Miles

LONDON: T. FISHER UNWIN, PATERNOSTER SQUARE, E.C.

THE STORY OF PARTHIA.

I.

GEOGRAPHICAL—PARTHIA PROPER, AND THE PARTHIAN EMPIRE.

PARTHIA Proper, the earliest home (so far as our knowledge extends) of the Parthian people, was, like Persia Proper and Macedonia Proper, a tract of some-what scanty dimensions. From the south-eastern corner of the Caspian Sea there extends, in a direction a little south of east, a narrowish mountain region, connected at one extremity with the lofty Elburz range, which skirts the Caspian on the south, and, at the other, with the Paropamisus, or Hindu Kush. On either side, northwards and southwards, stretch for hundreds of miles extensive sandy or gravelly deserts, that to the north known as the desert of Khorasan or Khiva, and that to the south as the Great Salt Desert of Iran. Between these is a comparatively rich and productive tract, reaching from the fifty-fourth to the sixty-first meridian, a distance of some seven degrees, or about three hundred miles, with a breadth varying from two to three degrees, and averaging about one hundred and

seventy miles. This region, in the earliest times of
which we have any distinct historical knowledge, was
parcelled out into two countries, belonging to two
different peoples, and known respectively as Parthia
and Hyrcania. The exact line of demarcation which
separated the two, it is impossible to trace ; but there
is sufficient proof, that, while Hyrcania lay towards
the north and west, the Parthians held the districts
towards the east and south. The valleys of the Ettrek
and the Gurghan belonged to the former, while the
regions south and east of these valleys, the skirt of
the southern mountains from Damaghan to Shebri-
No, and the valleys of the Tejend and the river of
Nishapur, constituted the country of the latter.

If the limits of Parthia Proper be thus defined, it
will have corresponded nearly to the modern Persian
province of Khorasan—that is to say, it will have
extended from about Damaghan (long. 54° 20′) upon
the west to the Heri-rud, or river of Herat, upon the
east, and have comprised the modern districts of
Damaghan, Shah-rud, Sebzawar, Nishapur, Meshed,
Tersheez, and Shebri-No. Its length from east to
west will have been about three hundred miles, and
its average width about a hundred or a hundred and
twenty. It will have contained an area of about
33,000 square miles, being thus about equal in size
to Ireland, Bavaria, or St. Domingo.

The general character of the region is, as has been
observed, rich and productive. The mountain formation consists of four or five distinct ranges, having
between them latitudinal valleys, with glens transverse to their courses. The valleys are often well

wooded ; the flat ground at the foot of the outer
ranges of hills is fertile ; water abounds ; and the
streams gradually collect into rivers which are of a
considerable size. Of these the principal are the
Tejend, or river of Meshed, and the river of Nishapur.
The Tejend rises from several sources in the central
mountain range, anciently known as Labus or Labuta,
and now as Alatagh, and runs with a course considerably south of east, past Meshed, to a point
a little beyond the sixtieth meridian, where it de-
flects towards the left, and runs east and a little
north of east to the Heri-rud. Having absorbed the
Heri-rud, it makes a second, and still sharper, turn to
the left, and flows with a northerly and north-westerly
course past Sarrakhs—now a Russian post—along the
foot of the northern Parthian range, now known as
 the Hills of the Kurds," to a marsh, in which it is
swallowed up, between the fifty-seventh and fifty-
eighth parallels. The river of Nishapur is a smaller
stream. It rises from the mountains which on three
sides enclose that city, and flows southwards and
south-westwards towards the Iranian desert. At times
the water is entirely absorbed in the irrigation of the
fertile plain immediately south of Nishapur, but the
channel is always traceable, past Tersheez into the
desert, and in some seasons it carries a certain quantity of water into that parched and arid region.

The valleys of these two streams are among the
most fertile and productive portions of the entire
territory ; but anciently the tract which was most
valued, and which supported the largest population,
seem to have been that which is now known as the

" Atak," or " Skirt "—the low cultivable country at the foot of the southern hills, intervening between them and the desert. Along this whole region, from Dama-ghan to Tersheez, the mountains send down a con-tinued succession of rills, rivulets, and rivers, which make it easy, at the expenditure of a little care and labour, to carry the life-giving element to a distance of four or five miles from their base. Some hus-banding of the water may be needed, together with the creation of a system of reservoirs and *kanats*, or underground channels ; but, if these be provided, the return is ample. The abundant remains of large cities, crumbled into dust, along the entire " Atak " is a sufficient indication of the beneficence of nature in this tract of country, if it be only seconded by a fair amount of human industry and skill.

On the other hand, the mountain tracts, of which the country so largely consists, offer a strong contrast to the valleys of the main streams, and to the southern strip of territory. They are for the most part barren and rugged, very scantily supplied with timber, and only in places capable of furnishing a tolerable pas-turage to flocks and herds. This is the more remark-able, as they do not attain any great elevation. While Mount Demavend in the Elburz range south of the Caspian exceeds 20,000 feet, and the same eleva-tion is reached, or exceeded, by many peaks in the Paropamisus, the greatest altitude of the Parthian ranges does not exceed ten thousand, or, at the utmost, eleven thousand feet. The northern range, called now the Daman-i-Koh, is the loftiest and the least known, the rudeness of the Kurdish tribes by which it is inhabited repelling travellers : the central range, called towards the west Alatagh, and towards the east Macrabea, is considerably lower ; while the southern range, called indifferently Djuvein and Jaghetai, is of about the same elevation.

The climate of Parthia Proper, according to ancient writers, was an extreme one, exceedingly hot in the low plains, and exceedingly cold in the mountains. But modern travellers are inclined to modify both statements. They tell us, that the winters, although protracted, are nowhere very inclement, the thermometer rarely sinking below ten or twelve degrees of Fahrenheit during the nights, and during the daytime rising, even in December and January, which are the coldest months, to forty or fifty. The winter, however, sets in early. Cold weather commences in October, and continues till nearly the end of March, when storms of sleet and hail are usual. A considerable quantity of snow falls in the earlier portion of the winter, and the valleys are scarcely clear of it till March. On the mountains it remains much longer, and forms the chief source of supply for the rivers during the spring and the early summer time. In the height of summer the heat is undoubtedly great, more especially in the region known as the "Atak," or "Skirt" ; and here the unwholesome wind, which blows from the southern desert, is felt from time to time as a terrible scourge. But in the upland country the heat is at no time very intense ; and the natives boast at the present day that they are not compelled by it to sleep upon their house-tops more than one month during the year.

The country, though reported by modern travellers to be only scantily clothed with wood, is still found to produce the pine, the walnut, the sycamore, the ash, the poplar, the willow, the vine, the mulberry, the apricot, and numerous other fruit trees. There is reason to believe that, in ancient times, if the variety of trees was not so great, the number of them was very much greater. Strabo calls the territory δασεῖα, or " densely wooded." Among indigenous plants are saffron, the assafœtida plant, and the gum ammoniac plant. Wheat, barley, and cotton are capable of being raised in large quantities ; and the fertility is such that the ordinary return on wheat and barley, under a bad system of cultivation, is reckoned at ten for one, while instances are said to have been known of the return of a hundred for one. The return from rice, according to one witness, is often four hundred for one ! Game abounds in the mountains, and fish in the underground watercourses. Among mineral products may be mentioned salt, iron, copper, and lead. The mountains contain precious stones of several kinds, especially that delicate and valuable gem, the turquoise.

Starting from. this narrow, but fairly productive region, the Parthians gradually brought under their dominion the greater portion of Western Asia. Very soon after establishing their own independence, they made an attack on their nearest neighbour to the west, Hyrcania. Hyrcania was a country geographically connected, in the closest way, with Parthia, very similar in general character, but richer, warmer, and altogether more desirable. It occupied the western

half of the mountain region already described (p. 2)
—extending from the Caspian Sea to the Heri-rud—
whereof the eastern half was Parthia. Mainly composed of the two fertile valleys of the Gurghan and
Ettrek, with the mountain chains enclosing and
dividing them, it was a picturesque and richly wooded
district almost as large as Parthia itself, and considerably more productive. Here, on the slopes of
the hills, grew the oak, the beech, the elm, the alder,
the wild cherry ; here luxuriant vines sprang from
the soil on every side, raising themselves aloft by the
aid of their stronger sisters, and hanging in wild
festoons from tree to tree ; beneath their shade the
ground was covered with flowers of various kinds,
primroses, violets, lilies, hyacinths, and others of unknown species ; while in the flat land at the bottom
of the valleys were meadows of the softest and ten-
derest grass, capable of affording to numerous flocks
and herds an excellent and never-failing pasture.
Vast quantities of game found shelter in the forests,
while towards the mouths of the rivers, where the
ground is for the most part marshy, large herds of
wild boars were frequent, and offered a variety to
sportsmen. Altogether Hyrcania was a most valuable and desirable region, and well deserved Strabo's
description of it as " highly favoured of heaven." Its
fertility was extraordinary. We are told that a single
vine in Hyrcania produced nine gallons of wine, and
a single fig-tree ninety bushels of figs, while corn
did not require to be sown by the hand, but sprang
sufficiently from the casual droppings of the last
year's crop.

Not very long after the absorption of Hyrcania, the Parthian arms were directed against the country of the Mardi. This region adjoined on Hyrcania towards the west, and consisted mainly of the mountain tract which shuts in the Caspian on the south, forming a continuation of the most southern of the three Parthian chains, and generally known under the appellation of Elburz. It is uncertain how far the Mardian territory extended towards the west, but probable that it was comprised within about two degrees, reaching from the neighbourhood of Dama-ghan to the great mountain of Demavend, or from E. long. 54° to 52° nearly. It is generally described as wholly rough and mountainous, but probably in-cluded the tract between the foot of the mountains and the Caspian—the eastern portion of the modern Mazanderan. This is a rich flat plain of alluvial soil, but little raised above the level of the neighbouring sea, from which rise gently-swelling hills, gradually increasing in elevation, and forming the supports of the lofty range, which was the heart of the Mardian territory. Here high rocky summits alternated with dense pathless woods, the mountains being clothed on their northern flank nearly to the top with dwarf oaks, or with shrubs and brushwood; while lower down their sides were covered with forests of elms, cedars, chestnuts, beeches, and cypress-trees. At the present day, the gardens and orchards of the natives, interspersed among the masses of primeval forest, are of the most superb character; the vegetation is luxuriant; lemons, oranges, peaches, pomegranates, besides other fruits, abound; rice, hemp, sugar-canes mulberries, are cultivated with success; vines grow wild; and the valleys are strewn with shrubs and flowers of rare fragrance, among which may be noted the rose, the honeysuckle, and the sweet-briar. Nature however—inexorably just, as usual—has balanced these extraordinary advantages with peculiar draw-backs; the tiger, scarcely known in any other part of Western Asia, here lurks in the jungles, ready to spring at any moment on the unwary traveller; inun-dations are frequent, and carry desolation far and wide; the waters, which thus escape from the river-beds, stagnate in marshes, and, during the summer and autumn heats, pestilential exhalations arise, which destroy the stranger, and bring even the acclimatised native to the brink of the grave. The Mardian territory was thus of no great value to the conquerors, except as conducting to other and healthier regions, a neces-sary link in the chain which was to unite East with West, and by means of which were to be re-knit in one the scattered fragments of the empire, which, built up originally by Cyrus, had been destroyed by Alexander.

The third tract which the Parthians annexed was a portion of Media. A strong spur runs out from the Elburz mountain range, about E. long. 52° 20′, which projects far into the desert, and forms a marked natural division between the regions west and east of it. The tract immediately to the west of the spur belonged to the ancient Media, and was known as Media Rhagiana from its capital city, Rhages, situ-ated in the angle between the spur and the main range, at no great distance from either. Parthia, soon after the conquest of the Mardians, invaded this territory, and effected a lodgment in it at a place called Charax, quite close to the spur, probably on the site now called Uewanikif. Hence, by degrees, the rest of Rhagiana was overrun, and the entire tract passed into the possession of the Parthians, as far probably as Kasvin westward, and southward as far as Kum. This was a district of a considerable size, a hundred and fifty miles long from the spur to Kasvin, and about eighty broad from the Elburz mountains to Kum. It was an elevated plain, from three thousand to four thousand feet above the sea level, having a climate dry and healthy, but a soil of indifferent quality. Portions of it belonged to the great central Iranian desert, and were absolutely unproductive, while the remainder could not boast any special fertility. It possessed, however, salt in abundance, was tolerably well watered, and could produce cereals and green crops in sufficient quantity to sustain a numerous population.

The next aggressive movement of the Parthians was in the opposite direction—towards the east. Here Parthia adjoined on the considerable state of Bactria, which had grown up simultaneously with herself, and had absorbed several extensive countries. Parthia's first aggression was on a small scale, and its result was merely the detachment from the Bactrian dominion of two inconsiderable provinces, known respectively as Turiun and Aspionus. The exact position of these tracts is unknown to us, but they must certainly be placed in the western portion of the Bactrian territory, and probably were districts north of the Paropamisus, either upon the Murghab, or upon the Ab-i-Kaisar river. The accession of territory gained by this conquest was insignificant.

But some extensive and most valuable conquests soon followed. Turning her attention once more towards the west, Parthia made war upon Media, the great country which had for a time held the first place in Western Asia, and exercised a dominion which reached from the Caspian Gates to the Halys, and from the mouth of the Araxes to the vicinity of Isfahan. Subjected first by Persia, and then by Alexander the Great, she had sunk back within much narrower limits, and had at the same time become split up into three provinces—Media Rhagiana, Media Magna, and Media Atropatêné. The Parthians had previously swallowed up, as already stated, Media Rhagiana : now they attacked Media Magna. This was an extensive tract situated between the thirty-second and thirty-seventh parallels, and reaching from the Great Salt Desert of Iran upon the east to the main chain of Mount Zagros upon the west. Its length from north to south was about five degrees, or nearly three hundred and fifty miles, and its width from west to east four degrees, or about two hundred and forty miles. The entire area cannot have been much under eighty thousand square miles, which is a little less than the size of Great Britain, and a little more than that of German Austria. The tract divides itself into two portions—the western and the eastern. The western, which is rather more than one half of the whole, lies within the limits of the broad mountain region known as Zagros, and is a country of alternate mountain and valley, with here and there a tolerably extensive plain, very productive, and for the most part picturesque and beautiful.   The loftiest of the mountains are bare and rugged towards their summits, but the inferior ranges are thickly clothed with forests quite to their top, while the valleys are full of magnificent orchards and gardens.   The walnut, the Oriental plane, the dwarf oak, the willow, and the poplar abound, while occasionally are to be seen the ash, and the terebinth, or turpentine tree.   The fruittrees in the orchards and gardens include, besides vines and mulberries, the apple, the pear, the quince, the plum, the almond, the nut, the chestnut, the olive, the peach, the nectarine, and the apricot.   With this western region, the eastern is in strong contrast.   East of Zagros, where the mountains sink down almost at once into the plain, lies a vast gravelly or sandy plateau, covered often with a saline efflorescence, called the "Kavir," and in places with a thick salt deposit, only scantily supplied with water from streams or wells which are often brackish, and crossed in places by bare rocky ridges, destitute of all vegetable mould, and incapable of nourishing even a bush or a tuft of grass.   Still, excepting where the salt efflorescence prevails, even the plateau can be made to produce good crops, if only water be supplied in sufficient quantity.   Hence the system of *kanats*, which is of great antiquity.   Everywhere the small streams and rills which descend from the mountains, and which, if left to themselves, would be almost immediately absorbed by the sands of the desert, are led into subterranean channels, which are placed at a

considerable depth below the surface, and conducted
for many miles across the plain. Openings are made
at intervals, from which water may be drawn by
means of a bucket for purposes of irrigation; and in
this way a considerable portion of the plateau is
brought into cultivation.

The conquest of Media Magna about doubled the
extent of the Parthian dominions, while it also soon
led to further acquisitions of a most important
character. On the western flank of Media Magna lay
the rich and valuable country, known originally as
Elam, and later on as Kissia or Susiana. This was an
extensive tract of very productive territory, interposed
between the main chain of Zagros and the lower
Tigris river, extending a distance of about five
degrees, or three hundred and fifty miles from north-
west to south-east, and having an average breadth of
about a hundred and fifty, or a hundred and sixty
miles, in the transverse direction. Like Media
Magna, it consisted of two strongly contrasted
regions. Towards the west was a broad tract of
fertile alluvium, intervening between the Tigris and
the mountains, well watered by numerous large
streams—the Jerahi, the Karun, the Kerkhah, the
Diala, and others—which are capable of giving an
abundant irrigation to almost the whole of the low
country. Above this region, towards the east and
the north-east, was a still more pleasant district, composed of alternate mountain, valley, and upland plain,
abounding in beautiful glens, richly wooded, and full
of gushing brooks and clear rapid rivers. Much of
this region is of course uncultivable mountain, range

succeeding range in six or eight nearly parallel lines, as the traveller advances towards the north-east ; and most of the ranges exhibiting vast tracts of bare and often precipitous rock, in the clefts of which snow rests till midsummer. Still the lower flanks of the mountains are, in general, cultivable ; while the valleys teem with orchards, and the plains furnish excellent pasture. The region closely resembles the western portion of Media Magna, whereof it is a continuation. As we follow it, however, towards the south-east, into the Bakhtiyari country, where it adjoins upon the ancient Persia, it deteriorates in character, the mountains becoming barer and more arid, and the valleys narrower and less fertile.

The fate of Susiana decided that of the adjoining countries of Babylonia and Persia, which seem to have submitted to Parthia without a struggle. Babylonia extended from the Persian Gulf on either side of the mouth of the Euphrates to the extreme northern limit of the alluvium, or to the vicinity of Hit on the Euphrates, and Samarah on the Tigris—a distance of about four hundred miles. The greatest width was about one hundred and eighty miles ; but the average width cannot be estimated at more than sixty or seventy, so that the area probably did not much exceed twenty-five thousand square miles. But the qualities of the soil were such as rendered the tract one of the chief granaries of the world. According to Herodotus and others, wheat, barley, and millet, which were the grains principally grown, yielded ordinarily a return of two hundred, and in some instances of three hundred, fold. Palm groves were numerous all along the courses of the rivers, and the dates which they produced were of first-rate quality. Under the early Achæmenian kings, when the food of the Court was supplied by each of the provinces in turn for a fixed portion of the year, Babylonia had the duty of furnishing the supplies during four months, so that it was reckoned equal, in respect of resources, to one-third of the empire. Irrigation was so easy in Babylonia that the whole country was brought under cultivation, and transformed into a garden. Here Parthia inherited all the advantages of an ancient civilisation, and had only to maintain the works of earlier times—canals, sluices, dams, embankments—in order to obtain from a single province a supply of food equal to the wants of almost her entire population.

Persia lay in the opposite direction from Babylonia, towards the east and the south-east. It stretched along the south-eastern shore of the Persian Gulf, from the inner recess of the Gulf near Mashur to Cape Jask, a little outside the straits of Ormuz, in E. long. 57° 40′. Inland it reached to the neighbourhood of Isfahan on the west, and to the deserts of Kerman and Yezd eastward. In length it thus extended to about eight degrees of longitude, a distance of six hundred and twenty miles, while in width it covered five degrees of latitude, or nearly three hundred and fifty miles. The entire area cannot have fallen much short of one hundred and fifty thousand square miles. The character of the region, speaking broadly, was far inferior to that of either Babylonia or Susiana. Along the coast, in the *Ghermsir,* or " warm country," as it is now called, was a sandy tract, often impregnated with salt, extending the whole length of the province, being a continuation of the flat region of Susiana, but falling very much short of that region in all the qualities which make a territory valuable. The soil is poor, consisting of alternate sand and clay —it is ill-watered, the entire tract possessing scarcely a single stream worthy of the name of river—and, lying only just outside of the northern tropic, the district is by its situation among the hottest in Western Asia. Fortunately, it was not very large in extent, since it reached inland a distance of only from ten to fifty miles, and thus did not constitute much more than one-eighth of the entire country. Of the other seven-eighths a considerable portion— perhaps as much as half—was very little superior, consisting of salt or sandy deserts, especially those of Kerman and Yezd, which were almost wholly unproductive by nature, and capable of only a very scanty cultivation. But, between these two arid districts, the stretch of hilly country which separated them was of a superior character, consisting of mountain, plain, and valley curiously intermixed, and for the most part fairly fertile. In places it is rich, picturesque, and romantic, almost beyond imagination, with lovely wooded dells, green mountain sides, and broad plains suited for the production of crops of almost any description. But, more commonly these features are absent, and there is a general look of sterility and barrenness which is unpleasant, or even forbidding. The supply of water is, almost everywhere, scanty. Scarcely any of the streams are strong enough to reach the sea. After short courses, they are either absorbed by the sand, or end in small salt lakes, from which the superfluous water is evaporated. Persia Proper deserves, on the whole, the description which its ancient inhabitants gave of it to Cyrus the Great—" a scant land and a rugged "— a land in which subsistence can only be obtained by strenuous and continual labour, and where the vicissitudes of climate are such as to brace and harden those who dwell in it.

Another country, probably subjugated about the same time as Media Magna, Susiana, Babylonia, and Persia Proper, was Assyria. Assyria, which had been long previously reduced nearly within its original limits, was at this period a smallish country, interposed between Mount Zagros and the Tigris, bounded on the east by Media Magna, on the north by Armenia, on the west by Mesopotamia, and on the south by Susiana or Elymaïs. Its greatest length was about three hundred and twenty miles, and its average width about a hundred. It would thus have had an area of about thirty-two thousand square miles, or have been equal in size to Ireland. But these narrow limits were amply compensated by the fertility of the soil. The tract between the Zagros mountains and the Tigris is principally an alluvium brought down by the rivers, which from time to time overflow their banks and spread themselves far and wide over the flat country. It produces excellent crops of wheat, barley, millet, and sesame ; besides growing palms in places, as well as walnuts, Oriental planes, sycamores, and poplars. The lower ranges of hills, outposts of

3

Zagros, bore olives, and in favoured situations the citron was largely cultivated ; while figs, vines, mulberries, pomegranates, and other fruit-trees were common. Of minerals, Assyria produced iron, copper, lead, bitumen, naphtha, petroleum, sulphur, alum, and salt.

The empire having been thus far extended towards the west, the time seemed to have arrived when something like an equivalent expansion towards the east was desirable. Bactria had hitherto stood in the way of any considerable Parthian advance in this direction ; and though Parthia had contrived to filch from her two small districts, yet no real impression had been made upon the powerful Bactrian kingdom, which at this time bore rule over the entire territory between the Tejend and the Hydaspes. But, soon after the time when the great expansion of the Parthian dominion towards the west was accomplished, Bactria began to decline in power, and may be said to have invited invasion. In the war which followed between the two countries, the success of the Parthian arms was marvellous. A few years sufficed for the subjugation of Bactria Proper, of Margiana, Aria, Sarangia or Drangiana, Sacastana, Arachosia, and perhaps we may add Sagartia and Chorasmia. It follows to give a short account of each of these countries.

Bactria Proper, the nucleus from which the Bactrian Empire had proceeded, may be considered as equivalent to the upper valley of the Oxus, or, in other words, to that valley from the remotest sources of the river towards the east down to its entrance on the great Chorasmian desert, in about E. long.

65° 30′, towards the west. The valley is enclosed on the north by the Hazaret Sultan, and Hissar mountains, while on the south it is bounded by the Paropamisus or Hindu Kush. Eastward it reaches to the Pamir table-land, whence several of its head-streams take their origin. Its length between the Pamir and the desert is about three hundred and sixty miles, while its width between the two mountain chains varies from a hundred and forty to two hundred and fifty miles. The area is probably twice as large as that of Parthia Proper, and may be estimated at about seventy thousand square miles. Much of the tract, being situated at a high elevation above the sea-level, is cold and infertile ; but the lower portion of the valley, especially the country about the ancient capital, Bactra, now Balkh, is fairly productive ; and the region between the Oxus and the Paropamisus— the southern moiety of the province, is regarded as among the most valuable portions of Affghanistan.

Margiana, or the district upon the Margus river (Marg-ab), adjoined Bactria upon the west, and, though geographically reckoned as distinct, was probably absorbed into it at an early period. It was mainly a narrow tract, shut in by deserts on either side, extending along the course of the Margus river for a distance of some two hundred miles, and then expanding suddenly into a broad oasis of the very highest fertility. Known in ancient, and again in modern times as Merv, it is still a region of some importance, and has recently been annexed by Russia, and connected by railway with Ashkabad and Bokhara.

Aria lay along the course of the River Arius, now the Heri-rud, which, rising on the south side of the Paropamisus in E. long. 67° nearly, runs westward, first through the mountains, and then along their southern flank, until, about E. long. 61°, it makes a sweep round to the north, and finding, or forcing, a way through the chain, joins the Tejend at Pul-i-Khatun, in lat. 36° nearly. The course of the stream, until it makes its great bend, measures between two hundred and seventy and two hundred and eighty miles ; and this may be regarded as the length of Aria from east to west. Its width between the Paropamisus and the tract known as Drangiana or Sarangia is difficult to determine, but was certainly not great. It may have averaged about fifty miles ; which would give for the entire area a size of about thirteen thousand square miles. The country was well watered, and tolerably fertile, but it was placed at too high an elevation to be more than moderately productive, Aria (or Herat), the capital, being more than three thousand feet above the sea-level, and the rest of the country being, for the most part, considerably more elevated.

Drangiana, or Sarangia, which adjoined on Aria towards the south, was a region of much greater extent, but of less fertility. It was ·the country watered by the streams which flow into the Hamun, or lake of Seistan, from the north-east and the north. On the west it verged upon the great Iranian desert, and partook of its character ; on the east it extended to the upper sources of the Kash river. It is difficult to determine its exact dimensions ; but it must have had an extent at least double that of Aria, and the entire superficies may not have fallen very much short of thirty thousand square miles.

Another country probably absorbed by Parthia at this time was Sacastana or Seistan. Sacastana was the country immediately south of the Hamun, or Great Salt Lake, in which the river Helmend ends. Except on the very banks of the Helmend, it was almost wholly unproductive, and incapable of habitation by any but a nomadic population. Portions of it were, however, liable to inundation, when the Helmend overflowed its banks ; and thus its general character was alternate reedy swamp and arid sandy desert. The extent was somewhat vague and indefinite, since there were no marked boundaries, unless the Helmend and Hamun may be reckoned such towards the north. Eastward it melted into Sattagydia, southward into Gedrosia, and westward into the desert of Kerman.

Dominion over Sarangia and Sacastana carried with it, almost necessarily, the sovereignty over Arachosia, which adjoined those countries upon the east. Arachosia, named from the river Arachotus (Argand-ab), a main tributary of the Helmend, consisted of the mountain tract about Candahar and a portion of the adjacent desert, now known as that of Registan. It was a large, but not very valuable country, and lay on the frontier of the Parthian Empire towards the south-east.

The power which held Hyrcania, Parthia, Aria, and Sarangia, was always predominant also in Sagartia, which coincided with the eastern and north-eastern portions of the Iranian desert. The Sagartians wandered freely over the greater part of the central region, where they found a scanty subsistence. Their country, notwithstanding its great extent, was almost valueless, being incapable of cultivation, and producing no mineral excepting salt.

An equally unproductive and undesirable territory, on the opposite side of the Parthian and Arian mountain chain, is commonly regarded as forming, together with Bactria, the limit of the Parthian dominion, east of the Caspian, towards the north. This is Chorasmia, or the country of the Chorasmians, known to moderns as the desert of Khorasan, which extends from the foot of the Bactrian, Parthian, and Hyrcanian hills to the old course of the Oxus, from its entrance on the desert to its ancient principal mouth. Chorasmia is thus a very extensive country, not less than six hundred miles in length by three hundred in breadth ; but its value is exceedingly slight, since, except along the course of the Oxus, or modern Amu Daria, it does not admit of cultivation.

By the absorption of these various countries and regions Parthia obtained her fullest extension towards the east and the north-east, but she was still able to make important additions to her dominions on the opposite side of her empire, especially towards the north-west. At a comparatively early period, certainly before her wars with Rome began, she made herself mistress of the extensive and valuable region of Mesopotamia Proper, which was the tract enclosed

between the Tigris and Euphrates rivers, bounded
on the north by Armenia, and on the south by the
Babylonian alluvium.   The length of this region
from north-west to south-east was at least three
hundred and fifty miles, while its breadth, where it
was broadest, cannot be estimated at much under two
hundred and sixty.   But as in some places the width
did not exceed fifty miles, the entire area, it is probable, fell short of fifty thousand square miles.   Much
of it was very unproductive, being a treeless plain,
the home of the wild ass, the bustard, and the gazelle;
but towards the north there was more fertility, and
the Mons Masius, together with its southern skirt,
and the valley of the Tigris north of it, were tracts
of some considerable value.   Masius produces abundant timber, together with manna and gall-nuts; the
pistachio grows wild in the district between Orfah and
Diabekr ; the Sinjar range of hills is noted for the
cultivation of the fig ; and the whole northern region
is favourable to the growth of fruit-trees, and produces
walnuts, oranges, lemons, pomegranates, apricots, and
mulberries.

During the period of the wars with Rome the
limits of the Parthian Empire fluctuated greatly.
Provinces were conquered and reconquered ; large
annexations were made and then relinquished ; whole
countries were ceded, and, after a time, recovered.
This is not the place for tracing out and placing on
record all these various changes.   We are concerned
only with the question of Parthia's extremest limits
at her most flourishing period.   In order, however, to
complete our sketch of this subject, we must bring

under the reader's notice two more districts—Media Atropatêné and Armenia.

Media Atropatêné, which became ultimately a dependency of Parthia, was the tract directly west of the lower Caspian Sea, extending from the River Araxes (Aras) towards the north to the borders of Media Magna and Media Rhagiana towards the south. Westward it bordered on Armenia, with which it was sometimes connected politically. Its southern boundary lay almost along the line of the thirty-sixth parallel. It was thus very nearly a square, extending from east to west for the space of two hundred and forty, and from north to south for the space of about two hundred and twenty miles. The area did not fall much short of fifty thousand square miles. Its chief rivers were the Aras and the Sefid-rud ; and it further contained within it the remarkable lake of Urumiyeh. The tract was mountainous, but fairly fertile, with a cold climate in the winter, but a delicious one during the summer months. It was a region of considerable value, and is still much prized by its possessors, the modern Persians.

Armenia, which, to the west of the Caspian, closed in the Parthian territory towards the north when the empire had reached its acme, lay north-west and partly north of Atropatêné. It reached from the Caspian at the mouth of the Aras to the elbow of the Euphrates, in lat. 38° 30′, long. 38° 25′ nearly, a distance of about six hundred miles, and extended from Iberia on the north to Mount Niphates on the south, a distance of rather more than two hundred miles. But Armenia was lozenge-shaped, narrowing gradually towards both extremities; and thus the area did not much exceed sixty thousand square miles. The character of the region closely resembled that of Atropatêné, but was on the whole superior; and Armenia is found to have been a productive territory, which exported wine to Babylon, and traded in the markets of Phœnicia with horses and mules (Ezek. xxvii. 14).

It would seem, then, that the Parthian Empire, when at the highest pitch of prosperity, extended fully two thousand miles from east to west between the Pamir upland and the Euphrates, while it had a general width of about five or six hundred miles between its northern and southern frontiers. It included the whole of modern Persia, the greater part of Affghanistan, much of Turkey in Asia, and some large regions which are now in the possession of the Russians. As Persia is said to extend over five hundred thousand square miles, and Affghanistan over two hundred thousand, while the Russian and Turkish provinces which were once Parthian cannot be estimated to contain less than one hundred thousand square miles, the whole territory included within the empire of the Parthians at its greatest extent can scarcely have fallen far short of eight hundred thousand square miles. It would thus have been about equal in extent to France, Germany, Austria, and Turkey in Europe put together.

The boundaries of the empire were, upon the north, Iberia, the river Kur or Cyrus, the Caspian, the Oxus, and the Hazaret Sultan, and Hissar ranges; on the east, the Pamir, the Bolor Chain, and the valley of the Indus; on the south, Beluchistan and the Persian Gulf; on the west, Cappadocia and the Euphrates. Westward of the Euphrates lay the territory of Rome; northward of the Oxus were the wild tribes of Scythia, Alani, Massagetæ, Yue-chi, and others; on the eastern frontier were the Indo-Scyths, a weak and divided people. Only two neighbours seemed to be of much account—Rome upon the west, and the Scythic tribes upon the north and north-east. With each of these enemies Parthia had important and dangerous wars, but her destruction came from neither. Revolt within her own borders brought the Parthian dominion to an end, and substituted in its place the Second Persian or Sassanian monarchy.

II.

ETHNOGRAPHICAL—TURANIAN CHARACTER OF THE PARTHIAN PEOPLE.

THE Parthians do not appear in history as a people until the time of Darius, the son of Hystaspes (B.C. 521–515). There is no mention of them in the Old Testament, or in the Assyrian Inscriptions, or in the Zendavesta. We first find any record of their existence in the great Inscription of Darius, at Behistun. They are there called the "Parthva," or "Parthwa," and appear in close connection with the "Varkana," or people of Hyrcania. Darius regards them as his subjects, and speaks of their "revolting" against his father, Hystaspes, who seems to have been at the time their satrap, and fighting a battle with him within the limits of their own country. They were defeated with the loss of about ten thousand men in killed and prisoners; after which they submitted, and returned to their allegiance.

Through the rest of the Achæmenian period (B.C. 515–331) we never hear of them but as faithful Persian subjects. They were assigned by Darius to his sixteenth satrapy, and united in it with the Arians, the Sogdians, and the Chorasmians. They took part in the expedition of his son, Xerxes, against Greece. They fought at Issus and at Arbela. We never hear of their joining in any revolt after their one attempt in the time of general disturbance at the beginning of the reign of Darius. If they did not offer a very strenuous resistance to Alexander, it was probably because the Persian Empire had collapsed, and the conqueror appeared to be irresistible.

This fidelity to the Persian rule, combined with the fact that geographically Parthia was situated in the midst of a group of purely Arian tribes—the Hyrcanians, Chorasmians, Margians, Arians of Herat, Bactrians, Sagartians, and Sarangians—has led some writers on ethnography to maintain that the Parthians, like all the other people of the Iranian plateau, belonged to the Iranian family. They certainly affected, to a large extent, Persian names —*e.g.*, Mithridates, Tiridates, Artabanus, Orobazus, Rhodaspes, Chosroës, if that is a form of Cyrus (*Kurush* in Persian)—and some of the appellations peculiar to them are explainable by Arian etymologies. "Priapatius," for instance, has been ingeniously compared with the Zendic "Frijapaitis," which means, like the Greek "Philopator," "Lover of his father." But conjectural explanations of names are an exceedingly unsafe basis for ethnological speculations. And it is certain that the Parthian names do not, as a general rule, suggest the idea of derivation from Arian sources.

If we ask what the ancient writers have left on record with respect to the Parthian nationality, we

shall find, in the first place, a general *consensus* that
they were Scyths. "The Parthian race is Scythic,"
says Arrian. "The Parthians," says Justin, in his
"Epitome of Trogus Pompeius," "were a race of
Scyths, who at a remote date separated themselves
from the rest of the nation, and occupied the
southern portion of the Chorasmian desert, whence
they gradually made themselves masters of the
mountain region adjoining it." Strabo adds to this,
that the particular Scythic tribe whereto they
belonged was that of the Dahæ; that their own
proper and original name was Parni, or Aparni;
and that they had migrated at a remote period from
the country to the north of the Palus Mæotis (Sea of
Azov), where they left the great mass of their fellow-
tribesmen. Some time after this the theory was
started that they were Scyths whom Sesostris, on
his return from his supposed Scythian expedition,
brought into Asia and settled in the mountain tract
south-east of the Caspian. We cannot put much
faith in the details of any of these various statements, since, in the first place, they are contradictory,
and, in the second, they are, most of them, highly
improbable. Sesostris, for instance, if there ever
was such a king, no more made an expedition into
Scythia than into Lapland or Kamskatka. No
Egyptian monarch ever penetrated further north
than the mountain chains of Taurus and Niphates.
Arrian's story is a mere variant of the tale told to
Herodotus and Diodorus, and believed by them, of
the planting of Scythian colonists in Colchis by the
hypothetical Sesostris; and it is even more impro-

bable, since it makes the returning conqueror depart from his natural course, and go a thousand miles out of his way, to plant for no purpose a colony in a region which he was never likely to visit again. Strabo's migration tale is less incredible, since the tribes to the north of the Euxine and Caspian lived in a constant state of unrest, and migratory movements on their part, far exceeding the supposed Parthian movement in the distance traversed, are among the most certain facts of ancient history. But it is difficult to see what trustworthy authority Strabo could even suppose that he had for his assertions, since the migration of which he speaks must have taken place at least six hundred years before his own time, and migratory races rarely retain any tradition of their origin for so much as a century. Strabo, moreover, admits it to be doubtful whether there ever were any Dahæ among the Scyths of the Mæotis, and thus seems to cut the ground from under his own feet.

The utmost that can be safely gathered from these numerous and discrepant notices is the conclusion that the Parthians were felt by the Greeks and Romans who first came into contact with them to be an alien nation, intruded among the Arian races of these parts, having their congeners in the great steppe country which lay north of the Black Sea, the Caucasus, the Caspian, and the Oxus river. These nations were nomadic, uncivilised, coarse, not to any brutal, in their habits ; of a type very much inferior to that of the races which inhabited the more southern regions, felt by them to be barbarians, and feared as

a continual menace to their prosperity and civilisation.   There is always an underlying idea of dis-
praise and disparagement whenever a Greek or a
Roman calls any race, or people, or custom "Scythic"—
the term connotes rudeness, grossness, absence of
culture and refinement—it is not perhaps strictly
ethnic, since it designates a life rather than a descent,
habits rather than blood—but it points to such a life
and such habits as have from the remotest antiquity
prevailed, and as still prevail, in the vast plain country
which extends from the Caucasus, the Caspian, and
the mountain chains of the Central Asian regions to
the shores of the great Arctic Sea.

It is certain that the inhabitants of this tract
have belonged, from a remote antiquity, to the ethnic
family generally known as Turanian.   In the south
they are of the Tâtar or Turkish type ; in the north,
of the Finnish, or Samoeidic.   Their language is
agglutinate, and wanting in inflections; their physique
is weak, languid, anæmic, unmuscular ; they have
large fleshy bodies, loose joints, soft swollen bellies,
and scanty hair.   They live chiefly on horseback or
in waggons.   Still, as enemies, they are far from
contemptible.   Admirable horsemen, often skilled
archers, accustomed to a severe climate and to ex-
posure in all weathers ; they have proved formidable
foes to many warlike nations, and still give serious
trouble to their Russian masters.

The Scythian character of the Parthians, vouched
for on all hands, and their derivation from Upper
Asia, or the regions beyond the Oxus, furnish a
strong presumption of their belonging to the Turanian

family of nations. This presumption is strengthened by the little that we know of their language. Their names, when not distinctly Persian, which they would often naturally be from conscious and intentional imitation, are decidedly non-Arian, and have certain Turanian characteristics. Among these may be mentioned, first of all, the guttural termination, found in Arsac-es, Sinnac-es, Parrhac-es, Vasac-es, Sana-trœc-es, Phraatac-es, Valarsac-es, &c.—a termination which characterises the primitive Babylonian, the Basque, and most of the Turanian tongues. Beyond this, it would not be difficult to suggest Turanian etymologies for a large number of Parthian names, but as such suggestions could only be " guesses at truth," not very much weight would attach to them.

The main argument for the Turanian character of the Parthian people is to be found in their physical and mental type, and in their manners and customs. Their sculptures give them the large ill-formed limbs, the heavy paunches, and the general flaccid appearance which characterise Turanian races. Their history shows them to have had the merits and defects of the Turanian type of character. They were covetous, grasping, ready to take the aggressive, and, on the whole, tolerably successful in their wars against weak races. But they were wanting in dash, in vigorous effort, and in perseverance. They were stronger in defence than in attack; and, as time went on, became more and more unenterprising and lethargic. In the arts they were particularly backward, devoid of taste, and wanting in originality. Considering the patterns that they had before their eyes in the architecture and sculptures of Pasargadæ, Nakhsh-i-Rustam, Istakr, and Persepolis, it is simply astonishing that they could rise no higher than the mean palace at Hatra, and the grotesque tablets at Behistun, Sir-pul-i-Zohab, and Tengh-i-Saoulek. Greek art, moreover, was not unknown to them ; and they imitated it upon their coins ; but the travesty is painful, and often verges on the ridiculous. In their manners and customs there was much that was markedly Turanian. Like the Turkoman and Tâtar tribes generally, they passed almost their whole lives on horseback, conversing, transacting business, buying and selling, even eating, while mounted on their horses. They practised polygamy, secluded their women from the sight of men, punished unfaithfulness with extreme severity, delighted in hunting, and rarely ate any flesh but that which they obtained in this way, were moderate eaters but great drinkers, did not speak much, but yet were very unquiet, being constantly engaged in stirring up trouble either abroad or at home. A small portion of the nation only was free ; the remainder were the slaves of the privileged few. Nomadic habits continued to prevail among a portion of those who remained in their primitive seats, even in the time of their greatest national prosperity ; and a coarse, rude, semi-barbarous character attached always—even to the most advanced part of the nation—to the king, the court, and the nobles generally, a character which, despite a certain varnish of civilisation, was constantly showing itself in their dealings with each other, and with foreign nations. " The Parthian monarchs," as Gibbon justly observes, "like the

4

Mogul sovereigns of Hindustan, delighted in the pastoral life of their Scythian ancestors, and the imperial camp was frequently pitched in the plain of Ctesiphon, on the eastern bank of the Tigris." Niebuhr seems even to doubt whether the Parthians dwelt in cities at all. He represents them as maintaining from first to last their nomadic habits, and regards the insurrection by which their empire was brought to an end as a rising of the inhabitants of towns—the Tadjiks of those times—against the Ilyats or wanderers, who had oppressed them for centuries. This is, no doubt, an over-statement ; but it has a foundation in fact, since wandering habits, and even tent life, were affected by the Parthians during the most flourishing period of their empire.

Another respect in which the Parthians resembled some, at any rate, of the principal Turanian tribes was in their combination of the rudeness and coarseness already mentioned with great vigour of administration and government. Like the early (or Accadian) Babylonians, like the Mongols under Jenghis Khan and his successors, like the Turks of the Middle Ages, and to some extent even of modern times, the Parthians possessed, to a large amount, the governing or ruling faculty. They rapidly developed a great power ; and they held together for nearly four centuries a heterogeneous mass of subject nations, who could have had no love for their rule, yet were constrained by their energy and other sterling qualities to render them, for the most part, a cheerful and steady obedience. Their governmental system was not refined, but it was effective ; they never permanently lost a province; and, at the dissolution of the empire, its limits were as extensive as they had ever been.

On the whole, it may be said, that the Turanian character of the Parthian people, though not absolutely proved, appears to be in the highest degree probable. If we accept it, we must regard them as in race closely allied to the vast hordes which, from a remote antiquity, have roamed over the steppe region of Upper Asia, from time to time bursting upon the south, and harassing or subjugating the comparatively unwarlike inhabitants of the warmer countries. We must view them as the congeners of the Huns, Bulgarians, Avars, Komans of the ancient world; of the Kalmucks, Ouigurs, Eleuts, Usbegs, Turkomans, &c., of the present day. Perhaps their nearest representatives will be, if we look to their primitive condition at the founding of their empire, the modern Turkomans, who occupy nearly the same districts; if we regard them at the period of their highest prosperity, the Osmanli Turks. Like the Turks, they combined great military prowess and vigour with a capacity for organisation and government not very usual among Asiatics. Like them, they remained at heart barbarians, though they put on an external appearance of civilisation and refinement. Like them, they never to any extent amalgamated with the subject peoples, but continued for centuries an exclusive dominant race, encamped in the countries which they had overrun.

III.

CONDITION OF WESTERN ASIA IN THE THIRD
CENTURY B.C.—ORIGIN OF THE PARTHIAN STATE.

THE grand attempt of Alexander the Great to
unite the East and West in a single universal
monarchy, magnificent in conception, and carried out
in act with extraordinary energy and political wisdom,
so long as he was spared to conduct his enterprise in
person, was frustrated, in the first place, by the
unfortunate circumstance of his premature decease;
and, secondly, by the want of ability among his
" Successors." Although among them there were
several who possessed considerable talent, there was
no commanding personality of force sufficient to
dominate the others, and certainly none who inherited
either Alexander's grandeur of conception or his powers
of execution, or who can be imagined as, under any
circumstances, successfully accomplishing his projects.
The scheme, therefore, which the great Macedonian
had conceived, unhappily collapsed, and his effort to
unite and consolidate led only to increased division
and disintegration. He left behind him at least
twelve rival claimants of his power, and it was only
by partition that the immediate breaking out of civil

war among the competitors was prevented. Partition itself did but stave off the struggle for a few years, and the wars of the " Successors," which followed, caused further change, and tended to split the empire into minute fragments. After a while the various collisions produced something like a "survival of the fittest," and about the close of the fourth century, after the great battle of Ipsus (B.C. 301), that division of the Macedonian Empire was made into four principal parts, which thenceforward for nearly three centuries formed the basis of the political situation in Eastern Europe and Western Asia. Macedonia, Asia Minor, Syria, and Egypt became the great powers of the time, and on the fortunes of these four powers, their policies, and lines of action, depended the general course of affairs in the Oriental world for the next two hundred years at any rate.

Of these four great monarchies the one with which the interests of Parthia were almost wholly bound up was the Syrian kingdom of the Seleucidæ. Originally, Seleucus received nothing but the single satrapy of Babylonia. But his military genius and his popularity were such, that his dominion kept continually increasing until it became an empire worthy of comparison with those ancient Oriental monarchies, which, in remoter times, had attracted, and almost monopolised, the attention of mankind. As early as B.C. 312, he had added to his original government of Babylonia the important countries of Media, Susiana, and Persia. After Ipsus he received, by the agreement then made among the " Successors," the districts of Cappadocia, Eastern Phrygia, Upper Syria, Mesopotamia, and the

entire valley of the Euphrates ; while, about the same
time, or rather earlier, he, by his own unassisted
efforts, obtained the adhesion of all the eastern
provinces of Alexander's Empire, Armenia, Assyria,
Sagartia, Carmania, Hyrcania, Parthia, Bactria, Sogdiana, Aria, Sarangia, Arachosia, Sacastana, Gedrosia,
and probably part of India. The empire thus established extended from the Mediterranean on the west
to the Indus valley and the Bolor mountain chain
upon the east, while it stretched from the Caspian
and the Jaxartes towards the north to the Persian
Gulf and the Indian Ocean southwards. Its entire
area could not have been much less than 1,200,000
square miles. Of these some 300,000 or 400,000 may
have been desert ; but the remainder was generally
fertile, and comprised within its limits some of the
very most productive regions in the whole world.
The Mesopotamian lowland, the Orontes valley, the
tract between the Southern Caspian and the mountains, the regions about Merv and Balkh, were among
the richest in Asia, and produced grain and fruit in
incredible abundance. The fine pastures of Media
and Armenia furnished excellent horses. Bactria
gave an inexhaustible supply of camels. Elephants
in large numbers were readily procurable from India.
Gold, silver, copper, iron, lead, tin were furnished by
several of the provinces, and precious stones of various
kinds abounded. Moreover, for above ten centuries,
the precious metals and the most valuable kinds of
merchandise had flowed from every quarter into the
region ; and though the Macedonians may have carried
off, or wasted, a considerable quantity of both, yet the

accumulations of ages withstood the strain; and the hoarded wealth, which had come down from Assyrian, Babylonian, and Median times, was to be found in the days of Seleucus chiefly within the limits of his empire.

It might have seemed that Western Asia was about to enjoy under the Seleucid princes as tranquil and prosperous a condition as had prevailed throughout the region for the two centuries which had intervened between the founding of the Persian Empire by Cyrus (B.C. 538) and its destruction by Alexander (B.C. 323). But the fair prospect was soon clouded over. The Seleucid princes, instead of devoting themselves to the consolidation of their power in the vast region between the Euphrates and the Indus, turned all their attention towards the West, and frittered away in petty quarrels for small gains with their rivals in that quarter—the Ptolemies and the princes of Asia Minor—those energies which would have been far better employed in arranging and organising the extensive dominions whereof they were already masters. It was symptomatic of this leaning to the West, that the first Seleucus, almost as soon as he found himself in quiet possession of his vast empire, transferred the seat of government from Lower Mesopotamia to Upper Syria, from the banks of the Tigris to those of the Orontes. This movement had fatal consequences. Already his empire contained within itself an element of weakness in its over-great length, which cannot be estimated at less than two thousand miles. To counteract this disadvantage a fairly central position for the capital was almost a necessity. The empire of Seleucus might have been

conveniently ruled from the old Median capital of
Ecbatana, or the later Persian one of Susa. Even
Babylon, or Seleucia, though further to the west, were
not unsuitable sites ; and had Seleucus been content
with either of these, no blame would attach to him.
But when, to keep watch upon his rivals, he removed
the seat of government five hundred miles further westward, and placed it almost on his extreme western
frontier, within a few miles of the Mediterranean, he
intensified the weakness which required to be counter-
acted, and made the disruption of his empire within
no great length of time certain. The change loosened
the ties which bound the empire together, offended
the bulk of the Asiatics, who saw their monarch withdraw from them into a remote corner of his dominions,
and particularly weakened the grasp of the government on those more eastern districts which were at
once furthest from the new metropolis, and least
assimilated to the Hellenic character. Among the
causes which led to the disintegration of the Seleucid
kingdom, there is none which deserves so well to be
considered the main cause as this. It was calculated
at once to produce the desire to revolt, and to render
the reduction of revolted provinces difficult, if not
impossible.

The evil day, however, might have been indefinitely
postponed, if not even escaped altogether, had the
Seleucid princes either established and maintained
throughout their empire a vigorous and efficient administration, or abstained from entangling themselves
in wars with their neighbours upon the West—the
Ptolemies, the kings of Pergamus, and others.

But the organisation of the Seleucid Empire was unsatisfactory. Instead of pursuing the system inaugurated by Alexander, and seeking to weld the heterogeneous elements of which his kingdom was composed into a homogeneous whole, instead of at once conciliating and elevating the Asiatics by uniting them with the Macedonians and the Greeks, by promoting intermarriage and social intercourse between the two classes of his subjects, educating the Asiatics in Greek ideas and Greek schools, opening his court to them, promoting them to high employments, making them feel that they were as much valued and as much . cared for as the people of the conquering race, the first Seleucus, and after him his successors, fell back upon the older, simpler, and ruder system—the system pursued before Alexander's time by the Persians, and before them perhaps by the Medes—the system most congenial to human laziness and human pride—that of governing a nation of slaves by means of a clique of victorious aliens. Seleucus divided his empire into satrapies, seventy-two in number. He bestowed the office of satrap on none but Macedonians and Greeks. The standing army, by means of which he maintained his authority, was indeed composed in the main of Asiatics, disciplined after the Greek model; but it was officered entirely by men of Greek or Macedonian parentage. Nothing was done to keep up the self-respect of the Asiatics, or to soften the unpleasantness which must always attach to being governed by foreigners. Even the superintendence over the satraps seems to have been insufficient. According to some writers, it was a gross outrage offered by a satrap to

an Asiatic subject that stirred up the Parthians to
their revolt.   The story may not be true ; but the
currency given to it shows of what conduct to those
under their rule the satraps of the Seleucidæ were
thought, by those who lived near the time, to have
been capable.   It may be said that this treatment
was no worse than that whereto the subject races
of Western Asia had been accustomed for many
centuries under their Persian, Median, or Assyrian
masters, and this statement may be quite consonant
with truth ; but a new yoke is always more galling
than an old one ; in addition to which we must take
into consideration the fact, that the hopes of the
Asiatics had been raised by the policy of assimilation
avowed, and to some extent introduced, by Alexander;
so that they may be excused if they felt with some
bitterness the disappointment of their very legitimate
expectations, when the Seleucidæ revived the old
satrapial system, unmodified, unsoftened, with all its
many abuses as pronounced and as rampant as ever.

An entire abstention on the part of the Seleucidæ
from quarrels with the other "Successors of Alexander,"
would perhaps scarcely have been possible.   Their
territory bordered on that of the Ptolemies and the
kings of Pergamus, and was liable to invasion from
either quarter.   But by planting their capital on the
Orontes they aggravated the importance of the attacks
which they could not prevent, and became mixed up
with Pergamenian and Egyptian, and even Macedonian,
politics far more than was necessary.   Had they but
made Seleucia permanently their metropolis, and held
lightly by their dominion to the west of the Euphrates,

they might certainly have avoided to a large extent the entanglements into which they were drawn by their actual policy, and have been free to give their main attention to the true sources of their real strength—the central and eastern provinces. But it may be doubted whether the idea of abstention ever presented itself to the mind of any one of the early Seleucid princes. It was the fond dream of each of them, as of the other " Successors," that possibly in his person might one day be re-united the whole of the territories which had been ruled by the Great Conqueror. Each Seleucid prince would have felt that he sacrificed his dearest and most cherished hopes, if he had withdrawn from the regions of the west, and shunning engagements and adventures in that quarter, had contented himself with efforts to consolidate a great power in the more inland and more thoroughly Asiatic portions of the empire.

The result was that, during the first half of the third century (B.C. 300–250), the Seleucid princes were almost constantly engaged in disputes and wars in Asia Minor and Syria Proper, gave their personal super-intendence to those regions, and had neither time nor attention to spare for the affairs of the far East. So long as the satraps of these regions paid regularly their appointed tributes, and furnished regularly the required quotas of troops for service in the western wars, Seleucus and his successors, the first and second Antiochi, were content. The satraps were left to manage the affairs of their provinces at their own discretion ; and we cannot be surprised if the absence of a controlling hand led to various complications and disorders.

As time went on these disorders would naturally increase, and matters might very probably have come to a head in a few more years through the mere negligence and apathy of those who had the direction of the state; but a further impulse towards actual disintegration was given by the character of the second Antiochus, which was especially weak and contemptible. To have taken the title of " Theos "— never before assumed, so far as we know, by any monarch—was, even by itself, a sufficient indication of presumption and folly, and might justify us, did we know no more of him, in concluding that the calamities of his reign were the fruit of his unfitness to direct and rule an empire. But we have further abundant evidence of his incapacity. He was noted, even among Asiatic sovereigns, for luxury and de-bauchery; he neglected all state affairs in the pursuit of pleasure; his wives and his male favourites were allowed to rule his kingdom at their will, and their most flagrant crimes were neither restrained nor punished. The satraps, to whom the character and conduct of their sovereign could not but become known, would be partly encouraged to follow the bad example set them, partly provoked by it to shake themselves free from the rule of so hateful yet contemptible a master.

It may be added, that already there had been examples of successful revolts on the part of satraps in outlying provinces, which could not but have been generally known, and which must have excited

ambitious longings on the part of persons similarly
placed, from the very beginning of the Macedonian
period.   Even at the time of Alexander's great
conquests, a Persian satrap, Atropates, succeeded in
converting his satrapy of Upper Media—thenceforward called Media Atropatênê—into an independent
sovereignty.   Not long afterwards, Cappadocia had
detached itself from the kingdom of Eumenes (B.C.
326), and had established its independence under
Ariarathes, who became the founder of a dynasty.
Still earlier, Bithynia, Paphlagonia, and Pontus, once
Persian provinces, had revolted, and in each case the
revolt had issued in the recovery of autonomy.   Thus
already in Western Asia, beside the Greco-Macedonian kingdoms which had been established by the
" Successors of Alexander," there were existent some
five or six states which had had their origin in successful
rebellions.

Such were the circumstances under which, in or
about the year B.C. 256, which was the sixth year of
Antiochus Theus, actual disturbances broke out in
the extreme north-east of the Seleucid Empire.   The
first province to raise the standard of revolt, and proclaim itself independent, was Bactria.   This district
had from a remote antiquity been one with special
pretensions.   The country was fertile, and much of
it readily defensible ; the people were hardy and
valiant ; they had been generally treated with
exceptional favour by the Persian monarchs ; and
they seem to have had traditions which assigned
them a pre-eminence among the Arian nations at
some indefinitely distant period.   " Bactria with the

lofty banner " is celebrated in one of the most ancient portions of the Zendavesta. It remained unsubdued until the time of Cyrus. Cyrus is said by some to have left it as an appanage to his second son, Bardes, or Tanyoxares. Under the Persians, it had for satrap generally, or at any rate frequently, a member of the royal family. Alexander had conquered it with difficulty, and only by prolonged efforts. It was therefore natural that disintegration should make its first appearance in this quarter. The Greek satrap of the time, Diodotus, either disgusted with the conduct of Antiochus Theus, or simply seeing in his weakness and general unpopularity an opportunity which it would be foolish to let slip, in or about the year B.C. 256, assumed the style and title of king, struck coins stamped with his own name, and established himself without any difficulty as king over the entire province. Theus, engaged in war with the Egyptian monarch, Ptolemy Philadelphus, did not even make an effort to put him down, and the Bactrian ruler, without encountering any serious opposition, passed into the ranks of autonomous sovereigns.

The example of successful revolt thus set could not well be barren of consequences. If one Seleucid province might throw off the yoke of its feudal lord with absolute impunity, why might not others ? There seemed to be actually nothing to prevent them. Syria, so far as we can discern, allowed Bactria to go its way without any effort whatever either to check the revolt or to punish it. For eighteen years no Syrian force came near the country. Diodotus was permitted to consolidate his kingdom and rivet his authority on his subjects, without any interference, and the Bactrian monarchy became thus a permanent factor in Asiatic politics for nearly two centuries.

It was about six years after the establishment of Bactrian independence that the Parthian satrapy followed the pattern set it by its neighbour, and detached itself from the Seleucid Empire. The circumstances, however, under which the severance took place were very different in the two cases. History by no means repeated itself. In Bactria the Greek satrap took the lead ; and the Bactrian kingdom was, at any rate at its commencement, as thoroughly Hellenic as that of the Seleucidæ. But in Parthia Greek rule was from the first cast aside. The native Asiatics rebelled against their masters. A people of a rude and uncivilised type, coarse and savage, but brave and freedom-loving, rose up against the polished but comparatively effeminate Greeks, who held them in subjection, and claimed and succeeded in establishing their independence. The Parthian kingdom was thoroughly anti-Hellenic. It appealed to patriotic feelings, and to the hate universally felt towards the stranger. It set itself to undo the work of Alexander, to cast out the Europeans, to recover for the native race the possession of its own continent. "Asia for for the Asiatics," was its cry. It was naturally almost as hostile to Bactria as to Syria, although danger from a common enemy might cause it sometimes to make a temporary alliance with the former kingdom. It had, no doubt, the general sympathy of the populations in the adjacent countries, and represented to them the cause of freedom and autonomy. Arsaces effected for Parthia that which Arminius strove to effect for Germany, and which Tell accomplished for Switzerland, and Victor Emmanuel for Lombardy.

The circumstances of the revolt of Parthia are variously narrated by ancient authors. According to a story reported by Strabo, though not accepted as true by him, Arsaces was a Bactrian, who did not approve of the proceedings of Diodotus, and, when he was successful, quitted the newly-founded kingdom, and transferred his residence to Parthia, where he stirred up an insurrection against the satrap, and, succeeding in the attempt, induced the Parthians to accept him as their sovereign. But it is intrinsically improbable that an entire foreigner would have been accepted as king under such circumstances, and it is fatal to the narrative that every other account contradicts the Bactrian origin of Arsaces, and makes him a Parthian, or next door to a Parthian. Arrian states that Arsaces and his brother, Tiridates, were Parthians, descendants of Phriapites, the son of Arsaces ; that they revolted against the satrap of Antiochus Theus, by name Pherecles, on account of a gross insult which he had offered to one of them ; and that finally, having murdered the satrap, they declared Parthia independent, and set up a government of their own. Strabo, while giving currency to more than one story on the subject, lets us see that, in his own mind, he accepts the following account : " Arsaces was a Scythian, a chief among the Parnian Dahæ, who inhabited the valley of the Ochus (Attrek ?). Soon after the establishment of Bactrian independence, he entered Parthia at the head of a body of his country-

men, and succeeded in making himself master of it."
Finally, Justin, who no doubt, here as elsewhere, follows
Trogus Pompeius, a writer of the Augustan age, ex-
presses himself as follows: "Arsaces, having been
long accustomed to live by robbery and rapine,
attacked the Parthians with a predatory band, killed
their satrap, Andragoras, and seized the supreme
authority." This last account seems fairly probable,
and does not greatly differ from Arrian's. If Arsaces
was a Dahan chief, accustomed to make forays into
the fertile hill country of Parthia from the Chorasmian desert, and, in one of them, fell in with the Greek
satrap, defeated him, and slew him, it would not be
unlikely that the Parthians, who were of a kindred
race, might be so delighted with his prowess as to
invite him to place himself at their head. An oppressed people gladly adopts as ruler the chieftain of
an allied tribe, if he has shown skill and daring, and
promises them deliverance from their oppressors.

The date of the Parthian revolt was probably B.C.
250, which was the eleventh year of Antiochus Theus.
Antiochus was at that time engaged in a serious
conflict with Ptolemy Philadelphus, King of Egypt,
which, however, was brought to a close in the following year by his marriage with Berenice, Ptolemy's
daughter. It might have been expected that, as soon
as his hands were free, he would have turned his
attention towards the East, and have made an effort,
at any rate, to regain his lost territory. But Antiochus lacked either the energy or the courage to engage
in a fresh war. He was selfish and luxurious in his
habits, and seems to have preferred the delights of

repose amid the soft seductions of Antioch to the perils and hardships of a campaign in the rough Caspian region. At any rate, he remained quietly at home, while Arsaces consolidated his power, chastised those who for one reason or another resisted his authority, and settled himself firmly upon the throne. His capital appears to have been Hecatompylus, which had been built by Alexander in the valley of the Gurghan river. According to some late authors of small account, he came to a violent end, having been killed in battle by a spear-thrust, which penetrated his side. It is certain that he had a short

COIN OF TIRIDATES I.

reign, since he was succeeded in B.C. 248 by his brother, Tiridates, the second Parthian monarch.

Tiridates, on ascending the throne, followed a practice not very uncommon in the East, and adopted his brother's name as a "throne-name," reigning as Arsaces the Second. He is the first Parthian king of whom we possess contemporary memorials. The coins struck by Arsaces II. commence the Parthian series, and present to us a monarch of strongly-marked features, with a large eye, a prominent, slightly aquiline nose, a projecting chin, and an entire absence of hair. He wears upon his head a curious cap, or helmet, with lappets on either side that reach to the shoulders, and has around his fore-head and above his ears a coronal of pearls, apparently of a large size. On the reverse side of his coins he exhibits the figure of a man, seated on a sort of stool, and holding out in front of him a strung bow, with the string uppermost. This may be either a representation of himself in his war costume, or an ideal figure of a Parthian god, but is probably the former. Tiridates takes upon his coins the title either of " King," or of " Great King." The legend which they bear is Greek, as is that of almost all the kings his successors. The coins follow the Seleucid model.

Tiridates was an able and active monarch. He had the good fortune to hold the throne for a period of above thirty years, and had thus ample space for the development of his talents, and for completing the organisation of the kingdom. Having received Parthia from his brother in a somewhat weak and unsettled condition, he left it a united and powerful monarchy, enlarged in its boundaries, strengthened in its defences, in alliance with its nearest and most formidable neighbour, and triumphant over the great power of Syria, which had hoped to bring it once more into subjection. He witnessed some extra-ordinary movements, and conducted affairs during their progress with prudence and moderation. He was more than once brought into imminent danger, but succeeded in effectually protecting himself. He made a judicious use of the opportunities which the disturbed condition of Western Asia in his time presented to him, and might well be considered, as he was by many, a sort of second founder of the State.

It was within two years of the accession of Tiridates to the Parthian throne that one of those vast, but transient, revolutions to which Asia is subject, but which are rare occurrences in Europe, swept over Western Asia. Ptolemy Euergetes, the son of Philadelphus, having succeeded to his father's kingdom in B.C. 247, made war on Syria in B.C. 245, to avenge the murder of his sister Berenicé, to whose death the Syrian king, Seleucus II., had been a party. In the war which followed he at first carried everything before him. Having taken Antioch, he crossed the Euphrates, and, in the course of a couple of years, succeeded in effecting the conquest of Mesopotamia, Assyria, Babylonia, Susiana, Media, and Persia, while the smaller provinces, as far as Parthia and Bactria, submitted to him without resistance. He went in person, as he tells us, as far as Babylon, and, regarding his power as established, proceeded somewhat hastily to gather the fruits of victory, by compelling the conquered countries to surrender all the most valuable works of art which were to be found in them, and sending off the treasures to Egypt, for the adornment of Alexandria. He also levied heavy contributions on the countries which had submitted to him, and altogether treated them with a severity that was impolitic. Bactria and Parthia cannot but have felt considerable alarm at his victorious progress. Here was a young warrior who, in a single campaign, had marched the distance of a thousand miles from the banks of the Nile to those of the Lower Euphrates, without so much as receiving a check, and who was threatening to repeat the career of Alexander. What

resistance could the little Parthian state hope to offer
to him? It must have rejoiced the heart of Tiridates
to hear that, while the conqueror was reaping the
spoils of victory in his newly-subjugated provinces,
dangerous disturbances had broken out in his own
land, which had forced him to withdraw his troops
suddenly (B.C. 243), and evacuate the territory which
he had overrun. Thus his invasion proved to be a
raid rather than a real conquest, and, instead of
damaging Parthia, had rather the effect of improving
her position, and contributing to the advance of her
power. On Ptolemy's departure, Syria recovered her
sway over her lost provinces, and again stood forward
as Parthia's principal enemy; but she was less formidable than she had been previously; her hold over
her outlying dominions was relaxed, her strength was
crippled, her prestige lost, and her honour tarnished.
Tiridates saw in her depression his own opportunity,
and, suddenly invading Hyrcania, his near neighbour,
and Syria's most distant dependency, succeeded in
overrunning it and detaching it from the empire of
the Seleucidæ.

The gauntlet was thus thrown down to the Syrian
king, and a challenge given, which he was compelled
to accept, unless he was prepared to yield unresist-
ingly, one after another, all the fairest of his remaining
provinces. It was not likely that he would so act.
Seleucus II. was no coward. He had been engaged
in wars almost continuously from his accession, and,
though more than once defeated in battle, had never
shown the white feather. On learning the loss of
Hyrcania, he proceeded immediately to patch up a

peace with his brother, Antiochus Hierax, against whom he was at the time contending, and having collected a large army, marched away to the East. He did not, however, at once invade Parthia, but, deflecting his course to the right, entered into negotiations with the revolted Bactrian king, Diodotus, and made alliance with him against Tiridates. It may be supposed that he represented Tiridates as their common foe, as much a danger to Bactria as to Syria, the head of a movement, which was directed against Hellenism, and which aimed as much at putting down Bactrian rule as Syrian. At any rate, he succeeded in gaining Diodotus to his side ; and the confederate monarchs, having joined their forces, proceeded to invade the territory of the Parthian sovereign. Tiridates did not await their onset. Regarding himself as overmatched, he quitted his country, and fled northwards into the region between the Oxus and the Jaxartes, where he took refuge with a Scythic tribe, called the Aspasiacæ, which was powerful at this period. The Aspasiacæ, probably lent him troops, for he did not remain long in retirement ; but, hearing that the first Diodotus, the ally of Seleucus, had died, he contrived to draw over his son, Diodotus II., to his alliance, and, in conjunction with him, gave Seleucus battle, and completely defeated his army. Seleucus retreated hastily to Antioch, and resumed his struggle with his brother, whom he eventually overcame ; but, having learned wisdom by experience, he made no further attempts against either the Bactrian or the Parthian power.

This victory was with reason regarded by the Parthians as a sort of second beginning of their independence. Hitherto the kingdom had existed precariously, and as it were by sufferance. From the day that the revolt took place, it was certain that, some time or other, Syria would reclaim, and make an attempt to recover, its lost territory. Until a battle had been fought, until the new monarchy had measured its strength against that of its former mistress, it was impossible for any one to feel secure that it would be able to maintain its existence. The victory gained by Tiridates over Seleucus Callinicus put an end to these doubts. It proved to the world at large, as well as to the Parthians themselves, that they had nothing to fear—that they were strong enough to preserve their freedom. If we consider the enormous disproportion between the military strength and resources of the narrow Parthian state and the vast Syrian Empire—if we remember that the one comprised at this time about fifty thousand, and the other above a million of square miles ; that the one had inherited the wealth of ages, while the other was probably as poor as any province in Asia ; that the one possessed the Macedonian arms, training, and tactics, while the other knew only the rude warfare of the Steppes—the result of the struggle cannot but be regarded as surprising. Still, it was not without precedent ; and it has not been without repetition. It adds another to the many instances, where a small but brave people, bent on resisting foreign domination, have, when standing on their defence in their own territory, proved more than a match for the utmost force that a foe of overwhelming strength could bring against them. It reminds us of Marathon,

of Bannockburn, of Morgarten. We may not sympa-
thise wholly with the victors, for Greek civivisation,
even of the type introduced by Alexander into Asia,
was ill replaced by Tâtar coarseness and barbarism ;
but we cannot refuse our admiration to the spectacle
of a handful of gallant men determinedly resisting in
the fastnesses of their native land a host of aliens,
and triumphing over their would-be oppressors. The
Parthians themselves were so impressed with the importance of the conflict, that they preserved the memory
of it by a solemn festival on the anniversary of their
victory, which was still celebrated in the days of the
historian Trogus Pompeius.

It is possible that Seleucus would not have accepted
his defeat as final, or desisted from his attempt
to reduce Parthia to obedience, if he had felt perfectly free to continue or discontinue the Parthian
war at his pleasure. But, on his return to Antioch,
he found much to occupy him. His brother, Antiochus
Hierax, was still a rebel against his authority, and
the proceedings of Attalus, King of Pergamus, were
threatening. Seleucus was engaged in contests with
these two enemies from the time of his return from
Parthia (B.C. 237) almost to his death (B.C. 226). He
was thus compelled to leave Tiridates to take his own
course, and either occupy himself with fresh conquests,
or devote himself to the strengthening and adorning of
his existing kingdom, as he pleased. Tiridates chose
the latter course ; and during the remainder of his
long reign, for the space of above twenty years,
employed his leisure in useful labours within the
limits of his own territories. He erected a number

of strong forts, or castles, in suitable positions, fortified the Parthian towns generally, and placed garrisons in them, and carefully selected a site for a new city, which he probably intended to make, and perhaps actually made, his capital. The situation chosen was one in the mountain range known as Zapavortenon, where a hill was found, surrounded on all sides by precipitous rocks, and placed in the middle of a plain of extraordinary fertility. Abundant wood and copious streams of water existed in the neighbourhood. The soil was so rich that it scarcely required cultivation, and the woods were so full of game as to afford endless amusement to hunters. The city itself was called Dara, which the Greeks and Romans elongated into Dareium. Its exact site is undiscovered; but it seems to have lain towards the east, and was probably not very far from the now sacred city of Meshed.

We may account for the desire of Tiridates to establish a new capital by the natural antipathy of the Parthians to the Greeks, and the fact that Hecatompylos, which had been hitherto the seat of government, was a thoroughly Greek town, having been built by Alexander the Great, and peopled mainly by Grecian settlers. The Parthians disliked close contact with Hellenic manners and Hellenic ideas. Just as, in their most palmy days, they rejected Seleucia for their capital, and preferred to build the entirely new town of Ctesiphon in its immediate vicinity, as the residence of the Court and monarch, so even now, when their prosperity was but just budding, an instinctive feeling of repulsion caused them to shrink from sharing a locality with the Greeks, and make the experiment of having for their headquarters a city wholly their own. The experiment did not altogether succeed. Either Hecatompylos had natural advantages even greater than those of Dara, or, as the growth of the Parthian power was mainly towards the west, the eastward position of the latter was found inconvenient. After a short trial, the successors of Tiridates ceased to reside at Dara, and Hecatompylos became once more the Parthian capital and the seat of Parthian government.

Tiridates, having done his best, according to his

COIN OF ARTABANUS I.

lights, for the security of Parthia from without, and for her prosperity within, died peaceably after a reign which is reckoned at thirty-four years, and which lasted probably from B.C. 248 to B.C. 214. He left his throne to a son, named Artabanus, who, like his father, took the "throne-name" of Arsaces, and is known in history as Arsaces the Third.

Artabanus I., if we may judge by his coins, was not unlike his father in appearance, having the same projecting and slightly aquiline nose, and the same large eye ; but he differed from his father in possessing abundance of hair, and wearing a long beard. He has discarded, moreover, the cap of Tiridates, and, instead of it, wears his own hair, which he confines with a band (the diadem), passing from the forehead to the occiput, there knotted, and flowing down behind. He takes the later legend of his father—ΒΑΣΙΛΕΩΣ ΜΕΓΑΛΟΥ ΑΡΣΑΚΟΥ—"Arsaces, the Great King."

It was the aim of Artabanus to pursue his father's aggressive policy, and further enlarge the limits of the kingdom. He was scarcely settled upon the throne, when he declared war against Antiochus the Great, the second son of Seleucus Callinicus, who had inherited the Syrian crown in B.C. 223, and was entangled in a contest with one of the satraps of Asia Minor, named Achæus. Proceeding westward along the skirts of the mountains, he made his way to Ecbatana in Media, receiving the submission of the various countries as he went, and (nominally) adding to his dominions the entire tract between Hyrcania and the Zagros mountain chain. From this elevated position he threatened the low-lying countries of the Mesopotamian plain, and seemed likely, unless opposed, in another campaign to reach the Euphrates. The situation was most critical for Syria; and Antiochus, recognising his peril, bent all his energies to meet and overcome it. Fortunately he had just crushed Achæus, and was able, without greatly exposing himself to serious loss in the West, to collect and lead a vast expedition against the East. With an army of a hundred thousand foot and twenty thousand horse, he set out for Media in the spring of B.C. 213, recovered Ecbatana without a battle, and thence pressed eastward after his startled enemy, who retreated as he advanced. In vain Artabanus attempted to hinder his progress by stopping, or poisoning, the wells along the route which he had necessarily to take; Antiochus caught the poisoners at their work, and brushed them from his path. He then marched rapidly against Parthia, and entering the enemy's country, took and occupied without a battle the chief city, Hecatompylos.

Artabanus, bent on avoiding an engagement, re-treated into Hyrcania, perhaps flattering himself that his adversary would not venture to follow him into that rugged and almost inaccessible region. If so, however, he soon found that he had underrated the perseverance and tenacity of the Syrian king. Antiochus, after resting his army for a brief space at Hecatompylos, set out in pursuit of his enemy, crossed by a difficult pass, chiefly along the dry channel of a mountain torrent, obstructed by masses of rock and trunks of trees, the high ridge which separated be-tween Parthia and Hyrcania—his advance disputed by the Parthians at every step—fought and won a battle at the top, and thence descending into the rich Hyrcanian valley, endeavoured to take possession of the entire country. But Artabanus, brought to bay by his foe, defended himself with extraordinary courage and energy. One by one the principal Hyrcanian towns were besieged and taken, but the monarch himself was unsubdued. Carrying on a guerilla warfare, moving from place to place, occupy-ing one strong position after another, he continued his resistance with such dogged firmness that at length the patience of Antiochus was worn out, and he came to terms with his gallant adversary, conced-

ing to him that which was the real bone of contention, his independence. Parthia came out of the
struggle with the Great Antiochus unscathed : she did
not even have to relinquish her conquered dependency
of Hyrcania. Artabanus moreover had the honour of
being admitted into the number of the Great King's
allies. As for Antiochus, he turned his attention to
the affairs of Bactria, and the remoter East, and
having arranged them to his satisfaction, returned
by way of Arachosia, Drangiana, and Kerman to his
western possessions (B.C. 206).

The retirement of Antiochus, however honourable

COIN OF PRIAPATIUS.

to Parthia, must have left her weakened and exhausted by her vast and astonishing efforts. She
had been taxed almost beyond her strength, and must
have needed a breathing-space to recruit and recover
herself. Artabanus wisely remained at peace during
the rest of his reign ; and his son and successor, Priapatius, followed his example. It was not till B.C.
181 that the fifth Arsaces, Phraates I., son of Priapatius, having mounted the throne, resumed the policy
of aggression introduced by Tiridates, and further
extended the dominion of Parthia in the region south

of the Caspian. The great Antiochus was dead. His successor, Seleucus IV. (Philopator), was a weak and unenterprising prince, whom the defeat of Magnesia had cowed, and who regarded inaction as his only security. Aware probably of this condition of affairs, Phraates, early in his reign, invaded the country of the Mardi, which lay in the mountain tract south of the Caspian Sea, overran it, and added it to his territories. Successful thus far, he proceeded to make an encroachment on Media Rhagiana, the district between the Caspian Gates and Media Atropatêné, by occupying the tract immediately west of the Gates, and building there the important city of Charax, which he garrisoned with Mardians. This was an advance of the Parthian Terminus towards the west by a distance of nearly two hundred miles—an advance, not so much important in itself as in the indication which it furnished, at once of Parthian aggressiveness and of Syrian inability to withstand it. The conquests of Phraates added little either to the military strength or to the resources of his kingdom, but they were prophetic of the future. They foreshadowed that gradual waning of the Syrian and advance of the Parthian state, which is the chief fact of West Asian history in the two centuries immediately preceding our era, and which was to make itself startlingly apparent within the next few years, during the reign of the sixth Arsaces.

IV.

FIRST PERIOD OF EXTENSIVE CONQUEST—REIGN OF MITHRIDATES I.

MITHRIDATES THE FIRST, a brother of Phraates, was nominated to the kingly office by his predecessor, who had shown his affection for him during his life by assuming the title of "Philadelphus" upon his coins, and at his death passed over in his favour the claims of several sons. Undoubtedly, he was a born

COIN OF MITHRIDATES I.

"king of men"—pointed out by nature as fitter to rule than any other individual among his contemporaries. He had a physiognomy which was at once intelligent, strong, and dignified. He was ambitious, but not possessed of an ambition which was likely to "o'erleap itself"—strict, but not cruel—brave, energetic, a good general, an excellent administrator, a firm ruler. Parthia, under his government, advanced " by leaps and bounds." Receiving at his accession a kingdom but of narrow dimensions, confined apparently between the city of Charax on the one side and the river Arius, or Heri-rud, on the other, he transformed it, within the space of thirty-seven years—which was the time that his reign lasted—into a great and flourishing empire. It is not too much to say that, but for him, Parthia might have remained to the end a mere petty state on the outskirts of the Syrian kingdom, and, instead of becoming a rival to Rome, might have sunk after a short time into insignificance and obscurity.

To explain the circumstances under which this vast change—this revolution in the Asiatic balance of power — became possible, it is necessary that we should cast our eye over the general condition of Western Asia in the early part of the second century before our era, and especially consider the course of events in the two kingdoms between which Parthia intervened, the Bactrian and Syrian monarchies.

The Bactrian kingdom, as originally established by Diodotus, lay wholly to the north of the Paropamisus, in the long and broad valley of the Oxus, from its sources in the Pamir to its entrance on the Kharesmian Desert. The countries to the south of the range continued to be Syrian dependencies, and were reckoned by Seleucus Nicator as included within the limits of his dominion. But it was not long before the empire of Alexander in these parts began to crumble and decay. Indian princes, like Sandra-

cottus (Chandragupta) and Sophagasenus, asserted
their rights over the Region of the Five Rivers
(Punjab), and even over the greater portion of
Affghanistan. Greek dominion was swept away.
At the time when Bactria, having had its independence acknowledged by Antiochus the Great, felt
itself at liberty to embark in ambitious enterprises,
as Parthia had done, the Greco-Macedonian sway
over the tracts between Parthia and the Sutlej was
either swept away altogether, or reduced to a mere
shadow ; and Euthydemus, the third Bactrian
monarch, was not afraid of provoking hostilities
from Syria, when, about B.C. 205, he began his
aggressions in this direction. Under him, and under
his son and successor, Demetrius, in the twenty years
between B.C. 205 and B.C. 185, Bactrian conquest was
pushed as far as the Punjab region, Cabul and Candahar were overrun, and the southern side of the
mountains occupied from the Heri-rud to the Indus.
Eucratidas, who succeeded Demetrius (about B.C. 180),
extended his sway still further into the Punjab region,
but with unfortunate results, so far as his original
territories were concerned. Neglected, and comparatively denuded of troops, these districts began to slip
from his grasp. The Scythian nomads of the Steppes
saw their opportunity, and bursting into Bactria,
harried it with fire and sword, even occupying portions, and settling themselves in the Oxus valley.

While matters were thus progressing in the East,
and the Bactrian princes, attempting enterprises
beyond their strength, were exhausting rather than
advantaging the kingdom under their sway, the

Seleucid monarchs in the West were also becoming more and more entangled in difficulties, partly of their own creation, partly brought about by the ambition of pretenders. Antiochus the Great, shortly after his return from the eastern provinces, became embroiled with the Romans (B.C. 196), who dealt his power a severe blow by the defeat of Magnesia (B.C. 190), and further weakened it by the support which they lent to the kings of Pergamus, which was now the ruling state in Asia Minor. The weakness of Antiochus encouraged Armenia to revolt, and so lost Syria another province (B.C. 189). Troubles began to break out in Elymaïs, consequent upon the exactions of the Seleucidæ (B.C. 187). Eleven years later (B.C. 176) there was a lift of the clouds, and Syria seemed about to recover herself through the courage and energy of the fourth Antiochus (Epiphanes) ; but the hopes raised by his successes in Egypt (B.C. 171–168) and Armenia (B.C. 165) were destroyed by his unwise conduct towards the Jews, whom his persecuting policy permanently alienated, and erected into a hostile state upon his southern border (B.C. 168–160). Epiphanes having not only plundered and desecrated the Temple, but having set himself to eradicate utterly the Jewish religion, and completely Hellenise the people, was met with the most determined resistance on the part of a moiety of the nation. A patriotic party rose up under devoted leaders, who asserted, and in the end secured, the independence of their country. Not alone during t⁻ ⁻⁻maining years of Epiphanes, but for half a centu.y ⸱⸱⸱ death, throughout seven reigns, the struggle continued ; Judæa taking advantage of every trouble and difficulty in Syria to detach herself more and more completely from her oppressor, and being a continued thorn in her side, a constant source of weakness, preventing more than anything else the recovery of her power. The triumph which Epiphanes had obtained in the distant Armenia, where he defeated and captured the king, Artaxias, was a poor set-off against the foe which he had created for himself at his doors through his cruelty and intolerance. Nor did the removal of Epiphanes (B.C. 164) improve the condition of affairs in Syria. The throne fell to his son, Antiochus V. (Eupator), a boy of nine, according to one authority, or, according to another, of twelve years of age. The regent, Lysias, exercised the chief power, and was soon engaged in a war with the Jews, whom the death of the oppressor had encouraged to fresh efforts. The authority of Lysias was further disputed by a certain Philip, whom Epiphanes, shortly before his death, had made tutor to the young monarch. The claim of this tutor to the regent's office being supported by a considerable portion of the army, a civil war arose between him and Lysias, which raged for the greater part of two years, terminating in the defeat and death of Philip (B.C. 162). But Syrian affairs did not even then settle down into tranquillity. A prince of the Seleucid house, Demetrius by name, the son of Seleucus IV., and consequently the first cousin of Eupator, was at this time detained in Rome as a hostage, having been sent there during his father's lifetime, as a security for his fidelity. Demetrius, with some reason, regarded

his claim to the Syrian throne as better than that of
his cousin, who was the son of the younger brother;
and, being in the full vigour of early youth, he determined to assert his pretensions in Syria, and to make
a bold stroke for the crown.   Having failed to obtain
the Senate's consent to his quitting Italy, he took his
departure secretly, crossed the Mediterranean in a
Carthaginian vessel, and landing in Asia, succeeded
within a few months in establishing himself as Syrian
monarch.

From this review of the condition of affairs in the
Syrian and Bactrian kingdoms during the first half
of the second century before Christ, it is sufficiently
apparent, that in both countries the state of things
was favourable to any aspirations which the power
that lay between them might entertain after dominion
and self-aggrandisement.   The kings of the two
countries indeed, at the time of the accession of
Mithridates to the Parthian throne (B.C. 174), were,
both of them, energetic and able princes, but the
Syrian monarch was involved in difficulties at home
which required all his attention, while the Bactrian
was engaged in enterprises abroad which equally
engrossed and occupied him.   Mithridates might
have attacked either with a good prospect of success.
Personally, he was at least their equal, and though
considerably inferior in military strength and resources, he possessed the great advantage of having
a perfectly free choice both of time and place, could
seize the most unguarded moment, and make his
attack in the quarter where he knew that he would
be least expected and least likely to find his enemy

on the alert. Circumstances, of which we now cannot appreciate the force, seem to have determined him to direct his first attack against the territories of his eastern neighbour, the Bactrian king, Eucratidas. These, as we have seen, were left comparatively unguarded, while their ambitious master threw all his strength into his Indian wars, pressing through Cabul into the Punjab region, and seeking to extend his dominion to the Sutlej river, or even to the Ganges. Naturally, Mithridates was successful. Attacking the Bactrian territory where it adjoined Parthia, he made himself master, without much difficulty, of two provinces—those of Turiûa and of Aspionus. Turiûa recalls the great but vague name of "Turanian," which certainly belongs to these parts, but can scarcely be regarded as local. Aspionus has been regarded as the district of the Aspasiacæ; but the two words do not invite comparison. It is best to be content with saying that we cannot locate the districts conquered, but that they should be looked for in the district of the Tejend and Heri-rud, between the Paropamisus and the great city of Balkh.

It does not appear that Eucratidas attempted any retaliation. Absorbed in his schemes of Indian conquest, he let his home provinces go, and sought compensation for them only in the far East. Meantime Mithridates, having been successful in his Bactrian aggression, and thus whetted his appetite for territorial gain, determined on a more important expedition. After waiting for a few years, until Epiphanes was dead, and the Syrian throne occupied by the boy king, Eupator, while the two claimants of the regency, Lysias and Philip, were contending in arms for the supreme power, he suddenly marched with a large force towards the West, and fell upon the great province of Media Magna, which, though still nominally a Syrian dependency, was under the rule of a king, and practically, if not legally, independent. Media was a most extensive and powerful country. Polybius calls it "the most powerful of all the kingdoms of Asia, whether we consider the extent of the territory, or the number and quality of the men, or the goodness of the horses produced there. For these animals," he says, "are found in it in such abundance, that almost all the rest of Asia is supplied with them from this province. It is here also that the Royal horses are always fed, on account of the excellence of the pasture." The capital of the province was now, as in the more ancient times, Ecbatana, situated on the declivity of Mount Orontes (Elwand), and, though fallen from its former grandeur, yet still a place of much importance, second only in all Western Asia to Antioch and perhaps Babylon. The invasion of Mithridates was stoutly resisted by the Medes, and several engagements took place, in which sometimes one and sometimes the other side had the advantage ; but eventually the Parthians prevailed. Mithridates seized and occupied Ecbatana, which was at the time an unwalled town, established his authority over the whole region, and finally placed it under the government of a Parthian satrap, Bacasis, while he himself returned home, to crush a revolt which had broken out.

The scene of the revolt was Hyrcania. The Hyrcanian people, one markedly Arian, had probably from the time of their subjugation chafed under the Parthian yoke, and seeing in the absence of Mithridates, with almost the whole of his power, in Media a tempting opportunity, had resolved to make a bold stroke for freedom before the further growth of Parthia should render such an attempt hopeless. We are not told that they had any special grievances ; but they were brave and high-spirited ; they had enjoyed exceptional privileges under the Persians ; and no doubt they found the rule of a Turanian people galling and oppressive. They may well have expected to receive support and assistance from the other Arian nations in their neighbourhood, as the Mardi, the Sagartians, the Arians on the Heri-rud, &c., and they may have thought that Mithridates would be too fully occupied with his Median struggle to have leisure to direct his arms against them. But the event showed that they had miscalculated. Media submitted to Mithridates without any very protracted resistance ; the Parthian monarch knew the value of time, and, quitting Media, marched upon Hyrcania without losing a moment ; the other Arian tribes of the vicinity were either apathetic or timid, and did not stir a step for their relief. The insurrection was nipped in the bud ; Hyrcania was forced to submit, and became for centuries the obedient vassal of her powerful neighbour.

The conquest of Media had brought the Parthians into contact with the important country of Susiana or Elymaïs, an ancient seat of power, and one which had flourished much during the whole of the Persian period, having contained within it the principal Persian capital, Susa. This tract possessed strong attractions for a conqueror ; and it appears to have been not very long after he had succeeded in crushing the Hyrcanian revolt, that Mithridates once more turned his arms westward, and from the advantageous position which he held in Media, directed an attack upon the rich and flourishing province which lay to the south. It would seem that Elymaïs, like Media, though reckoned a dependency of the Seleucid Empire, had a king of its own, who was entrusted with its government and defence, and expected to fight his own battles. At any rate we do not hear of any aid being rendered to the Elymæans in this war, or of Mithridates having any other antagonist to meet in the course of it, besides " the Elymæan king." This monarch he defeated without difficulty, and, having overrun his country, apparently in a single campaign, added the entire territory to his dominions.

Elymaïs was interposed between two regions of first-rate importance, Babylonia and Persia. The thorough mastery of any one of the three, commonly carried with it in ancient times dominion over the other two. So far as can be gathered from the scanty materials which we possess for Parthian history at this period, the conquest of Elymaïs was followed almost immediately by the submission of Babylonia and Persia to the conqueror. Media and Elymaïs having been forced to submit, the great Mithridates was very shortly acknowledged as their sovereign lord by all the countries that intervened between the Paropamisus and the Lower Euphrates.

Thus gloriously successful in this quarter, Mithridates, who may fairly be considered the greatest monarch of his day, after devoting a few years to repose, judged that the time was come for once more embarking on a career of aggression, and seeking a similar extension of his dominions towards the East to that which he had found it so easy to effect in the regions of the West. The Bactrian troubles had increased. Eucratidas, after greatly straining the resources of Bactria in his Indian wars, had been waylaid and murdered on his return from one of them by his son Heliocles, who chose to declare him a public enemy, drove his chariot over his corpse, and ordered it to be left unburied. This ill beginning inaugurated an unfortunate reign. Attacked by Scythians from the north, by Indians and Sarangians on the east and the south-east, Heliocles had already more on his hands than he could conveniently manage, when Mithridates declared war against him, and marched into his country (about B.C. 150). Already exhausted by his other wars, Heliocles could bear up no longer. Mithridates rapidly overran his dominions, and took possession of the greater part of them. According to some he did not stop here, but pressing still further eastward invaded India, and carried his arms over the Punjab to the banks of the Hydaspes. But this last advance, if it ever took place, was a raid rather than an attempt at conquest. It had no serious results. Indo-Bactrian kingdoms continued to exist in Çabul down to about B.C. 80, when Hellenism in this quarter was finally swept away by the Yue-chi and other Scythic tribes. The Parthian Empire never included any portion of the Indus region, its furthest provinces towards the east being Bactria, Aria, Sarangia, Arachosia, and Sacastana.

The great increase of power which Mithridates had obtained by his conquests could not be a matter of indifference to the Syrian monarchs. But their domestic troubles—the contentions between Philip and Lysias, between Lysias and Demetrius Soter, Soter and Alexander Balas, Balas and Demetrius II., Demetrius II. and Tryphon—had so engrossed them for twenty years (from B.C. 162 to B.C. 142), that they had felt it impossible, or hopeless, to attempt any expedition towards the East, for the protection or recovery of their provinces. Mithridates had been allowed to pursue his career of conquest unopposed, so far as the Syrians were concerned, and to establish his sway from the Hindu Kush to the Euphrates. A time, however, at last came when home dangers were less absorbing, and a prospect of engaging the terrible Parthians with success seemed to present itself. The second Demetrius had not, indeed, altogether overcome his domestic enemy, Tryphon ; but he had so far brought him into difficulties as to believe that he might safely be left to be dealt with by his wife, Cleopatra, and by his captains. At the same time, the condition of affairs in the East seemed to invite his interference. Mithridates ruled his new conquests with some strictness, probably suspecting their fidelity, and determined that he would not by any remissness allow them to escape from his grasp.

The native inhabitants could scarcely be much attached to the Syro-Macedonians, who had certainly not treated them with much tenderness ; but a possession of one hundred and ninety years' duration confers prestige in the East, and a strange yoke may have galled more than one to whose pressure they had become accustomed. Moreover, all the provinces which the Parthians had taken from Syria contained Greek towns, and their inhabitants might at all times be depended on to side with their countrymen against the Asiatics. At the present conjuncture, too, the number of the malcontents was swelled by the addition of the recently subdued Bactrians, who hated the Parthian yoke, and longed for an opportunity of recovering their freedom.

Thus, when Demetrius II., anxious to escape the reproach of inertness, determined to make a great expedition upon the formidable Parthian monarch, who ruled over all the countries between the Paropamisus and the Lower Euphrates, he found himself welcomed as a deliverer by a considerable number of his enemy's subjects, whom the harshness or the novelty of the Parthian rule had offended. The malcontents joined his standard as he advanced ; and supported, as he thus was, by Persian, Elymæan, and Bactrian contingents, he engaged and defeated the Parthians in several battles. Mithridates at last, recognising his inferiority in military strength, determined to have recourse to stratagem, and having put Demetrius off his guard by proposals of peace, made a sudden attack upon him, completely defeated his army, and took him prisoner. The conquered monarch was at

first treated with some harshness, being conveyed
about to the several nations which had revolted, and
paraded before each in turn, to show them how
foolish they had been in lending him their aid ; but
when this purpose had been answered, Mithridates
showed himself magnanimous, gave his royal captive
the honours befitting his rank, assigned him a
residence in Hyrcania, and even gave him the hand
of his daughter, Rhodoguné, in marriage. It was
policy, however, still more than clemency, which
dictated this conduct. Mithridates nurtured designs against the Syrian kingdom itself, and saw
that it would be for his advantage to have a Syrian
prince in his camp, allied to him by marriage, whom
he could put forward as entitled to the throne, and
whom, if his enterprise succeeded, he might leave to
govern Syria for him, as tributary monarch. These
far-reaching plans might perhaps have been crowned
with success, had the head which conceived them
been spared to watch over and direct their execution.
But Providence decreed otherwise. Mithridates had
reached an advanced age, and, being attacked by
illness soon after his capture of Demetrius, found his
strength insufficient to battle with his malady, and,
to the great grief of his subjects, succumbed to it
(B.C. 136), after an eventful and glorious reign of
thirty-eight years.

V.

GOVERNMENTAL SYSTEM OF MITHRIDATES I.— LAWS AND INSTITUTIONS.

THE Parthian institutions had, no doubt, their roots in that early condition of society among the inhabitants of the Caspian region, which belongs to the twilight, rather than to the dawn of history, and which has to be conjectured or divined rather than worked out from the statements of ancient writers. From time immemorial this region has been mainly occupied by nomadic tribes, for whom alone it is fitted, and has been divided up among a number of races more or less closely allied, and generally very similar in character. Constant wars and raids occupy such races. Every man has to be a warrior ; and their conduct in war marks out a comparatively few for leaders, the mass for mere soldiery. Hence, something like a feudal organisation naturally prevails. The leader in war is the chieftain or noble in peace. An aristocracy forms itself, round which the " villeins " or " serfs " are grouped. When, in course of time, some specially perilous war threatens, or some enterprise is taken in hand of more than usual magnitude and gravity, the need of a directing hand

is felt—the confederacy of chiefs recognises the
weakness of a confederacy—and by common consent
a single individual is selected as King, Great Khan,
Dictator, Governor, Commander-in-chief. Thus, in
such a state of society as has been described,
monarchy makes its appearance. The fittest to
command and direct is placed at the head of affairs,
given some title or other implying authority, and
accepted by the general body of chiefs as their
suzerain.

But in conceding this authority to the necessities
of the case, the chiefs are careful to reserve to themselves considerable powers, and the result is thus a
limited monarchy. In Parthia, the king was permanently advised by two councils, consisting of
persons not of his own nomination, whom rights,
conferred by birth or office, entitled to their high
positions. One of these was a family conclave
(*concilium domesticum*), or assembly of full-grown
males of the Royal House; the other was a Senate
comprising both the spiritual and the temporal chiefs
of the nation, the " Sophi," or " Wise Man," and the
" Magi," or " Priests." Together these two bodies
constituted the Megistanes, the "Nobles," or " Great
Men "—the privileged class which, to a considerable
extent, checked and controlled the monarch. The
monarchy was elective, but only in the house of the
Arsacidæ; and the concurrent vote of both councils
was necessary to the election of a new king. Practically, the ordinary law of hereditary descent appears
to have been commonly followed, unless in the case
where a king left no son of sufficient age to exercise

the royal office. Under such circumstances, the Megistanes usually nominated the late king's next brother to succeed him, or, if he had left no brother, went back to an uncle. When the line of succession had once been changed, the right of the elder branch was lost, and did not revive, unless the branch preferred died out or possessed no member qualified to rule. When a king had been duly nominated by the two councils, the right of placing the crown upon his head belonged to the Surena, the "Field-Marshal," or "Commander-in-chief of the Parthian armies." The Megistanes further claimed, and sometimes exercised, the right of deposing a monarch whose conduct displeased or dissatisfied them ; but an attempt to exercise this privilege naturally, and almost necessarily, led to a civil war, since no monarch was likely to accept his deposition without a struggle ; and thus it was force, and not right, which practically determined whether a deposed king should lose his crown or no.

After a monarch had been once elected, and firmly fixed upon the throne, the power which he wielded appears to have been very nearly despotic. At any rate, he could put to death without a trial whomsoever he chose ; and adult members of the Royal House, who ventured to provoke the reigning monarch's jealousy, were constantly so treated. But probably it would have been more risky to arouse the fears of the "Sophi" or "Magi." The latter especially were a powerful body, consisting of an organised hierarchy which had come down from ancient times, and was feared and venerated by all

classes of the people. Their numbers at the close of
the empire, counting adult males only, are reckoned
at eighty thousand ; they possessed considerable
tracts of fertile land, and were the sole inhabitants of
many large towns or villages, which they were permitted to govern as seemed good to them. The
arbitrary power of the monarchs must, in practice,
have been largely checked by the privileges of this
numerous priestly class, of which it would seem that,
in the later times, they became jealous, thereby
preparing the way for their own downfall.

The dominion of the Parthians over the provinces,
which Mithridates and earlier kings had conquered,
was maintained by reverting to the system which had
prevailed generally throughout the East before the
accession of the Achæmenian Persians to power, and
which is the simplest and rudest of all possible
empire organisations. This was the system of
establishing in the various countries either viceroys,
holding office for life, or else dependent dynasties of
kings. In either case, the rulers, so long as they paid
their tribute regularly to the Parthian monarchs, and
furnished the contingents required of them for the
wars in which Parthia was almost always engaged,
were allowed to govern the people under their sway
at their pleasure. Among monarchs, in the higher
sense of the term, who nevertheless were vassals to
Parthia, may be enumerated the kings of Persia,
Elymaïs, Adiabênê, Osrhoënê, and of Armenia and
Media Atropatênê, when they formed, as they sometimes did, portions of the Parthian Empire. The
viceroys, who governed the other provinces, bore the

title of Vitaxæ, or Bistakes, and were fourteen or fifteen in number. The remark has been made by perhaps the greatest of English historians, Gibbon, that the system thus established " exhibited under other names, a lively image of the feudal system, which has since prevailed in Europe." The comparison is of some value, as pointing out an analogy which might otherwise have been overlooked ; but, like most historical parallels it is inexact, the points of difference between the Parthian and the feudal systems being probably more numerous than those of resemblance, but the points of resemblance being very main points, not few in number, and striking. It was with special reference to the system thus established that the Parthian monarchs took the title of " King of Kings "—ΒΑΣΙΛΕΥΣ ΒΑΣΙΛΕΩΝ—so frequent upon their coins—a title exchanged, but in one instance only, for " Satrap of Satraps "—ΣΑΤΡΑΠΗΣ ΤΩΝ ΣΑΤΡΑΠΩΝ. The title " King of Kings " naturally appears first on the coins of Mithridates.

In the Parthian system there was one anomaly of a very curious character. The Grecian cities which were scattered in large numbers throughout the empire, foundations of Alexander or his successors, enjoyed a municipal government of their own, and in some cases were almost independent communities, the Parthian kings exercising over them little or no control. The great city of Seleucia upon the Tigris was the most important of these places ; its population was estimated in the first century after Christ at six hundred thousand souls ; it had strong walls, and was surrounded by a most fertile territory. Tacitus tells us that it had its own senate, or municipal council of three hundred members, elected by the inhabitants to rule over them, from among the wealthiest and best educated of the citizens. Under ordinary circumstances it enjoyed the blessing of complete self-government, and was entirely free from Parthian interference, paying no doubt its appointed tribute, but otherwise holding the position of a " free city." It was only in the case of internal dissensions that these advantages were lost, and the Parthian soldiery, invited within the walls, arranged the quarrels of parties, and settled the constitution of the State at its pleasure. Privileges of a similar character, though probably less extensive, belonged, it would seem, to most of the other Greek cities, at least seventy in number, contained within the empire. The Parthian monarchs thought it politic to favour them ; and their practice in this respect justified the title of " Phil-Hellene," which they were fond of assuming upon their coins. On the whole, the policy may have been wise, but it diminished the unity of the empire, and there were times when serious danger arose from it. The Syro-Macedonian monarchs could always count with certainty on having powerful friends in Parthia, anxious to render them assistance, whatever portion of it they invaded ; and even the Romans, though their ethnic connection with the cities was not so close, were sometimes indebted to them for aid of an important kind.

Another anomaly of a similar character, but of less importance, since the number of persons which it affected cannot have been nearly so great, was the position occupied by the Jewish communities within the Parthian state. These, though far less numerous than the Grecian, were still not infrequent, and their location in some of the most considerable cities of the empire gave them a consequence which makes it necessary that they should not be overlooked. In Babylon, in Seleucia, in Ctesiphon, and in other principal towns, as Susa probably, and Rhages, there was so large a Jewish element in the population, that it had been thought best to give them municipal independence, the power to elect magistrates, and perhaps a special quarter in each town to dwell in. There were also a certain number of places the inhabitants of which were wholly Jews, and these enjoyed similar privileges with the "free towns" of the Greeks. Hence another element of weakness in the organisation of the empire, wherein an amalgamation of races, or even a thorough consolidation was impossible. The worst results showed themselves in the towns with mixed populations, where, from time to time, the most fearful disturbances broke out, often terminating in horrible massacres.

A Greek author of the Augustan age tells us, that the Great Mithridates, after effecting his conquests, made a collection of the best laws which he found to prevail among the various subject peoples, and imposed them on the Parthian nation. This statement is, no doubt, an exaggeration; but we may attribute to Mithridates with some reason, the introduction at this time of various practices and usages, whereby the Parthian Court was assimilated to those of the earlier Great Monarchies of Asia, and became

in the eyes of foreigners the successor and representative of the old Assyrian and Persian kingdoms.
The assumption of new titles and of a new state—the
organisation of the Court on a new plan—the bestowal
of a new character on the subordinate officers of the
empire, were suitable to the new phase of its life on
which the monarchy had now entered, and may with
the highest probability, if not with absolute certainty,
be assigned to this period.

It has been already noticed that Mithridates I.
appears to have been the first Parthian sovereign
who took the sounding title of " King of Kings." The
title had been a favourite one with the old Assyrian
and Persian monarchs, but was not adopted either by
the Seleucidæ or by the Greek kings of Bactria. Its
revival implied a distinct pretension to that mastery
of Western Asia, which had belonged of old to the
Assyrians and Persians, and which was, in later times,
formally claimed by Artaxerxes, the son of Babek,
the founder of the New Persian Kingdom. Previous
Parthian monarchs had been content to call themselves " the King," or " the Great King "—Mithridates
I. is " the King of Kings, the great and illustrious
Arsaces " — ΒΑΣΙΛΕΩΣ ΒΑΣΙΛΕΩΝ ΜΕΓΑΛΟΥ
ΑΡΣΑΚΟΥ ΕΠΙΦΑΝΟΥΣ.

At the same time Mithridates appears to have
assumed the tiara, or tall stiff crown which, with
certain modifications in its shape, had been the mark
of sovereignty, both under the Assyrians and under
the Persians. Previously the royal headdress had
been either a mere cap of a Scythic type, pointed, but
lower than the Scyths usually wore it, or the ordinary

diadem, which was a band encircling the head, and
terminating in two long ribbons or ends, that hung
down behind the head on the back. According to
Herodian, the diadem, in the later times, was double;
but the coins of Parthia do not exhibit this peculiarity.
The cap of the first king is ornamented with pendant
pearls in front; the stiff tiara of Mithridates has three
rows of pearls sewn on to it.

Ammianus Marcellinus tells us that among the
titles assumed by the Parthian monarchs was that
of "Brother of the Sun and Moon." The Shahs of
modern Persia still claim the epithet. It is ordinarily
used, not so much by themselves, as by their courtiers
and subjects, in the language of compliment, and this
may have been to some extent the case in Parthia.
Still, there is reason to believe that in the minds of
men at the time, something of a divine character was
regarded as attaching to the Arsacid race. In the
civil contentions, which form so main a feature of the
later history, combatants abstained from lifting their
hands knowingly against one of the royal stock,
since to kill or wound one was looked upon as a
sacrilege. The actual name of Θεὸς, "God," was even
assumed as a title by at least one of the kings, and a
favourite epithet upon the coins is θεοπάτωρ, which
implies the divinity of the king's father. After his
death the monarch seems generally to have been the
object of a qualified worship; statues were erected
to him in the temples, where they were apparently
associated with the images of the Sun-God and the
Moon-God.

No account of the Parthian Court has come down

to us that is either complete or altogether trustworthy ; but some particulars may be gathered of it from the scattered notices of various ancient writers, on which we may place reliance. The best authorities are agreed that it was not stationary, but migrated at different times of the year to different cities of the empire, in this respect resembling the Court of the Achæmenians. It is not quite clear, however, which of the cities were thus honoured. Ctesiphon was undoubtedly one of them. All writers agree that it was the chief city of the empire, and the ordinary seat of the government. Here, according to Strabo, the kings passed the winter months, delighting in the excellence of the air. The town was situated on the left bank of the Tigris, opposite to Seleucia, twelve or thirteen miles below the modern Baghdad. Pliny says that it was built by the Parthians in order to reduce Seleucia to insignificance, and that when it failed of its purpose, they built another city, Vologesocerta, in the same neighbourhood with the same object ; but the account of Strabo is more probable— namely, that it grew up gradually out of the wish of the Parthian kings to spare Seleucia the unpleasantness of having the rude soldiery, which followed the Court from place to place, quartered upon them. The remainder of the year, according to the same authority, was spent by the Parthian monarchs either at the Median city of Ecbatana, which is the modern Hamadan, or in the province of Hyrcania. In Hyrcania the palace, Strabo says, was at Tapé ; and between this place and Ecbatana he appears to have regarded the monarchs as spending the whole time which was not passed at Ctesiphon. Athenæus, however, declares that Rhages, near the Caspian Gates, was the spring residence of the Parthian kings; and it seems not unlikely that this famous city, which Isidore of Charax, writing in Parthian times, calls "the greatest in Media," was among the occasional residences of the Court. Parthia itself was, it would seem, deserted; but still a city of that region preserved in one respect a royal character, being the place where all the earlier monarchs were interred. Ultimately Arbela became the royal burying-place.

The pomp and grandeur of the Parthian kings are described only in the vaguest terms by the Greek and Roman writers. No author of repute, whose remains have come down to us, appears to have visited the Parthian Court. We may perhaps best obtain a true notion of the splendour of the sovereign from the accounts which have reached us of his relations and great officers, who can have reflected only faintly the magnificence of the sovereign. Plutarch tells us that the general whom Orodes deputed to conduct the war against Crassus came into the field accompanied by two hundred litters wherein were contained his concubines, and by a thousand camels which carried his baggage. His dress was the long flowing robe of the ancient Medes; he wore his hair parted down the middle, and had his face painted with cosmetics. A body of ten thousand horse, composed entirely of his clients and slaves, followed him in battle. We may conclude from this picture, and from the general tenor of the classical notices, that the Arsacidæ revived and maintained very much such a Court as that of the old Achæmenian princes, falling probably somewhat below their model in general politeness and refinement, but equalling it in luxury, in extravagant expenditure, and in display. Moreover, in one respect, an advance was made beyond the limits of Achæmenian civilisation. The theatrical representations introduced into Asia by the Greeks proved extraordinarily attractive to the semi-barbaric race, unacquainted hitherto with any such performances. The Greek language and literature were so far studied as to render the representation of Greek dramas intelligible to the upper classes. " An exotic literature and a gaudy theatre flourished at Seleucia under the royal patronage, the ritual ceremonies of the most graceful of superstitions were too closely interwoven with the forms of the Grecian drama not to follow in its train. The Court of Seleucia presented a motley combination of the manners of different ages and countries, only to be paralleled, perhaps, in the semi-European fashions of St. Petersburg and Moscow." [1]

But if, at their Court, the Parthian kings thus tolerated, or even encouraged, luxurious habits and enervating amusements, among the bulk of the nation the very opposite characteristics prevailed. The taint of their Scythian origin always clung to the Parthian people. They had always about them, as Strabo notes, "much that was barbaric and Scythic." The organisation of their army was very rude. Each chieftain brought into the field, like the nobles of the Middle Ages, an indefinite and probably uncounted contingent of retainers, armed as their means allowed

[1] See Merivale, " Roman Empire," vol. ii. pp. 3, 4.

them—some, the richest, in coats of scale or chain armour, and mounted on steeds similarly protected, carrying, besides the universal bow and arrows, a long spear or pike—others lightly equipped, without armour, and carrying nothing but a bow and arrows, with a short sword or knife. Of these last, a portion only were mounted, while the remainder served on foot. When the contingents united, the troops were simply massed together, according to their character, into three bodies—the heavy cavalry, the light cavalry, and the foot. There were no divisions corresponding to the Roman legions, or our regiments ; and, apparently, no petty officers, each contingent simply obeying its chief. When he went out to battle with his army, the king was, of course, Commander-in-chief. In his absence, his place was taken by a Surena, or field-marshal, appointed by him to the command. There was, however a chief Surena, whose office was hereditary, and who, besides commanding in the field, was a great State official.

Such seems to have been the general character of those practices and institutions which distinguished the Parthians from the foundation of their empire by Mithridates. Some of them, it is probable, he rather adopted than invented ; but there is no good reason for doubting that of many he was the originator. He appears to have been one of those rare individuals to whom it has been given to unite the powers and capacities which form the conqueror with those which constitute the successful organiser of a State. Brave and enterprising in war, prompt to seize an occasion and skilful to turn it to the best advantage, not even averse to severities when they seemed to be required, he yet felt no acrimony towards those who had resisted his arms, but was ready to befriend them as soon as their resistance ceased. Mild, clement, philanthropic, he conciliated those whom he subdued almost more easily than he subdued them, and by the efforts of a few years succeeded in welding together a dominion which lasted without suffering serious mutilation for nearly four centuries. Though not formally dignified with the epithet of "Great," he was beyond all question the greatest of the Parthian monarchs. Later times did him more justice than his contemporaries ; and, when the names of almost all the other kings had sunk into oblivion, retained his in honour, and placed it on a par with that of the original founder of Parthian independence. "The Parthians,' says Agathias, "though a subject nation, and previously of very little reputation, put an end to the dominion of the Macedonians, and subsequently became lords of the whole empire except Egypt, Arsaces first of all beginning the rebellion, and Mithridates not very long afterwards exalting the Parthian name to a high pitch of glory."

VI.

LAST STRUGGLE WITH SYRIA—DEFEAT AND DEATH OF ANTIOCHUS SIDETES.

THE death of Mithridates, and the accession of a comparatively unenterprising successor, Phraates II., encouraged Syria to make one more effort to thrust the Parthians back into their native wilds, and to recover the dominion of Western Asia. So great a position was not a thing to be surrendered without

COIN OF PHRAATES II.

a final, even if it were a despairing, struggle ; and in the actual position of affairs it was quite open to question whether, on the whole, Parthia or Syria were the stronger. The dominion of both countries was comparatively recent ; neither had any firm hold on its outlying provinces ; neither could claim to have conciliated to itself the affections of the Western Asiatics generally, or to rest its power on any other basis than that of military force. And in military force it was uncertain which way the balance inclined. Both countries had a nucleus of native troops, on which absolute reliance might be placed, which was brave, faithful, stanch, and would contend to the death for their respective sovereigns. But, beyond this, both had also a fluctuating body of unwilling subjects or subject-allies, unworthy of implicit trust, and likely to gravitate to one side or the other, according as hope, or fancy, or the merest caprice might decide. The chances of victory or defeat turned mainly on this fluctuating body, the instability of which had been amply proved in the wars of the last half-century. Those wars themselves, taken as a whole, had manifested no decided preponderance of either people over the other; at one time Parthia, at another Syria, had been hard pressed; and it was natural for the leaders on either side to believe that accidental circumstances, rather than any marked superiority of one of the two peoples over the other, had brought about the results that had been reached.

In the last war that had been waged success had finally rested with Parthia. An entire army had been destroyed, and the Syrian monarch captured. Demetrius " the Conqueror," as he called himself, was expiating in the cold and rugged region of Hyrcania, the rashness which had led him to deem himself a match for the craft and strategic skill of Mithridates. But now a new and untried monarch was upon the throne—one who was clearly without his father's ambition, and probably lacked his ability. Settled in his kingdom for the space of six years, he had not only attempted nothing against Syria, but had engaged in no military enterprise whatever. Yet the condition of Syria had been such as to offer the strongest possible temptation to a neighbour possessed of courage and energy. Civil war had raged, and exhausted the resources of the country, from B.C. 146 to 137, after which there had been a protracted struggle between the Syrians and the Jews (B.C. 137–133), in which the Syrian arms had at first been worsted, but had at length asserted their superiority. Had Phraates II., the son and successor of Mithridates, inherited a tenth part of his father's military spirit, he would have taken advantage of this troubled time to carry the war into Syria Proper, and might have shaken the Syrian throne to its base, or even wholly overturned it. In the person of the captured Demetrius, he possessed one whom he might have set up as a pretender with a certainty of drawing many Syrians to his side, and whom he might, if successful, have left to rule as Vitaxa, or subject king, the country of which he had once been actual monarch. But Phraates had no promptitude, no enterprise. He let all the opportunities which offered themselves escape him, content to keep watch on Demetrius—when he escaped from confinement, to pursue and retake him—and to hold him in reserve as a force of which he might one day make use, when it seemed to him that the fitting time was come for it.

The result of his long procrastination was, that the war, when renewed, was renewed from the other side. Antiochus Sidetes, who had succeeded to the Syrian throne on the captivity of his brother, Demetrius, and had taken to wife his brother's wife, Cleopatra, having crushed the pretender, Tryphon, with her assistance, and then with some difficulty enforced submission on the Jews, felt himself, in B.C. 129, at liberty to resume the struggle with Parthia, and, having made great preparations, set out for the East with the full intention of releasing his brother, and recovering his lost provinces.

It is impossible to accept without considerable reserve the accounts that have come down to us of the force which Antiochus collected. According to Justin, it consisted of no more than eighty thousand fighting men, to whom were attached the incredible number of three hundred thousand camp-followers, the majority. of them consisting of cooks, bakers, and actors ! As in other extreme cases the camp-followers do but equal, or a little exceed, the number of men fit for actual service, this estimate, which makes them nearly four times as numerous, is entitled to but little credit. The late historian, Orosius, corrects the error here indicated ; but his account seems to err in rating the supernumeraries too low. According to him, the armed force amounted to three hundred thousand, while the camp-followers, including grooms, sutlers, courtesans, and actors, were no more than a third of the number. From the two accounts, taken together we are perhaps entitled to conclude that the entire host did not fall much short of four hundred thousand men. This estimate receives a certain amount of confirmation from an independent statement made incidentally by Diodorus, with respect to the number on the Syrian side that fell in the campaign, which he estimates at three hundred thousand.

The army of Phraates, according to two consentient accounts, numbered no more than a hundred and twenty thousand. An attempt which he made to enlist in his service a body of Scythian mercenaries from the regions beyond the Oxus failed, the Scyths being quite willing to lend their aid, but arriving too late at the rendezvous to be of any use. At the same time a defection on the part of the subject princes deprived the Parthian monarch of contingents which usually swelled his numbers, and threw him upon the support of his own countrymen, chiefly or solely. Under these circumstances it is more surprising that he was able to collect a hundred and twenty thousand men than that he did not succeed in bringing into the field a larger number.

The Syrian troops were magnificently appointed. The common soldiers had their military boots fastened with buckles or studs of gold ; and the culinary utensils, in which the food of the army was cooked, were in many instances of silver. It seemed as if banqueting, rather than fighting, was to be the order of the day. But to suppose that this was actually so would be to do the army of Antiochus an injustice. History, from the time of Sardanapalus to that of the Crimean War of 1854–6, abounds with instances of the somewhat strange combination of luxurious habits with valour of the highest kind. No charge of poltroonery can be established against the Syrian soldiery, who, on the contrary, seem to have played their part in the campaign with credit. They were accompanied by a body of Jews under John Hyrcanus, the son of Simon and grandson of the first Maccabee leader, who had been forced to take up temporarily the position of a Syrian feudatory. As they advanced through the Mesopotamian region after crossing the Euphrates, they received continually fresh accessions of strength by the arrival of contingents from the Parthian tributary states, which, disgusted with Parthian arrogance and coarseness, or perhaps attracted by Syrian luxury and magnificence, embraced the cause of the invader.

Phraates, on his part, instead of awaiting attack in the fastnesses of Parthia or Hyrcania, advanced to meet his enemy across the Assyrian and Babylonian plains, and, either in person or by his generals, engaged the Syrian monarch in three pitched battles, in each of which he was worsted. One of these was fought upon the banks of the Greater Zab or Lycus, in Adiabênê, not far from the site of Arbela, where Antiochus met and defeated the Parthian general, Indates, and raised a trophy in honour of his victory. The exact scene of the other two engagements is unknown to us, and in no case have we any description of the battles, so that we have no means of judging whether it was by superiority of force or of strategy that the Syrian monarch thus far prevailed, and obtained almost the whole for which he was fighting. The entire province of Babylonia, the heart of the empire, where were situated the three great cities of

Babylon, Seleucia, and Ctesiphon, fell into his hands, and a further defection of the tributary countries from the Parthian cause took place, a defection so wide-spread, that the writer who records it says, with a certain amount of rhetoric, no doubt—" Phraates had now nothing left to him beyond the limits of the original Parthian territory." He maintained, however, a position somewhere in the Lower Babylonian plain, and still confronted Antiochus with an army, which, though beaten, was bent on resistance.

When affairs were in this state, Phraates, recognis-ing the peril of his position, came to the conclusion that it was necessary to attempt, at any rate, a diver-sion. He had still what seemed to him a winning card in his hand, and it was time to play it. Deme-trius, the brother of Antiochus, and *de jure* the king of Syria, was still in his possession, watched and carefully guarded in the rough Hyrcanian home, from which he had twice escaped, but only to be re-captured. He would send Demetrius into Syria under an escort of Parthian troops, who should conduct him to the frontier and give him the opportunity of recovering his kingdom. It would be strange if one, entitled to the throne by his birth, and its actual occupant for the space of six years, could not rally to himself a party in a country always ready to welcome pretenders, and to accept, as valid, claims that were utterly baseless. Let troubles break out in his rear, let his rule over Syria be threatened in Syria itself, and Antiochus would, he thought, either hasten home, or, at the least, be greatly alarmed, have his attention distracted from his aggressive designs, and be afraid of plunging

8

deeper into Asia, lest, while grasping at the shadow of power, he should lose the substance.

Demetrius and his Parthian escort set out, but the distance to be traversed was great, and travelling is slow in Asia. Moreover, the winter time was approaching, and each week would increase the difficulties of locomotion. The scheme of Phraates hung fire. No immediate effect followed from it. Antiochus may not have received intelligence of the impending danger, or he may have thought his wife, Cleopatra, whom he had left at Antioch, capable of coping with it. In any case, it is certain that his movements were in no way affected by the bolt which Phraates had launched at him. Instead of withdrawing his troops from the occupied provinces and marching them back into Syria, thus relinquishing all that he had gained by his successful campaign, he resolved to maintain all the conquests that he had made, and to keep his troops where they were, merely dividing them, on account of their numbers, among the various cities which he had taken, and making them go into winter quarters. His design was carried out ; the army was dispersed ; discipline was probably somewhat relaxed ; and the soldiery, having no military duties to perform, amused themselves, as foreign soldiers are apt to do, by heavy requisitions, and by cavalier treatment of the native inhabitants.

Some months of the winter passed in this way. Gradually the discontent of the civil populations in the cities increased. Representations were made to Phraates by secret messengers, that the yoke of the Syrians was found to be intolerable, and that, if he

would give the signal, the cities were ripe for revolt.
Much hidden negotiation must have taken place before
a complete arrangement could have been made, or a
fixed plan settled on.   As in the "Saint Bartholomew,"
as in the "Sicilian Vespers," as in the great outbreak
against the Roman power in Asia Minor under
Mithridates of Pontus, the secret must have been
communicated to hundreds, who, with a marvellous
tenacity of purpose, kept it inviolate for weeks or
months, so that not a whisper reached the ears of the
victims.   Sunk in a delicious dream of the most
absolute security, careless of the feelings, and deaf to
the grumblings of the townsmen, the Syrian soldiers
continued to enjoy their long and pleasant holiday,
without a suspicion of the danger that was impending.
Meanwhile Phraates arranged all the details of his
plan, and communicated them to his confederates.   It
was agreed that, on an appointed day, all the cities
should break out in revolt ; the natives should take
arms, rise against the soldiers quartered upon them,
and kill all, or as many as possible.   Phraates
promised to be at hand with his army, to prevent the
scattered garrisons from giving help to each other.
It was calculated that, in this way, the invaders might
be cut off almost to a man without the trouble of
even fighting a battle.

But, before he proceeded to these terrible extremities, the Parthian prince, touched perhaps with compassion, determined to give his adversary a chance
of escaping the fate prepared for him by timely concessions.   The winter was not over ; but the snow was
beginning to melt through the increasing warmth of

the sun's rays, and the day appointed for the general
rising was probably drawing near. Phraates felt that
no time was to be lost. Accordingly, he sent ambassadors to Antiochus to propose peace, and to inquire
on what terms it would be granted him. The reply
of Antiochus, according to Diodorus, was as follows:
" If Phraates would release his prisoner, Demetrius,
from captivity, and deliver him up without ransom, at
the same time restoring all the provinces which had
been taken by Parthia from Syria, and consenting to
pay a tribute for Parthia itself, peace might be had;
but not otherwise." To such terms it was, of course,
impossible that any Parthian king should listen; and
the ambassadors of Phraates returned, therefore,
without further parley.

Soon afterwards, the day appointed for the outbreak arrived. Apparently, even yet no suspicion had
been excited. The Syrian troops were everywhere
quietly enjoying themselves in their winter quarters,
when, suddenly and without any warning, they found
themselves attacked by the natives. Taken at disadvantage, it was impossible for them to make a successful resistance; and it would seem that the great bulk
of them were massacred in their quarters. Antiochus,
and the detachment stationed with him, alone, so far
as we hear, escaped into the open field, and contended
for their lives in just warfare. It had been the
intention of the Syrian monarch, when he quitted his
station, to hasten to the protection of the division
quartered nearest to him; but he had no sooner commenced his march than he found himself confronted
by Phraates, who was at the head of his main army,

having, no doubt, anticipated the design of Antiochus and resolved to frustrate it. The Parthian prince was anxious to engage at once, as his force far out-numbered that commanded by his adversary ; but the latter might have declined the battle had he so willed, and have at any rate greatly protracted the struggle. He had a mountain region—Mount Zagros, probably —within a short distance of him, and might have fallen back upon it, so placing the Parthian horse at great disadvantage ; but he was still at an age when caution is apt to be considered cowardice, and temerity to pass for true courage. Despite the advice of one of his captains, he determined to accept the battle which the enemy offered, and not to fly before a foe whom he had three times defeated. But the determi-nation of the commander was ill seconded by the army which he commanded. Though Antiochus fought strenuously, he was defeated, since his troops were without heart and offered but a poor resistance. Athenæus, the general who had advised retreat, was the first to fly, and then the whole army broke up and dispersed itself. Antiochus himself perished, either slain by the enemy or by his own hand. His son, Seleucus, and a niece, a daughter of his brother, Demetrius, who had accompanied him in his expe-dition, were captured. His troops were either cut to pieces or made prisoners. The entire number of those slain in the battle, and in the general massacre, was reckoned at three hundred thousand.

Such was the issue of this great expedition. It was the last which any Seleucid monarch conducted into these countries—the final attempt made by Syria to repossess herself of her lost Eastern provinces. Henceforth, Parthia was no further troubled by the power that had hitherto been her most dangerous and most constant enemy, but was allowed to enjoy, without molestation from Syria, the conquests which she had effected.   Syria, in fact, had received so deep a wound that she had from this time a difficulty in preserving her own existence.   The immediate result of the destruction of Antiochus and his host was the revolt of Judæa, which henceforth maintained its independence uninterruptedly to the time of the Romans.   The dominions of the Seleucidæ were reduced to Cilicia, and Syria Proper, or the tract west of the Euphrates between the chain of Amanus and Palestine.   Internally, the Syrian state was agitated by constant commotions from the claims of various pretenders to the sovereignty ; externally, it was kept in continual alarm by the Egyptians, the Romans, and the Armenians.   During the sixty years that elapsed between the return of Demetrius to his kingdom (B.C. 128) and the conversion of Syria into a Roman province (B.C. 65) she ceased wholly to be formidable to her neighbours.   Her flourishing period was gone by, and a rapid decline set in, from which there was no recovery.   It is surprising that the Romans did not step in earlier, to terminate a rule which was but a little removed from anarchy.   Rome, however, had other work on her hands—-civil troubles, social wars, and the struggle with Mithridates ; and hence the Syrian state continued to exist till the year B.C. 65, though in a feeble and moribund condition.

In Parthia itself the consequences of Syria's defeat

and collapse were less important than might have been expected. One would naturally have looked to see, as the immediate result, a fresh development of the aggressive spirit, and a burst of energy and enterprise parallel to that which had carried the arms of Mithridates I., from his Parthian fastnesses to the Hydaspes on the one hand and to the Euphrates on the other. But no such result followed. We hear indeed of Phraates *intending* to follow up his victory over Antiochus by a grand attack upon Syria—an attack to which, if it had taken place, she must almost certainly have succumbed—but, in point of fact, the relations between the two countries continued for many years after the Great Massacre, peaceful, if not even friendly. Phraates celebrated the obsequies of Antiochus with the pomp and ceremony befitting a powerful king, and ultimately placed his remains in a coffin of silver, and sent them into Syria, to find their last resting-place in their native country. He treated Seleucus, the son of Antiochus, who had been made prisoner in the final battle, with the highest honour, and took to wife Antiochus's niece, who fell into his hands at the same time. The royal houses of the Seleucidæ and the Arsacidæ became thus doubly allied ; and, all grounds for further hostilities having been removed, peace and amity were established between the former rivals. No doubt a powerful motive influencing Parthia in the adoption of this policy was that revelation of a new danger which will form the chief subject of the ensuing section.

VII.

PRESSURE OF THE NORTHERN NOMADS UPON PARTHIA — SCYTHIC WARS OF PHRAATES II. AND ARTABANUS II.

THE Turanian or Tâtar races by which Central and Northern Asia are inhabited, have at all times constituted a serious danger to the inhabitants of the softer South. Hordes of wild barbarians wander over those inhospitable regions, increase, multiply, exert a pressure on their southern neighbours, and are felt as a perpetual menace. Every now and then a crisis arrives. Population has increased beyond the means of subsistence, or a novel ambition has seized a tribe or a powerful chief, and the barrier, which has hitherto proved a sufficient restraint, is forced. There issues suddenly out of the frozen bosom of the North a stream of coarse, uncouth savages—brave, hungry, countless— who swarm into the fairer southern regions determinedly, irresistibly ; like locusts winging their flight into a green land. How such multitudes come to be propagated in countries where life is with difficulty sustained, we do not know ; why the impulse suddenly seizes them to quit their old haunts and

move steadily in a given direction, we cannot say ;
but we see that the phenomenon is one of constant
recurrence, and we have thus come to regard it as
being scarcely curious or strange at all. In Asia,
Cimmerians, Scythians, Comans, Mongols, Turks ; in
Europe, Gauls, Goths, Huns, Avars, Vandals, Burgundians, Lombards, Bulgarians, have successively
illustrated the law, and made us familiar with its
operation. " Inroads of the northern barbarians "
has become a common-place with writers of history,
and there is scarcely any country of the South,
whether in Asia or in Europe, that has not experienced them.

Such inroads are very dreadful when they take
place. Hordes of savages, coarse and repulsive in
their appearance, fierce in their tempers, rude in their
habits, not perhaps individually very brave or strong,
but powerful by their numbers, and sometimes by a
new mode of warfare, which it is found difficult to
meet, pour into the seats of civilisation, and spread
havoc around. On they come (as before observed)
like a flight of locusts, countless, irresistible—finding
the land before them a garden, and leaving it behind
them a howling wilderness. Neither sex nor age is
spared. The inhabitants of the open country and of
the villages, if they do not make their escape to high
mountain tops or other strongholds, are ruthlessly
massacred by the invaders, or, at best, forced to
become their slaves. The crops are consumed, the
flocks and herds swept off or destroyed, the villages
and homesteads burnt, the whole country made a
scene of desolation. Walled towns perhaps resist

them, as they have not often patience enough for sieges ; but sometimes, with a dogged determination, they sit down before the ramparts, and by a prolonged blockade, starve the defenders into submission. Then there ensues an indescribable scene of havoc, rapine, and bloodshed. Ancient cities, rich with the accumulated stores of ages, are ransacked and perhaps burnt ; priceless works of art often perish ; civilisations which it has taken centuries to build up are trampled down. Few things are more terrible than the devastation and ruin which such an inroad has often spread over a fair and smiling kingdom, even when it has merely swept over it, like a passing storm, and has led to no permanent occupation.

Against a danger of this kind the Parthian princes had had, almost from the first, to guard. They were themselves of the nomadic race—Turanians, if our hypothesis concerning them be sound—and had established their kingdom by an invasion of the type above described. But they had immediately become settlers, inhabitants of cities ; they had been softened, to a certain extent, civilised ; and now they looked on the nomadic hordes of the North with the same dislike and disgust with which the Persians and the Greco - Macedonians had formerly regarded them. In the Scythians of the Trans-Oxianian tract they saw an unceasing peril, and one, moreover, which was, about the time of Phraates, continually increasing and becoming more and more threatening.

Fully to explain the position of affairs in this quarter, we must ask the reader to accompany us into the remoter regions of inner Asia, where the Turanian tribes had their headquarters. There, about the year B.C. 200, a Turanian people called the Yue-chi were expelled from their territory on the west of Chen-si by the Hiong-nu, whom some identify with the Huns. "The Yue-chi separated into two bands: the smaller descended southwards into Thibet; the larger passed westwards, and after a hard struggle, dispossessed a people called 'Su,' of the plains west of the river of Ili. The latter advanced to Ferghana and the Jaxartes; and the Yue-chi not long afterwards retreating from the U-siun, another nomadic race, passed the 'Su' on the north, and occupied the tracts between the Oxus and the Caspian. The 'Su' were thus in the vicinity of the Bactrian Greeks; the Yue-chi in the neighbourhood of the Parthians."[1] On the particulars of this account, which comes from the Chinese historians, we cannot perhaps altogether depend; but there is no reason to doubt the main fact, testified by an eye-witness, that the Yue-chi, having migrated about the period mentioned from the interior of Asia, had established themselves sixty years later (B.C. 140) in the Caspian region. Such a movement would necessarily have thrown the entire previous population of those parts into commotion, and would probably have precipitated them upon their neighbours. It accounts satisfactorily for the unusual pressure of the northern hordes at this period on the Parthians, the Bactrians, and even the Indians; and it completely explains the crisis of Parthian history

[1] See Wilson, " Ariana Antiqua," p. 303.

which we have now reached, and the necessity which
lay upon the nation of meeting, and if possible overcoming, a new danger.

In fact, one of those occasions of peril had arisen
to which we have before alluded, and to which, in
ancient times, the civilised world was always liable
from an outburst of northern barbarism. Whether
the peril has altogether passed away or not, we need
not here inquire, but certainly in the old world there
was always a chance that civilisation, art, refinement,
luxury, might suddenly and almost without warning
be swept away by an overwhelming influx of savagery
from the North. From the reign of Cyaxares, when
the evil, so far as we know, first showed itself, the
danger was patent to all wise and far-seeing governors
both in Europe and Asia, and was from time to time
guarded against. The expeditions of Cyrus against
the Massagetæ, of Darius Hystaspis against the
European Scyths, of Alexander against the Getæ, of
Trajan and Probus across the Danube, were designed
to check and intimidate the northern nations, to break
their power, and diminish the likelihood of their
taking the offensive. It was now more than four
centuries since in this part of Asia any such effort
had been made ; and the northern barbarians might
naturally have ceased to fear the arms and discipline
of the South. Moreover, the circumstances of the
time scarcely left them a choice. Pressed on continually more and more by the newly-arrived "Su" and
Yue-chi, the old inhabitants of the Trans-Oxianian
regions were under the necessity of seeking new
settlements, and could only attempt to find them in

the quarter towards which they were driven by the new-comers. Strengthened probably by daring spirits from among their conquerors themselves, they crossed the rivers and the deserts by which they had been hitherto confined, and advancing against the Parthians, Bactrians, and Arians, threatened to carry all before them. In Bactria, soon after the establishment of the Greco-Bactrian kingdom, they began to give trouble. Province after province was swallowed up by the invaders, who occupied Sogdiana, or the tract between the Lower Jaxartes and the Lower Oxus, and hence proceeded to make inroads into Bactria itself. The rich land on the Polytimetus, or Ak-Su, the river of Samarkand, and even the highlands between the Upper Jaxartes and Upper Oxus, were permanently occupied by Turanian immigrants ; and, if the Bactrians had not compensated themselves for their losses by acquisitions of territory in Affghanistan and India, they would soon have had no kingdom left. The hordes were always increasing in strength through the influx of fresh tribes. Bactria was pressed to the south-eastward, and precipitated upon its neighbours in that direction.

Presently, in Ariana, the hordes passed the mountains, and proceeding southwards, occupied the tract below the great lake wherein the Helmend terminates, which took from them the name of Sacastana—"the land of the Saka or Scyths"—a name still to be traced in the modern Seistan. Further to the east they effected a lodgment in Cabul, and another in the southern portion of the Indus valley, which for a time bore the name of Indo-Scythia. They even

crossed the Indus, and attempted to penetrate into
the interior of Hindustan, but here they were met
and repulsed by a native monarch, about the year
B.C. 56.

The people engaged in this great movement are
called in a general way by the classical writers Sacæ
or Scythæ, *i.e.*, Scyths.   They consisted of a number
of tribes, similar for the most part in language, habits,
and mode of life, and allied more or less closely to
the other nomadic races of Central and Northern
Asia.   Of these tribes the principal were the
Massagetæ ("great Jits or Jats"), the former adversaries of Cyrus, who occupied the country on both
sides of the lower course of the Oxus; the Dahæ,
who bordered the Caspian above Hyrcania, and
extended thence to the longitude of Herat ;   the
Tochari, who settled in the mountains between the
Upper Jaxartes and the Upper Oxus, where they gave
name to the tract known as Tokharistan ; the Asii
or Asians, who were closely connected with the
Tochari ; and the Sacarauli, who are found connected
with both the Tochari and the Asians.   Some of
these tribes contained within them further sub-
divisions, as the Dahæ, who comprised the Parni or
Aparni, the Pissuri, and the Xanthii ; and the Massagetæ, who included among them Chorasmii, Attasii,
and others.

The general character of the barbarism, in which
these various races were involved, may be best learnt
from the description given of one of them, with but
few differences, by Herodotus and Strabo.   According
to these writers, the Massagetæ were nomads who

moved about in waggons or carts, like the modern Kalmucks, accompanied by their flocks and herds, on whose milk they chiefly sustained themselves. Each man had only one wife, but all the wives were held in common. They were good riders, and excellent archers, but fought both on horseback and on foot, and used, besides their bows and arrows, lances, knives, and battle-axes. They had little or no iron, but made their spear and arrow-heads, and their other weapons, of bronze. They had also bronze breastplates, but otherwise the metal with which they adorned and protected their own persons and the heads of their horses, was gold. To a certain extent they were cannibals. It was their custom not to let the aged among them die a natural death, but, when life seemed approaching its term, to offer them up in sacrifice, and then boil the flesh and feast upon it. This mode of ending life was regarded as the best and most honourable; such as died of disease were not eaten, but buried, and their friends bewailed their misfortune. It may be added to this, that we have sufficient reason to believe, that the Massagetæ and the other nomads of these parts regarded the use of poisoned arrows in warfare as legitimate, and employed the venom of serpents and the corrupted blood of men, to make the wounds which they inflicted more deadly.

Thus, what was threatened by the existing position of affairs was not merely the conquest of one race by another cognate to it, like that of the Medes by the Persians, or of the Greeks by Rome, but the obliteration of such art, civilisation, and refinement as

Western Asia had attained to in the course of ages
by the successive efforts of Babylonians, Assyrians,
Medes, Persians, and Greeks—the spread over some
of the fairest regions of the earth of a low type of
savagery—a type which in religion went no further
than the worship of the Sun ; in art knew but the
easier forms of metallurgy and the construction of
carts ; in manners and customs, included cannibalism,
the use of poisoned weapons, and a relation between
the sexes destructive alike of all delicacy and all
family affection.   The Parthians were, no doubt, rude
and coarse in their character as compared with the
Persians ; but they had been civilised to some extent
by three centuries of subjection to the Persians and
the Greeks before they rose to power ; they affected
Persian manners ; they patronised Greek art ; they
had a smattering of Greek literature ; they appreciated
the advantages of having in their midst a number of
Grecian states.   Many of their kings called themselves upon their coins " Phil-Hellenes," or " lovers of
the Hellenic people." [1]   Had the Massagetæ and
their kindred tribes of Sacæ, Tochari, Dahæ, Yue-chi,
and Su, which now menaced the Parthian power,
succeeded in sweeping it away, the gradual declension
of all that is lovely or excellent in human life would
have been marked. Scythicism would have overspread
Western Asia.   No doubt the conquerors would have
learnt something from those whom they subjected to
their yoke ; but it cannot be supposed that they
would have learnt much.   The change would have
been like that which passed over the Western Roman

---

[1] Lindsay, " History and Coinage of the Parthians," p. 213.

Empire, when Goths, Vandals, Burgundians, Alans, Heruli, depopulated its fairest provinces and laid its civilisation in the dust. The East would have been barbarised ; the gains of centuries would have been lost ; the work of Cyrus, Darius, Alexander, and other great benefactors of Asiatic humanity, would have been undone ; Western Asia would have sunk back into a condition not very much above that from which it had been raised two thousand years previously by the primitive Chaldæans and the Assyrians.

The first monarch to recognise the approach of the crisis and its danger was Phraates II., the son of Mithridates I., and the conqueror of Antiochus Sidetes. Not that the danger presented itself to his imagination in its full magnitude ; but that he first woke up to the perception of the real position of affairs in the East, and saw that, whereas Parthia's most formidable enemy had hitherto been Syria, and the Syro-Macedonian power, it had now become Scythia and the Sacæ. No sooner did the pressure of the nomads begin to make itself felt on his north-eastern frontier, than, relinquishing all ideas of Syrian conquests, if he had really entertained them, he left his seat of empire in Babylonia to the care of a viceroy, Hymerus, or Evemerus, and marched in person to confront the new peril. The Scythians, apparently, had attacked Parthia Proper from their seats in the Oxus region. Phraates, in his haste to collect a sufficient force against them, enlisted in his service a large body of Greeks—the remnants mainly of the defeated army of Antiochus—and taking with him also a strong body of Parthian troops, marched at his

9

best speed eastward. A war followed in the mountain region, which must have lasted for some years, but of which we have only the most meagre account. At last there was an engagement in which the Scythians got the advantage, and the Parthian troops began to waver and threaten to break, when the Greeks, who had been from the first disaffected, and had only waited for an occasion to mutiny, went over in a body to the enemy, and so decided the battle. Deserted by their allies, the Parthian soldiery were cut to pieces, and Phraates himself was among the slain. The event proved that he had acted rashly in taking the Greeks with him, but he can scarcely be said to have deserved much blame. It would have been surprising if he had anticipated so strange a thing as the fraternisation of a body of luxurious and over-civilised Greeks with the utter barbarians against whom he was contending, or had imagined that in so remote a region, cut off from the rest of their countrymen, they would have ventured to take a step which must have thrown them entirely on their own resources.

We have no information with regard to the ultimate fate of the Greek mutineers. As for the Scythians, with that want of energy and of a settled purpose which characterised them, they proceeded to plunder and ravage the portion of the Parthian territory which lay open to them, and, when they had thus wasted their strength, returned quietly to their homes.

The Parthian nobles appointed as monarch, in place of the late king, an uncle of his, named Artabanus, who is known in history as " Artabanus the

Second." He was probably advanced in years, and might perhaps have been excused, had he folded his arms, awaited the attack of his foes, and stood wholly on the defensive. But he was brave and energetic ; and, what was still more important, he appears to have appreciated the perils of the position. He was not content, when the particular body of barbarians, which had defeated and slain his predecessor, having ravaged Parthia Proper, returned home, to sit still and wait till he was attacked in his turn. According to the brief but emphatic words of Justin, he assumed the aggressive, and invaded the country of

COIN OF ARTABANUS II.

the Tochari, one of the most powerful of the Scythian tribes, which was now settled in a portion of the region that had, till lately, belonged to the Bactrian kingdom. Artabanus evidently felt that what was needed was, not simply to withstand, but to roll back the flood of invasion, which had advanced so near to the sacred home of his nation ; that the barbarians required to be taught a lesson ; that they must at least be made to understand that Parthia was to be respected ; if this could not be done, then the fate of the empire was sealed. He therefore, with a gallantry and boldness that we cannot sufficiently admire—a boldness that seemed like rashness, but

was in reality prudence—without calculating too
closely the immediate chances of battle, led his troops
against one of the most forward of the advancing
tribes. But fortune, unhappily, was adverse. How
the battle was progressing we are not told ; but it
appears that, in the thick of an engagement, Artabanus, who was leading his men, received a wound in
the fore-arm, from the effect of which he died almost
immediately. The death of the leader on either side
decides in the East, almost to a certainty, the issue of a
conflict. We cannot doubt that the Parthians, having
lost their monarch, were repulsed ; that the expedition
failed ; and that the situation of affairs became once
more at least as threatening as it had been before
Artabanus made his attempt. Two Parthian monarchs had now fallen, within the space of a few years,
in combat with the aggressive Scyths—two Parthian
armies had suffered defeat. Was this to be always so ?
If it was, then Parthia had only to make up her mind
to fall, and, like the great Roman, to let it be her care
that she should fall grandly and with dignity.

VIII.

MITHRIDATES II. AND THE NOMADS—WAR WITH ARMENIA—FIRST CONTACT WITH ROME.

ARTABANUS II. was succeeded on the throne by his son, Mithridates II., about the year B.C. 124. His military achievements were considerable, and procured him the epithet of "the Great," though that title was perhaps better deserved by Mithridates the First, his uncle. However, the reign of the second Mithridates was undoubtedly a distinguished one, and it is most unfortunate that the accounts of it, which have come down to us, are so meagre and unsatisfactory. We can but trace the history of Parthia during his time in its general outline, with very scanty details, and those not always altogether trustworthy.

There seems, however, to be no doubt, that his earliest efforts after mounting the throne were directed to the quarter where the great danger pressed—the danger which had proved fatal to his two immediate predecessors, his cousin and his uncle. Probably, in thus determining, he scarcely exercised any choice. The Scyths, after their double victory, would naturally take an attitude so menacing that unless immediately met and checked, all hope would have had to be

given up—absolute ruin would have had to be met
and faced—Parthia would have been overrun, and the
empire established by the first Mithridates would
have been extinguished, within twenty or thirty years
of its first appearance, under the second.   The young
king, perceiving his peril, bent every effort to meet
and repel it.   He employed the whole force of the
State upon his north-eastern frontier, and, in a series
of engagements, so effectually checked the advance
of the Scyths, that from his time the danger which
had been impending wholly passed away.   The
nomads gave up the hope of making any serious
impression on the Arsacid kingdom, and, turning
their restless energies in another direction, found a
vent for their superabundant population in the far
East, in Affghanistan and India, where they settled
themselves, and set up permanent governments.
Parthia was so completely relieved from their attacks,
that she was able once more to take the aggressive in
this region, and to extend her sway at the expense of
the nation before which she had so lately trembled.
The acquisition of parts of Bactria from the Scyths,
which is attested by Strabo, belongs, in all probability,
to this reign ; and it is even possible that the extension of Parthian dominion over Sacastané, or Seistan,
dates from the same period.   We are assured that
the second Mithridates "added many nations to the
Parthian Empire."   As these were decidedly not on
the western side of the empire, where Mithridates
did not even succeed in *conquering* Armenia, it would
seem that they must have lain towards the East, in
which case it would be almost certain that they must

have been outlying tribes of the recent Scythic immigration.

The successes of Mithridates in this quarter left him at liberty, after a time, to turn his attention towards the west, where, though Syria was no longer formidable, troubles of various kinds had broken out, which could no longer be safely neglected. Hymerus, or Euemerus, the viceroy appointed to direct the affairs of the west from Babylon by Phraates II. when he marched eastward against the Scyths, had greatly misconducted himself in his government, and almost shaken himself free from the Parthian yoke. He had treated the inhabitants of Babylon with extreme cruelty, condemning many of them to slavery, and sending them into Media, besides burning the market-place, several temples, and other buildings of that great city. He had greatly encouraged luxury and extravagance, had offended many by his exactions, and affected the state, if he did not actually claim the title, of an independent monarch. Mithridates, on reaching the West, crushed the nascent rebellion of Hymerus, and having thus recovered dominion over those regions, proceeded to engage in war with a new enemy.

Armenia, the new enemy, was a territory of very considerable importance, and was henceforth so mixed up with Parthia in her various wars and negotiations, that some account of the country, and people, and of the previous history of the people seems to be necessary.

According to Justin, Armenia was a tract eleven hundred miles long by seven hundred broad; but this is an extravagant estimate. If we extend Armenia from the Caspian to the range of Taurus, we cannot make its length much more than seven hundred miles ; and if we even allow it to have reached from the Caucasus to Mount Masius and the lake of Urumiyeh, we cannot make its width more than four hundred miles. But, practically, its limits were almost always much narrower. Iberia and Albania were ordinarily independent countries, occupying the modern Georgia, and intervening between Armenia and the Caucasus ; the Euphrates was the natural boundary of Armenia on the west ; and Niphates, rather than Mons. Masius, shut it in upon the south. Its normal dimensions have been already estimated in this volume at six hundred miles in length by a little more than two hundred in breadth, and its area at about sixty or seventy thousand square miles. There is no reason to believe that, during the Parthian period, it ever much exceeded these dimensions, except it were during the fourteen years (B.C. 83 to 69) when, under Tigranes I., it held possession of the dwindled kingdom of the Seleucidæ.

Armenia was a country of lofty ridges, deep and narrow valleys, numerous and copious streams, and occasional broad plains—a country of rich pasture grounds, productive orchards, and abundant harvests. It occupied the loftiest position in Western Asia, and contained the sources of all the great rivers of these parts—the Euphrates, the Tigris, the Halys, the Araxes, and the Cyrus—which, rising within a space of two hundred and fifty miles long by a hundred wide, flow down in four directions to three different seas.

It was thus to this part of Asia what Switzerland is to Western Europe, an elevated fastness region containing within it the highest mountains, and yielding the waters which fertilise the subjacent regions. It contained also two large lakes, each occupying its own basin, and having no connection with any sea—those of Van and Urumiyeh—salt lakes of a very peculiar character. The mountain tracts yielded supplies of gold, silver, copper, lead, and other metals, beside emery and antimony. The soil in the valleys was fertile and bore several kinds of grain ; the flanks of the hills grew vines ; and the pastures produced horses and mules of good quality.

The Armenians of Parthian times were probably identical with the race, which, still under the same name, occupies the greater portion of the old country, and holds an important position among the inhabitants of Western Asia. They are a pale race, with a somewhat sallow complexion, marked features, and dark eyebrows and hair. By their language, which can be traced back to the fourth century of our era, it appears that they are an Arian people, but with a certain amount of Turanian admixture. Their relations are closer with the Persians than probably with any other race, but still they possess many notable points of difference. They are of a weaker physique than the Persians, slighter in their frames, less muscular and robust. They are subtle, wily, with a great talent for commerce, but wanting in strength, stamina, and endurance. In the earlier times they were strongly attached to their own independence, and, though seldom able to maintain it for long, were continually reasserting it whenever an opportunity seemed to offer. But they have now for many centuries been absolutely quiescent, and are patient under the harsh rule of the three races which hold them in subjection —the Russians, the Persians, and the Turks.

Historically, the Armenians of to-day cannot be traced further back than about the sixth century B.C., when they appear to have immigrated into the territory that they have from that time occupied. Previously their land was possessed by three powerful and warlike races, who are thought to have been Turanians, and who from the tenth to the seventh century B.C. were continually at war with the great Assyrian Empire. These were the Naïri, the Urarda, and the Mannai, or Minni—names which constantly recur in the cuneiform inscriptions. The Naïri were spread from the mountains west of lake Van, along both sides of the Tigris, to Bir on the Euphrates, and even further ; the Urarda, or people of Ararat, probably the Alarodii of Herodotus, dwelt north and east of the Naïri, on the Upper Euphrates, about the lake of Van, and probably on the Araxes ; while the Minni, or Mannai, whose country lay southeast of the Urarda, held the Urumiyeh basin, and the adjoining parts of Zagros. Of these three races, the Urarda were the most powerful, and it was with them that the Assyrians waged their most bloody wars. The capital city of the Urarda was Van, on the eastern shores of the lake, and here it was that the kings set up the most remarkable of their inscriptions. The language of these inscriptions is of a Turanian type, and, though it may have furnished the non-Arian element in the modern Armenian, cannot have been its real main progenitor. An immigration must have occurred between the end of the Assyrian and the early part of the Persian period, which changed the population of the mountain region, submerging the original occupants in a far larger number of Arian in-comers.

The first distinct knowledge that we obtain of this new people is from the inscriptions of Darius Hystaspis. Darius, after mentioning Armenia (Armina) among the twenty-three provinces into which his empire was divided, informs us that, in the second year of his reign (B.C. 520), while he was at Babylon, a great revolt broke out, in which Armenia participated, together with eight other districts. It was not till his third year that the revolt was put down, the Armenians, as well as the other confederates, making a most vigorous resistance. The names of the persons and of the places mentioned in this campaign seem to be Arian, as are the other Armenian names generally. On the suppression of the revolt, and the full establishment of the power of Darius, Armenia, together with some adjacent regions, became a satrapy of the Persian Empire—the thirteenth, according to Herodotus—and was rated in the Royal Books as bound to furnish a revenue of four hundred talents—about £96,000—annually. From this time its fidelity to the Persian monarchs was remarkable. Not only was the money tribute paid regularly, but a contribution of twenty thousand young colts was made each year to the Royal Stud, so far as appears, without any murmuring. Contingents of troops were also readily furnished whenever required by the Great Monarch; and, through the whole

Achæmenian period, after the reign of Darius, Armenia remained perfectly tranquil, and never caused the Persians the slightest alarm or anxiety.

After Arbela (B.C. 331) the Armenians submitted to Alexander without a struggle, or an attempt at regaining independence, and, when in the division of his dominions which followed upon the battle of Ipsus (B.C. 301), they were assigned to Seleucus, they acquiesced in the arrangement. It was not until Antiochus the Great suffered his great defeat at the hands of the Romans (B.C. 190), and all Western Asia was thrown into a ferment, that the Arian Armenians, after, at least, four centuries of subjection, raised their thoughts to independence, and succeeded in establishing an autonomous monarchy. Even then the movement seems to have originated rather in the ambition of a chief than in any ardent desire for liberty upon the part of the people. Artaxias had been governor of the Greater Armenia in the earlier portion of the reign of Antiochus, and seized the opportunity afforded by the defeat of Magnesia to change his title of satrap into that of sovereign. Antiochus was too much occupied at home to resist him ; and he was allowed at his leisure to establish his power, to build a new capital at Artaxata near the Araxes, and to reign in peace for a space of about twenty-five years. Then, however, he was attacked by Antiochus Epiphanes. This prince (about B.C. 165) resolved on an attempt at re-establishing the power of Syria over Armenia, and invading the country with a large army, forced Artaxias to an engagement, in which he defeated him and took him prisoner. Armenia, for the time, sub-

mitted ; but it was not long before fresh troubles broke
out.   When Mithridates I. overran the eastern provinces of Syria (about B.C. 150), and made himself
master in succession of Media, Babylonia, and Elymaïs,
Armenia was once more thrown into a state of excitement, and, partly by her own efforts, partly, it would
seem, by Parthian assistance, threw off for a second
time the Syrian yoke, and became again independent,
this time under an Arsacid prince, named Wagharshag
or Val-arsaces, a member of the Parthian royal family.
A reign of twenty-two years is assigned to this monarch,
whose kingdom is declared to have extended from the
Caucasus to Nisibis, and from the Caspian to the
Mediterranean.   He was succeeded by a son named
Arshag or Arsaces, who carried on wars with the
neighbouring state of Pontus, and had a reign of
thirteen years, probably from about B.C. 128 to B.C. 115.
Ardashes—the Ortoadistus of Justin—then became
king, and was firmly seated on the Armenian throne,
when Mithridates II., nephew of Mithridates I., having
brought the Scythic war to a successful termination,
determined (about B.C. 100) to make an attempt to add
Armenia to his dominions.

No account has come down to us of the war between
Ortoadistus and the invaders.   The relative power of
the two states was, however, such as to make it almost
certain that in a collision between the two Parthia
would have the advantage ; and a casual allusion in
Strabo appears to indicate pretty clearly, that in point
of fact, the advantage gained was not inconsiderable.
Strabo says that Tigranes, the eldest son of Ortoadistus,
was a hostage in the hands of the Parthians for some

time before his accession to the throne—a statement from which it may be confidently inferred, that Ortoadistus, having been worsted in battle by Mithridates, concluded with him an ignominious peace, and as security for the performance of its terms gave hostages to the Parthian monarch, his own son being among the number.   Still, it is also clear, from the fact recorded, that Armenia, if worsted, was far from being subjugated—she ended the war by a treaty of peace—she maintained her own monarch upon the throne—she was not even seriously reduced in strength, since within the space of the next twenty years she attained to the height of her power, absorbing the Syrian state, and really ruling for a time from the Gulf of Issus to the shores of the Caspian.

It cannot have been more than a few years after the termination of the Armenian war, which must have fallen about the close of the second, or the beginning of the first century before our era, that the Parthian state, while still under the rule of Mithridates II., was for the first time brought into contact with Rome.

Rome appears as a permanent factor in the politics of the East somewhat later than might have been expected.   When, towards the close of the second century B.C., the ambition of the Great Antiochus dragged her unwillingly into Asiatic quarrels, she disembarrassed herself, as speedily as she could, of all ties binding her to Asia, and made what was almost a formal retreat to her own continent, and renunciation of the heritage of another, which fortune pressed upon her.   For more than half a century the policy of abstention was pursued.   The various states of

Western Asia were left to follow their own schemes
of self-aggrandisement, and fight out their own quarrels
without Roman interference. But, in course of time,
the reasons for the policy of abstention disappeared.
Macedonia and Greece having been conquered and
absorbed, and Carthage destroyed (B.C. 148–146), the
conditions of the political problem seemed to be so far
changed as to render a further advance towards the
East a safe measure ; and accordingly, when it was
perceived that the line of the kings of Pergamus was
coming to an end, the Senate set on foot intrigues
which had for their object the devolution upon Rome
of the sovereignty belonging to those monarchs. By
dexterous management the third Attalus was induced,
in repayment of his father's obligations to the Romans,
to take the extraordinary and wholly unprecedented
step of bequeathing by will his entire dominions as a
legacy to the Republic. In vain did his illegitimate
half-brother, Aristonicus, dispute the validity of so
strange a testament ; the Romans, aided by Mithridates IV., then monarch of Pontus, easily triumphed
over such resistance as this unfortunate prince could
offer, and, having ceded to their ally the portion of
Phrygia which had belonged to the Pergamene kingdom, entered on the possession of the remainder.
Having thus become an Asiatic power, the Great
Republic was of necessity mixed up henceforth with
the various movements and struggles which agitated
Western Asia, and was naturally led to strengthen its
position among the Asiatic kingdoms by such alliances
as seemed at each conjuncture to be best suited to its
interests.

Hitherto no occasion had arisen for any direct dealings between Rome and Parthia. Their respective territories were still separated by considerable tracts, which were in the occupation of the Syrians, the Cappadocians, and the Armenians. Their interests had neither clashed, nor as yet sufficiently united them to give rise to any diplomatic intercourse. But the progress of the two empires in opposite directions was, slowly but surely, bringing them nearer to each other; and events had now reached a point at which the empires began to have—or to seem to have—such a community of interests as led naturally to an exchange of communications. A new power had been recently developed in these parts. In the rapid way so common in the East, Mithridates V. of Pontus, the son and successor of Rome's ally, had, between B.C. 112 and B.C. 93, built up an empire of vast extent, large population, and almost inexhaustible resources. He had established his authority over Armenia Minor, Colchis, the entire eastern coast of the Black Sea, the Chersonesus Taurica, or kingdom of the Bosporus, and even over the whole tract lying west of the Chersonese as far as the mouth of the Tyras, or Dniestr. Nor had these gains contented him. He had obtained half of Paphlagonia by an iniquitous compact with Nicomedes, King of Bithynia; he had occupied Galatia; and he was engaged in attempts to bring Cappadocia under his influence. In this last-mentioned project he was assisted by the Armenians, with whose king, Tigranes, the son of Ortoadistus, he had (about B.C. 96) formed a close alliance, at the same time giving him his daughter, Cleopatra, in marriage.   Rome, though she had not yet determined on war with Mithridates, was bent on thwarting his Cappadocian projects, and in B.C. 92 sent Sulla into Asia, with orders to put down the puppet king whom Mithridates V. and Tigranes were establishing, and to replace upon the Cappadocian throne a certain Ariobarzanes, whom they had driven from his kingdom.   In the execution of this commission, Sulla was brought into hostile collision with the Armenians, whom he defeated with great slaughter, and drove from Cappadocia, together with their puppet king. Thus, not only did the growing power of Mithridates of Pontus, by inspiring Rome and Parthia with a common fear, tend to draw them together, but the course of events had actually given them a common enemy in Tigranes of Armenia, who was equally obnoxious to both of them.

For Tigranes, who, during the time that he was a hostage in Parthia, had contracted engagements towards the Parthian monarch, which involved a cession of territory, and who, on the faith of his pledges, had been aided by the Parthians in seating himself on his father's throne, though he made the cession required of him in the first instance, had soon afterwards repented of his honesty, had gone to war with his benefactors, recovered the ceded territory, and laid waste a considerable tract of country lying within the admitted limits of the Parthian kingdom.   These proceedings had, of course, alienated Mithridates II.; and we may with much probability ascribe to them the step, which he now took, of sending an ambassador to Sulla.   Orobazus, the individual selected, was charged with the duty of proposing an alliance offensive and defensive between the two countries. The Roman general received the overture favourably, but probably considered that it transcended his powers to conclude a treaty ; and thus no further result was secured by the embassy than the establishment, at their first contact, of a friendly understanding between the two states.

Soon after this, Tigranes appears to have renewed his attacks upon Parthia, which in the interval between B.C. 92 and B.C. 83 he greatly humbled, depriving it of the whole of Upper Mesopotamia, at

COIN OF MITHRIDATES II.

this time called Gordyené, or the country of the Kurds, and under the rule of one of the Parthian tributary kings. Rome was too deeply engaged in the first Mithridatic war to lend Parthia any aid, even if she had been so disposed, and Parthia herself seems to have been suffering from domestic troubles, a time of confusion and disturbance having followed on the death of Mithridates II. about B.C. 89.

Mithridates the Second is commonly regarded as the most distinguished of all the Parthian monarchs after his uncle, Mithridates the First. He has a fine head upon his coins, with a large eye, and a pro-

minent Roman nose. He takes the epithets of
" Theopator " and " Nicator." The obverse of his
coins is commonly adorned with the sitting Parthian
figure with an outstretched bow ; but sometimes exhibits, instead of this, a Pegasus or winged horse. The
military exploits of the prince were undoubtedly remarkable, and it is unfortunate for him that the
record of them is so scanty. It is certain that he
made a deep impression upon the Scythian hordes,
and thus averted from his country a great danger. It
is probable that he considerably enlarged the limits of
his empire on the side of Bactria and India. But, on
the whole, perhaps his permanent fame will rest
mainly upon the two facts, that he was the first to
initiate those Armenian wars which occupied so large
a portion of the later Parthian history, and that he
was also the first to bring Parthia into contact with
the most formidable of all her external enemies, Rome,
and thus—though with far different intent—to pave
the way for those many bloody struggles with the
Great Imperial Power, which for nearly three centuries
—from the time of Crassus to that of Caracallus—
riveted the attention of mankind upon the East.

IX.

DARK PERIOD OF PARTHIAN HISTORY—ACCESSION OF SANATRŒCES—PHRAATES III. AND POMPEY.

THE death of Mithridates II. introduced into Parthian history, as has been already observed, a period of confusion and disturbance. Civil wars, according to one authority, raged during this period; according to another, there was a rapid succession of monarchs. It would seem that the ancient race of the Arsacidæ had pretty nearly died out; and, as the superstition still prevailed, that fatal consequences would follow, if any one in whose veins the old blood did not run were allowed to ascend the throne, very aged scions of the royal house had to be sought out, and the royal authority committed to hands that were quite unfitted for it. One king who has been thought to belong to the period is said to have died at the age of ninety-six[1]; another was eighty at his accession. Under these circumstances it may well have been that younger rivals sprang up, whether of the royal, or of some fresher and lustier stocks, who disputed the crown with the decrepit monarchs preferred to the position by the Megistanes, and threw the whole country into confusion. These quarrels fell out at an unfortunate

[1] See Appendix.

conjuncture. Rome had at last been forced into a contest with Mithridates of Pontus, and this pre-occupation of the two great powers had for the moment given Armenia a free hand. Armenia, under Tigranes, one of the most ambitious princes that ever lived, took immediate advantage of the occasion, and, while the Mithridatic war was impending, and also during the eleven years that it lasted (B.C. 85–74), employed herself in building up a powerful and extensive empire. Not content with recovering from Parthia the portion of territory which he had begun by ceding to her, Tigranes had, quite early in his reign, carried his aggressions much further, had made himself master of two most important Parthian provinces, Gordyené or Northern Mesopotamia, and Adiabêné or the tract about the Zab rivers, including Assyria Proper and Arbelitis, had conquered Sophené, or the lesser Armenia, which was independent under a king named Artanes, and had also brought under subjection the extensive and valuable country of Media Atropatêné, which had maintained its independence since the time of Alexander. Nor had these successes contented him. Invited into Syria, about B.C. 83, by the wretched inhabitants, who were driven to desperation by the never-ceasing civil wars between rival princes of the house of the Seleucidæ, he had found no difficulty in absorbing the last remnant of the Syro-Macedonian Empire, and establishing himself as king over Cilicia, Syria, and most of Phœnicia. About B.C. 80 he had determined on building himself a new capital in the recently-acquired province of Gordyené—a capital of a vast size, provided with all the luxuries required by an Oriental Court, and fortified with walls such as should recall the glories of the ancient cities of the Assyrians. Twelve Greek cities were depopulated to furnish Tigrano-certa—so the new capital was called —with a sufficiency of Hellenic inhabitants; three hundred thousand Cappadocians were at the same time transported thither; and the population was further swelled by contingents from Cilicia, Gordyené, Adiabêné, and Assyria Proper. A royal palace on a large scale was constructed in the immediate vicinity, together with extensive parks or "paradises," marshes well stocked with wild-fowl, and well-appointed hunting establishments. The walls of the city are declared to have been seventy-five feet in height; and the intention evidently was to constitute it a standing menace to Seleucia, Ctesiphon, Babylon, or whatever might be made the Parthian western capital. The supersession of Parthia by Armenia was clearly aimed at; and it was only a slight step in advance when finally Tigranes placed upon his coins the ancient title of the Great Sovereigns of Asia—recently claimed only by the Arsacid monarchs—the title of βασιλεὺς βασιλέων.

The emergence of Armenia into the position of a Great Power would, under any circumstances, have tended to throw Parthia into the shade; and now, occurring as it did when she was already under a cloud, rent with civil dissensions, and guided by the uncertain hands of aged and feeble monarchs, it produced her almost entire disappearance. For twenty years—from B.C. 89 to B.C. 69—amid the rapid movements that occupy the field of Oriental history, we scarcely obtain a glimpse of Parthia, which is jostled out of sight by the stronger and burlier forms that fill the space, and force themselves on our attention.

It is with difficulty that, by dint of careful search, we at length discover, or fancy we discover, among the fierce struggles of the times two shadowy forms of Parthian kings to place in this interval as links connecting the earlier with the later history. The first of these is a certain Mnasciras, of whom Lucian appears to speak, as a Parthian prince who reached

COIN OF SANATRŒCES.

the great age of ninety-six years, and whom it is impossible to insert at any other point.[1] The other is a somewhat better defined personage—a certain Sanatrœces, called also Sinatroces and Sintricus— who has left his name upon some of his coins, and is mentioned by several authors. This last-named monarch appears to have reigned from B.C. 76 to B.C. 69, and thus to have been contemporary

[1] Professor Gardner argues that the supposed Mnasciras is in reality a certain Kamnasciras, otherwise known to us, who was not a Parthian king at all, and did not belong to this period ("Coinage of Parthia," p. 8). His arguments must be allowed to have great force.

with Tigranes of Armenia, Mithridates of Pontus, and the Roman general, Lucullus. He was seventy-nine years old at his accession, and is said to have been indebted for his crown to aid lent him in the civil struggles, wherein he was engaged with rivals, by the Scythic tribe of the Sacauracæ. During his short reign it was his special endeavour to hold himself aloof from the quarrels of his neighbours, and thus escape the fate of the earthen pot when brought into collision with iron ones. He entirely declined the overtures of Mithridates for an alliance, which were made to him in B.C. 72 ; and when, in B.C. 69, the war had approached his own frontier, and, the most earnest appeals for assistance reaching him from both parties, he found it impossible to maintain the line of pure abstention, he had recourse to the expedient of amusing both sides with promises, while he lent no real aid to either. Plutarch tells us that this course of action so offended and enraged Lucullus, that at one time it almost induced him to defer to a more convenient season his quarrel with Mithridates and his ally, Tigranes, and direct the whole force at his command against Parthia. But the prolonged resistance of Nisibis, and the success of Mithridates in Pontus (B.C. 67) averted the danger, and, the war rolling northwards, Parthia was not yet driven to take a side, but found herself able to maintain her neutral position for a few years longer.

The turning point of the Mithridatic War was the recall of Lucullus (B.C. 66), and his replacement by one of the greatest Roman generals of the time, Cneius Pompeius. Pompey's generalship showed him at

once that, so long as Rome was obliged to contend
single-handed with two such powerful enemies as
Mithridates and Tigranes, success could not be
reasonably expected. The Pontine and Armenian
kings played into each other's hands, and between
them possessed such advantages in local position, in
men, and in resources, that the war might go on
indefinitely without any clear and decisive issue,
unless its conditions could be changed. He looked
about therefore to see whether a new factor could not
be called in, and a change in the balance of force be
thereby brought about. Might not Parthia, which
had rejected the cheap blandishments of Lucullus
and despised his coarse threats, be won over by somewhat more dexterous management, and more refined
diplomacy? A Parthian monarch was now seated
upon the throne who was untried, to whom overtures
had not yet been made, who at any rate had not
committed himself to the policy of abstention. Might
he not be prevailed upon? Might not Phraates the
Third, the son of Sanatrœces, who had just succeeded
his father upon the Parthian throne, be induced by
a sufficiently tempting promise, to join his forces with
those of Rome in the war, and so place the preponderance of military strength on the Roman side?
The main question was, what would be a sufficiently
tempting offer? Pompey thought it enough to
pledge himself, that, if Parthia embraced his cause
and gave him the assistance which he required,
Armenia should at the end of the war be compelled
to make restitution to her of her lost provinces—she
should be once more put in possession of Gordyené,

and Adiabênê. The bait took—Phraates came into the terms proposed—and Parthia for the first and last time became a Roman ally.

The general terms of the agreement made between the high contracting parties seem to have been, that, while Rome pressed the war against the Pontine monarch incessantly and without relaxing in her efforts, Phraates should enter Armenia, and find occupation for Tigranes in his own country. As Parthia and Armenia were conterminous along an extended line of frontier, Phraates could make his assault where he pleased, and how he pleased. It happened that he had at his Court an Armenian refugee of the highest consequence —no less a person than the Crown Prince of Armenia, or eldest living son of Tigranes, who, having quarrelled with his father, had raised a rebellion, and being defeated had been forced to fly, and seek a refuge in Parthia. Phraates determined to take advantage of this circumstance. Having completed his arrangements with Pompey, he, in the year B.C. 65, placed himself at the head of his troops, and, in conjunction with the Armenian prince, invaded the territory of Tigranes. The prince had a party in the country which desired to see a youthful monarch upon the throne, and was soon joined by a considerable body of supporters. The invading army penetrated deep into Armenia, advancing upon the capital, Artaxata, whither Tigranes had retreated. The Armenian monarch made, however, no stand, even at his metropolis ; but, when his foes still pressed forward, quitted the city, and fled to the neighbouring mountains. Artaxata was invested ; but, as the siege promised to be long, Phraates became tired of sitting before the place, and persuaded himself that he had done enough to satisfy Pompey, and might safely leave the young prince, with a contingent of Parthian troops and his own adherents, to carry on the war against his father. Accordingly, he retired, and the young prince remained in sole command. The result followed which might have been anticipated. Scarcely was Phraates withdrawn, when the old king, descending suddenly from his fastnesses, fell upon his son's army at unawares, defeated it, and drove it out of the country. He thus recovered full possession of Armenia, and was once more in a position to render help to Mithridates against Pompey ; but the time for giving effectual help was gone by. Pompey had made such good use of the interval during which the hands of Tigranes were fully employed, that in a single campaign he had broken the power of Mithridates, driven him in head-long flight from place to place, and finally forced him to seek a refuge beyond the Phasis, at Dioscurias, in the modern Mingrelia. Deprived of his ally, Tigranes was too weak to make further head against Rome, and his complete submission, in the autumn of B.C. 66, left Pompey at liberty to settle the affairs of the East at his pleasure.

The settlement made was not very greatly to the liking of the Parthian king. His old adversary, the elder Tigranes, who had propitiated Pompey by the gift of six thousand silver talents—nearly a million and a half of our money—though deprived of Syria, which was made into an actual Roman province, was

left in full possession of his ancestral kingdom of
Armenia, and not even mulcted of the valuable
province of Gordyené, which he had seized in the
time of the acute Parthian distress. His friend and
protégé, the younger Tigranes, was first offered the
petty principality of Sophené, and when he refused it
and remonstrated, was arrested, put in confinement,
and reserved by Pompey for his triumph. He himself
gained nothing by the Roman alliance but the
recovery of Adiabêné, of which he no doubt took
possession before invading Armenia in B.C. 66.
When he attemped, without Pompey's permission, to
repeat in Gordyené the process which had proved
successful on the other side of the Tigris, Pompey did
not scruple to resist him in open warfare—and this
notwithstanding that the province had been actually
promised to him as the price of his alliance. Phraates
learnt what Roman promises were worth, when, on
seeking to repossess himself of Gordyené, he was
met by Pompey's legate, Afranius, who, at the head
of an armed force, drove his troops from the country,
and proceeded to deliver it into the hands of the
Armenians.   Policy might, conceivably, have been
pleaded for this measure, which would tend to weaken
Parthia, Rome's most formidable rival in the East,
and strengthen Armenia, Rome's most convenient
ally, against her ; but no plea of policy could excuse
the useless insult offered to the Parthian monarch,
when Pompey in his written communications refused
him his generally recognised title of " King of
Kings."

There can be little doubt, but that, at this time,

Pompey was balancing in his mind, with an inclination to the affirmative side, the question whether he should, or should not, declare the Parthian prince, a Roman enemy, and direct the full force of the Republic against him. There was much to attract him to the formation of such a decision. His military career had been hitherto without a reverse. He had great confidence in his good fortune. If not as ambitious as his rival, Julius, he was at any rate thoroughly desirous of posing in the eyes of his countrymen as unmistakably the foremost man of his day. To engage a new enemy, and that enemy the recognised successor of Assyria and Persia in the inheritance of the Asian continent, to tread in the steps of Alexander, and carry the arms of the West to the shores of the ocean which shut in the world upon the East, would give him a prestige which would elevate him far above all rivals, and satisfy all the dreams that he had ever entertained of distinction and glory. But, on the other hand, prudence counselled abstention from a risky enterprise. As the war had not been formally committed to him, his enemies at Rome would make his having entered upon it a ground of accusation. He had seen, moreover, with his own eyes, that the Parthians were an enemy far from despicable, and his knowledge of campaigning told him that success against them was by no means certain. He feared to risk the loss of all the glory which he had hitherto gained by grasping greedily at more, and deemed it wiser to enjoy the fruits of the good luck which had hitherto attended him than to tempt fortune on a new field.

He therefore, after hesitating for a while, determined finally on a pacific course. He would not allow himself to be provoked into hostilities by the reproaches, the dictatorial words, or even the daring acts of the Parthian king. When Phraates demanded his lost provinces, he replied, that the question of borders was one which lay, not between Parthia and Rome, but between Parthia and Armenia. When he laid it down that the Euphrates properly and of right bounded the Roman territory, and charged Pompey not to cross it, the latter said he would keep to the just bounds, whatever they were. When Tigranes on his part complained, that, after having been received into the Roman alliance, he was still attacked by the Parthian armies, the reply of Pompey was, that he was quite willing to appoint arbitrators who should decide all the disputes between the two nations. The moderation and caution of these answers proved contagious. On hearing them, the monarchs addressed resolved to compose their differences, or at any rate to defer the settlement of them to a more convenient time, when Rome should have withdrawn from the neighbourhood. They accepted Pompey's proposal of an arbitration; and in a short time an arrangement was effected by which relations of amity were re-established between the two countries.

With the retirement of Pompey from Asia in the year B.C. 62, the East settled down into a state of comparative tranquillity. There was a general feeling that time was necessary to recruit the strength exhausted in the fierce and sanguinary wars of the last thirty years, and a general impression that further contention would only advantage the common enemy—Rome. Rome had now to be looked upon as a permanent neighbour, securely lodged in Cilicia, Syria, and Cappadocia, biding her time, and at any moment ready to take advantage of any false step which might be made by any of the Asiatic kingdoms. Parthia, as having the most to lose, had the most to fear; but Armenia was still more exposed to attack, and might expect to be assailed first. The other minor powers could only hope to escape destruction by remaining quiet, and offering no provocation to the stronger states in their vicinity.

But external tranquillity in Parthia was only too apt to be the precursor of domestic disturbance. Within two years of Pompey's departure from Asia, a conspiracy was formed against the life of Phraates, which resulted in his assassination. His two sons, Mithridates and Orodes, plotted and effected his destruction, for what reason, or on what pretext, we know not. Phraates had held the throne during a time of difficulty, and had ruled, if not with signal success, yet on the whole with prudence and vigour. He had shown himself an active commander, a fair strategist, a successful negotiator. He was apparently in the full possession of all his powers and faculties when he was struck down. It seems as if the motive of the parricide must have been mere personal ambition, that unnatural longing to thrust a parent from his rightful place which has too often produced such tragedies, more especially in the East.

Mithridates, the elder son, obtained the throne, but scarcely succeeded in establishing himself firmly upon it. Very early in his reign he became jealous of his brother and fellow-conspirator, Orodes, and drove him into banishment; while at the same time he treated a large number of the Parthian nobles with cruelty. The Megistanes consequently deposed him, and the hereditary commander-in-chief brought back Orodes from exile, and set him up as king in his brother's room. As some compensation for the loss of his independent sovereignty, Mithridates was given the government of the important province of Media Magna; and, had he been content to remain in this subordinate position he might probably have lived

COIN OF MITHRIDATES III.

out the full term of his natural life in peace and quietness. But there are temperaments which nothing but actual kingship will content, after they have once had a taste of it, and the temperament of Mithridates would appear to have been of this order. He was raising an army with a view to the recovery of his lost throne, when Orodes, having become aware of his intention, marched against him, and crushed his nascent rebellion. Mithridates had to cross the frontier, and place himself under the protection of the nearest Roman proconsul, who happened to be Gabinius, governor of Syria, who had obtained his post through the influence of Pompey. Gabinius, a man of moderate abilities, but of vast ambition, readily received the fugitive, and for a time contemplated an immediate invasion of the Parthian territory, and an attempt to force back Mithridates upon his unwilling subjects. The expedition would probably have taken place, had it not happened that, just at the time, the Syrian proconsul received another invitation from another quarter, which, on the whole, was more tempting. Ptolemy Auletes ("the Fluter"), expelled from Egypt by his exasperated subjects, having obtained the countenance and patronage of Pompey, presented himself before Gabinius in the spring of B.C. 55, and besought his powerful assistance in recovering his lost kingdom. The price which he was ready to pay for the boon named was a sum nearly equal to two and a half millions of our money (twelve and a half millions of dollars). This offer dazzled Gabinius, and almost persuaded him; but the opposition made by his officers was such as might perhaps have induced him to decline it, had not the influence of the young Mark Antony, who was in his camp, been exerted in favour of Auletes, and his representations turned the scale in favour of the Egyptian venture. Mithridates, whose hopes had been raised to the highest pitch, was thus left to bear as he might his cruel disappointment. It is surprising that he did not altogether succumb. But it would seem that he still fancied he saw a possible chance of success. The wild Arab tribes recently settled by Tigranes in Mesopotamia were willing to espouse his cause, and the great cities of Seleucia and Babylon appear to have also declared in his favour. Under these circumstances he threw himself into Babylon, and there endured a long siege at the hands of his brother. It was not until food failed the garrison that a surrender was determined on. Then at last Mithridates, trusting that the ties of blood would be taken into consideration by his adversary, and would cause him to be spared the usual penalty of rebellion, allowed himself to fall alive into Orodes' hands. But fraternal affection was not strongly developed among the Parthians. Orodes, having declared that he placed the claims of country above those of kindred, caused the traitor who had sought aid from Rome to be instantly executed in his presence. Such was the end of the third Mithridates, a weak and selfish prince, with whom it is impossible to feel any sympathy.

X.

GREAT EXPEDITION OF CRASSUS AGAINST PARTHIA,
AND ITS FAILURE — RETALIATORY RAID OF
PACORUS.

CRASSUS—or, to give him his full name, Marcus
Licinius Crassus—though one of the foremost Romans
of his day, was neither a great man, nor a great commander. Sprung from a noble stock, and the son of
a respectable father, he first became noted for his
skill and success in money-getting, an employment
to which for many years he devoted all his energies,
and which he pursued with an ardour and perseverance that made success certain. The times were
favourable for the quick accumulation of a fortune
by commercial methods. The civil struggles, through
which Rome was passing, were accompanied by a
continual succession of forfeitures, confiscations, and
forced sales, which gave an opportunity, even for
moderate capitalists, within a comparatively short
space, by judicious investments, to become men of
large wealth. Crassus allowed no considerations of
compassion, or friendship, or delicacy to hamper him
in his bargains ; and the result was that in course of
time he came to be the legal owner of the greater

portion of the soil on which Rome was built.   His
other possessions were in proportion.   He had mines
which were rich and productive, fertile and well-cultivated estates, and, above all, an enormous number of
valuable slaves.   His own estimate of the worth of
his property, shortly before he started on his expedition, rated it at above seven thousand talents, or more
than a million and seven hundred thousand English
pounds.

In Rome—or at any rate in the Rome of this time
—wealth led, almost of necessity, to political distinction.   An enormous expenditure was needed in order
to obtain the highest offices of the state, and these
offices became naturally the objects of contention
among the most opulent men.   The wealth of Crassus
thrust him into a prominent position, and the position
gradually awoke in him those ambitious longings
which do not seem to have troubled him during his
youth.   After a time he began to court popularity,
and to endeavour to outshine the other political
favourites of the hour.   He came forward as a pleader
in the courts, undertook causes which others declined,
and showed himself especially zealous and pains-
taking.   He threw his house open to all, lent money
freely to his friends without requiring interest, and
exercised a wide, if not a lavish, hospitality.   In this
way he crept on into office, and by degrees worked
his way up to the highest grades.   There, the talents
that he displayed, without being brilliant, were respectable.   He came to be reckoned shrewd and safe.
At last, he was put on a par with the highest candi-
dates for political power, and, though really quite

undeserving of the position, was "bracketed" with Cæsar and Pompey in the so-called "First Triumvirate." The consulship followed (B.C. 55) as a matter of course, and when, on the lots being cast, Syria came out as his "province," Crassus found himself exalted to what was, practically, the first position in the state.

There is reason to believe that, for many long years, the ambition of Crassus, and his jealousy of the other chief political leaders, especially of Pompey and Cæsar, had been growing and expanding. It was particularly in military renown that their reputation excelled his; and it was consequently in this respect that he was most anxious to place himself on their level, if not even, as he hoped, to excel and outdo them. In the position now assigned him he thought he saw his opportunity. The project of Gabinius had got wind, and it had flashed upon the imagination of Crassus how grand a thing it would be to reduce under the dominion of Rome a wholly new country, and that country the seat of ancient empires, and the scene of the highest triumphs of Alexander. Like many another man of dull and plodding temper, Crassus no sooner allowed the desire of glory to get a hold on him, than his unstable mind was carried all lengths, and indulged in flights of the most wild and irrational character. Instead of waiting till he had reached his province, and examined into the position of affairs, before deciding how he would act, or what enterprise he would undertake, Crassus immediately began to boast among his friends of his designs and intentions. He spoke of the wars which Lucullus had waged against Tigranes and Pompey against Mithridates of Pontus as mere child's play, and declared that he was not going to content himself with such paltry conquests as had satisfied them ; Syria did not bound his horizon, no, nor Parthia either ; it was his intention to carry the Roman arms to Bactria, India, and the Eastern Ocean. The more prudent among the statesmen of the Republic remonstrated, but in vain. His friends and flatterers applauded and encouraged him. Even Cæsar, nothing loth to help towards the downfall of a reputation, wrote to him from Gaul to fan the flame of his ambition and stimulate his hopes. Crassus hurried on his preparations, and, though the tribune Ateius endeavoured to deter him by a solemn curse, and even, had the other tribunes permitted, would have arrested his steps at the city gates, left Rome some weeks before his consulship had expired, and, despising alike warnings and omens, set sail with a large fleet from Brundusium.

The journey of Crassus from Brundusium to the Euphrates was prosperous on the whole and uneventful. He lost a certain number of his transports in crossing the Adriatic, which, as it was already mid-November, was not surprising. Landing at Dyrrhachium, he passed through Macedonia and Thrace to the Hellespont, and thence through Asia Minor into Syria where he established himself at Antioch. On his way he fell in with an old Roman ally, Deiotarus, King of Galatia, who happened to be building a new city on his line of route. As Deiotarus was far advanced in years, Crassus, forgetting his own age, indulged in a joke at his expense: "You begin to build, Prince," he said, "rather late in the day ";— whereto the other replied with the retort: "And you, too, Commander, are not beginning very early in the morning to attack the Parthians."

During the time that Crassus was making his preparations at Rome, and the further time that he spent upon his march, Orodes, the Parthian monarch, had an ample space for forming his general plan of campaign at his leisure, and making ready to receive

COIN OF ORODES I.

his enemy. Not only was he able to collect his native troops from all parts of the empire, and to arm, train, and exercise them, but he had an opportunity of gaining over certain chiefs upon his borders, who had hitherto held a semi-independent position, and might have been expected to welcome the Romans. The most important of these was Abgarus, prince of Osrhoëné, or the tract lying east of the Euphrates about the city of Edessa, who had been received into the Roman alliance by Pompey, and was thought by the Romans generally to be well disposed to their cause. Orodes, however, persuaded him, while still remaining professedly a Roman ally, to give in secret his best services to the Parthian side. Another chief, Alchandonius, an Arab sheikh of these parts, who had made his submission to Rome even earlier, becoming convinced that Parthia was the stronger power of the two, was at the same time gained over. Orodes held himself on the defensive, covering the important cities of Seleucia and Babylon with his troops, and waiting to see in what way Crassus would develop his attack, and by what route he would advance into the interior.

The proconsul was at first in no hurry. His old lust of gain came upon him, and after contenting himself with a mere reconnaissance in Mesopotamia, where he defeated a Parthian satrap at Ichnæ on the Belik, and received the voluntary submission of a number of small Greek towns, which he garrisoned, he retraced his steps ere the year was half out, and gave himself up to a series of discreditable but "very lucrative" transactions. At Hierapolis, or Bambycé, where was a famous temple of the Syrian goddess, Atergatis or Derketo, he entered the shrine, carefully weighed all the offerings in the precious metals, and then ruthlessly carried them off. Having tidings of the treasures still remaining in the Sanctuary of Jehovah at Jerusalem, notwithstanding Pompey's sacrilege, he paid the city a visit for the mere purpose of plunder, rifled the sacred treasury, carried off the golden ornaments, and possessed himself by a perjury of a beam of solid gold of 750 pounds weight. In the other cities and states he professed to make requisitions of men and supplies, but let it be understood that in all cases he was willing to accept, instead, a composition in money.   One Greek town in Mesopotamia, which resisted his arms, he took by storm and sacked, afterwards selling all the inhabitants, who survived the sack, as slaves.

Thus passed the autumn and winter of B.C. 54. The spring of B.C. 53 arrived, and the avaricious proconsul began to see that he must absolutely do something to justify his high boasts.   Cæsar had sent him from Gaul his eldest son, a gallant youth and good officer, who was burning to distinguish himself; and his quæstor, C. Cassius Longinus, was also a captain of repute, who would have been ashamed to return to Rome without having fleshed his sword upon some worthier enemy than a handful of miserable Greek colonists. Artavasdes too, the Armenian king, the son of the younger Tigranes, was anxious that so large a Roman army as had been collected, should not quit the neighbourhood without striking Parthia a blow that might seriously weaken, if not even permanently cripple her.   With the first appearance of spring he came into the camp of Crassus, and made him the offer of all the resources of his country. He promised the assistance of sixteen thousand cavalry, of whom ten thousand should be equipped in complete armour, and of thirty thousand infantry, at the same time strongly urging Crassus to direct his march through his own friendly territories, well supplied with water and provisions, and abounding with hills and streams, suited to baffle the manœuvres of the terrible Parthian horsemen. A march through Southern Armenia would conduct to the head streams of the Tigris, whence there was an easy route through a fertile and practicable country down the course of the river to Seleucia-Ctesiphon, the double Parthian capital. Seleucia might be expected to welcome the Romans as liberators ; and there were other Grecian cities upon the route that might lend important aid. The Armenian proposals had much that was tempting about them, and there were not wanting some, among the more sober of the proconsul's advisers, to recommend their acceptance ; but he himself felt hampered by the situation into which he had brought himself by his movements of the preceding year, which had led to his placing garrisons in the various cities of Osrhoëné, whom he could not now leave to the tender mercies of the enemy. He therefore felt compelled to decline the offers of Artavasdes ; and it was probably with some feeling of offence that that prince quitted his camp and returned hastily to his own country.

On the part of Orodes no important movement was made during the winter season except his despatch of an embassy to the proconsul, which seems to have been intended rather to exasperate him than to induce him to forego his attack. The Parthian monarch, it may be suspected, had begun to despise his enemy. He would naturally compare him with Lucullus and Pompey, and when the whole of the first year passed by without anything more important being undertaken then a raid into an outlying province and the occupation of few insignificant and disaffected towns, he would begin to understand that a Roman army, like any other, was formidable or the reverse, according as it was ably or feebly commanded. He would know that Crassus was a sexagenarian, and may have heard that he had never yet shown himself a captain or even a soldier. Perhaps he almost doubted whether the proconsul had any real intention of pressing the contest to a decision, and might not rather be expected, when he had enriched himself and his troops with Mesopotamian plunder, to withdraw his garrisons across the Euphrates. Under these circumstances, Orodes, in the early spring, sent an embassy to the Roman camp, with a message which was well calculated to stir to action the most sluggish and poor-spirited of commanders. " If the war," said his envoys, " was really waged by Rome, it must be fought out to the bitter end. But if, as they had good reason to believe, Crassus, against the wish of his country, had attacked Parthia and seized her territory for his own private gain, Arsaces would be moderate. He would have pity on the advanced years of the proconsul, and would give the Romans back those men of theirs, who were not so much keeping watch in Mesopotamia as having watch kept on them." Crassus, stung with the taunt, made the answer so significant of the pride that goes before a fall—" He would give the ambassadors his response in their capital." Wagises, the chief envoy, prepared for some such exhibition of feeling, and glad to heap taunt on taunt, replied, striking the palm of one hand with the fingers of the other : " Hairs will grow here, Crassus, before you see Seleucia."

Soon after this, before the winter could well be said to be over, the offensive was taken against the Roman garrisons and adherents in Mesopotamia. The towns occupied were attacked by the Parthians in force, and though it does not seem that any of them were recovered, yet all of them were menaced, and all suffered considerably. The more timid of the defenders made their escape from some of them and brought to the Roman camp an exaggerated account of the difficulties of Parthian warfare. " The enemy," they said, " were so rapid in their movements that it was impossible either to overtake them when they fled or to escape them when they pursued ; their arrows sped faster than sight could follow, and penetrated every kind of defence, while their mail-clad horsemen had weapons that would pierce through any armour, and armour that defied the thrust of every weapon." Considerable alarm was excited by these rumours, an alarm which was reflected in the reports of unfavourable omens issuing from the augural staff ; but the proconsul had by this time made up his mind that something must be risked, and that he could not face the storm of ridicule that would meet him at Rome, if he did not fight at least one great battle.

A second campaign was therefore resolved upon ; but it still remained to determine the line of march. Armenia had been already rejected, partly as too circuitous and involving an unnecessary waste of time, but mainly as implying the desertion, and so the sacrifice, of the troops which to the number of eight thousand had been left in Mesopotamia the year before. Crassus felt bound to support his garrisons, and so to make Mesopotamia, and not Armenia, the basis of his operations. But there were several lines of route through Mesopotamia. In the first place, there was the line best known to the Greeks, and through them best known to the Romans—that of the Euphrates—which had been pursued by Cyrus the Younger in the expedition against his brother, whereon he had been accompanied by the Ten Thousand. Along this line water would be plentiful; forage and other supplies might be counted on to a certain extent; and the advancing army, resting its right upon the river, could not be surrounded. Another was that which Alexander had taken against Darius Codomannus—the line along the foot of the Mons. Masius (Karajah Dagh), by Edessa and Nisibis to Nineveh. Here, too, water and supplies would have been readily procurable, and by clinging to the skirts of the hills the Roman infantry would have been able to set the Parthian cavalry at defiance. Between these two extreme courses to the right and to the left, were numerous slightly divergent lines across the Mesopotamian plain, all of them shorter than either of the two above-mentioned routes, and none offering any great advantage over the remainder.

The original inclination of Crassus seems to have been to follow in the track of the Ten Thousand. He crossed the Euphrates at Zeugma (Bir or Birehjik), in about latitude 37°, at the head of seven legions, four thousand cavalry, and an equal number of slingers and archers, and at first began his march along the river bank. No enemy appeared in sight; and his scouts brought him word that there was none to be seen for a long distance in front; the only traces that appeared were numerous tracks of horses in rapid retreat before his advancing squadrons. The news

was considered to be good, and the soldiers marched
forward cheerfully.   The same direction was maintained ; but presently, Abgarus, the Osrhoënian sheikh,
made his appearance, and had a conference with the
proconsul, wherein he professed the most friendly feelings, and strongly recommended an entire change of
tactics.   " The Parthians," he said, " did not intend to
make a stand ; they might do so later, when the king
had collected all his forces ; but at present they were
demoralised, and were thinking only of quitting Mesopotamia, and flying with their treasures to the remote
regions of Hyrcania and Scythia.   The king was
already far away ; the main host was in full retreat ;
only a rearguard under a couple of generals, Surenas
and Sillaces, still lingered in Mesopotamia, and might
be within striking distance. Crassus should give up his
cautious proceedings, and hurry on at his best speed ;
he would then probably succeed in overtaking and
cutting to pieces the rearguard of the great army,
a flying multitude encumbered with baggage, which
would furnish a rich spoil to the victors."   The crafty
Osrhoënian was believed ; and, though Cassius with
some other officers is said to have still counselled
a more cautious advance, the proconsul resolved on
giving himself up to the guidance of " the Bedouin,"
and altering the direction of the march in accordance
with his recommendations.   Accordingly, he turned
off from the Euphrates, and proceeded eastward over
the swelling hills and dry gravelly plains of Upper
Mesopotamia.

Here we shall leave him for the present, while we
consider the real disposition of his forces which the

Parthian monarch had made to meet the impending attack. He had, as already stated, come to terms with his outlying vassals, the prince of Osrhoëné and the sheikh of the Scenite Arabs, and had engaged especially the services of the former against his assailant. He had further, on considering the various possibilities of the campaign, come to the conclusion that it would be best to divide his forces, and while himself attacking Artavasdes in the mountain fastnesses of his own country, to commit the task of meeting and coping with the Romans to a general of approved talents. It was of the greatest possible importance to prevent the Armenians from effecting a junction with the Romans, and strengthening them in that arm in which they were especially deficient, the cavalry. Probably nothing short of an invasion of his kingdom by the Parthian monarch in person would have prevented Artavasdes from detaching a portion of his troops to act in Mesopotamia. And no doubt it is also true that Orodes had great confidence in his general, whom he may even have felt to be a better commander than himself. Surenas, as we must call him, since his personal appellation has not come down to us, was in all respects a person of the highest consideration. He was the second man in the kingdom for birth, wealth, and reputation. In courage and ability he excelled all his countrymen ; and he had the physical advantages of commanding height, and great personal beauty. When he went to battle, he was accompanied by a train of a thousand camels, which carried his baggage ; and the concubines in attendance on him required for their conveyance as many as two hundred chariots. A thousand mail-clad horsemen, and a still larger number of light-armed, formed his body-guard. At the coronation of a Parthian monarch, it was his hereditary right to place the diadem on the brow of the new sovereign. When Orodes was driven into banishment, it was he who had brought him back to Parthia in triumph. When Seleucia revolted, it was he who at the assault had first mounted the breach, and striking terror into the defenders, had taken the city. Though less than thirty years of age when he was appointed commander, he was believed to possess, besides these various qualifications, consummate prudence and sagacity.

The force which Orodes committed to his brave and skilful lieutenant consisted entirely of horse. This was not the ordinary character of a Parthian army, which often comprised four or five times as many cavalry as infantry. Whether it was to any extent the result of his own selection and military insight, is uncertain. Perhaps fortunate accident rather than profound calculation brought about the sole employment against the Romans of the cavalry arm. Horse would be wholly useless in the rugged and mountainous Armenia, while they would act with effect in the comparatively open and level Mesopotamian region. Footmen, on the other hand, were essential for the Armenian war, and perhaps the king thought that he needed as many as he could collect. In this case he would naturally take with him the whole of the infantry, and leave his general the troops which were not required for his own operations. It certainly does not appear, that Surenas was allowed any choice in the matter.

The Parthian horse, like the Persian, was of two kinds, standing in strong contrast the one to the other. The bulk of their cavalry was of the lightest and most agile description. Fleet and active coursers, with scarcely any caparison but a headstall and a single rein, were mounted by riders clad only in a tunic and trousers, and armed with nothing but a strong bow and a quiver full of arrows. A training begun in early boyhood and continued through youth made the rider almost one with his steed; and he could use his weapons with equal ease and effect whether his horse was stationary or at full gallop, or whether he was advancing towards or hurriedly retreating from his enemy. His supply of missiles was practically inexhaustible, since when he found his quiver empty, he had only to retire a short distance and replenish his stock from magazines, borne on the backs of camels, in the rear. It was his ordinary plan to keep constantly in motion when in the presence of an enemy, to gallop backwards and forwards, or round and round his square or column, never charging it, but at a moderate interval plying it with his keen and barbed shafts; which were driven by a practised hand from a bow of unusual strength. Clouds of this light cavalry enveloped the advancing or retreating foe, and inflicted grievous damage, without, for the most part, suffering anything in return.

But this was not the whole, nor the worst. In addition to these light troops, a Parthian army contained always a body of heavy cavalry, armed on an entirely different system. The strong chargers selected for this service were clad almost wholly in mail. Their head, neck, chest, even their sides and flanks, were protected by scale-armour of bronze or iron, sewn probably upon leather. Their riders had cuirasses and cuisses of the same materials, and helmets of burnished iron. For an offensive weapon they carried a long and strong spear or pike. They formed a serried line in battle, bearing down with great weight on the enemy whom they attacked, and standing firm as an iron wall against the charges that were made upon them. A cavalry, answering to this in some respects, had been employed by the later Persian monarchs, and was in use also among the Armenians at this period ; but the Parthian pike appears to have been considerably more formidable than the corresponding weapon borne by either of these nations.

As compared with these troops, the Romans, as Mommsen observes, were thoroughly inferior both in respect of number and of excellence. Their infantry of the line, excellent as they were in close combat, whether at a short distance with the heavy javelin, or in hand-to-hand combat with the sword, could not compel an army consisting wholly of cavalry to come to an engagement with them ; and they found, even when they did come to a hand-to-hand conflict, an equal or superior adversary in the iron-clad hosts of lancers. As compared with a force like that of Surenas, the Roman army was at a disadvantage strategically, be-cause the cavalry commanded the communications ; and at a disadvantage tactically, because every weapon of close combat must succumb to that which is wielded from a distance, unless the struggle becomes an in-dividual one man against man. The concentrated

position, on which the whole Roman method of war
was based, increased the danger in the presence of
such an attack, since the closer the ranks of the
Roman column, the less could the missiles fail to hit
their mark. Under ordinary circumstances, where
towns have to be defended, and difficulties of the
ground have to be considered, such a system of opera-
ting with mere cavalry against infantry could never
be completely carried out ; but in the Mesopotamian
plain region, where an army was almost like a ship on
the high seas, neither encountering an obstacle, nor
meeting with a basis for strategic dispositions during
many days' march, this mode of warfare was irresistible
for the very reason that circumstances allowed it to be
developed there in all its purity and therefore in all its
power. *There* everything combined to put the foreign
infantry at a disadvantage against the native cavalry.
Where the heavily-laden Roman foot soldier dragged
himself toilsomely over the steppe, and perished from
hunger, or still more from thirst, on a route marked
only by water-springs that were far apart and difficult
to find, the Parthian horseman, accustomed from child-
hood to sit on his fleet steed or camel, nay, almost to
spend his life in the saddle, easily traversed the desert,
whose hardships he had long learned how to lighten,
and in case of need to bear. *There* no rain fell to
mitigate the intolerable heat, and to slacken the bowstrings and leathern thongs of the enemy's archers and
slingers ; *there* in the light soil of some places ordinary
ditches and ramparts could hardly be formed for the
camp. Imagination can hardly conceive a situation in
which all the military advantages were more on the

one side, and all the disadvantages more thoroughly on the other.

The force entrusted by Orodes to Surenas comprised cavalry of both the kinds above described. No estimate is given us of their number; but, as they are called "a vast multitude," and "an immense body," we may assume that it was considerable. At any rate it was sufficient to induce him to make a movement in advance—to cross the Sinjar range and the river Khabour, and take up his position in the country between that stream and the Belik—instead of merely seeking to cover the capital. The presence of the traitor, Abgarus, in the camp of Crassus, became now of the utmost importance to the Parthian commander. Abgarus, fully trusted by the Romans, and at the head of a body of light horse, admirably adapted for outpost service, was allowed, upon his own request, to scour the country in front of the advancing legions, and had thus the means of communicating freely with the Parthian chief. He kept Surenas informed of all the movements and intentions of Crassus, while at the same time he suggested to Crassus such a line of route as suited the views and designs of his adversary. Our chief authority for the details of the expedition, Plutarch, tells us, that he led the Roman troops through an arid and trackless desert, across plains without tree, or shrub, or even grass, where the soil was composed of a light shifting sand, which the wind raised into a succession of hillocks that resembled the waves of an interminable sea. The soldiers, he says, fainted with the heat and with the drought, while the audacious Osrhoënian scoffed at their complaints and reproaches,

asking them whether they expected to find the border-
tract between Arabia and Assyria a country of cool
streams and shady groves, of baths and hostelries, like
their own delicious Campania.   But our knowledge of
the real geographical character of the region through
which the march lay makes it impossible for us to
accept this account as true.   The country between the
Euphrates and the Belik is one of alternate hill and
plain, neither destitute of trees, nor very ill-provided
with water.   The march through it can have presented
no very great difficulties. All that Abgarus could do to
serve the Parthian cause was, first, to induce Crassus
to trust himself to the open country instead of clinging either to a river or to the mountains ; and, secondly,
to bring him, after a hasty march, and in the full heat
of the day, into the presence of the enemy.   Both
these things he contrived to effect ; and Surenas was,
no doubt, so far beholden to him.   But the notion
that he enticed the Roman army into a trackless
desert, and gave it over, when it was perishing with
weariness, hunger, and thirst, into the hands of its
enraged enemy, being in contradiction with the topo-
graphical facts, must be regarded as a fiction of Roman
apologists, and is one not even consistently maintained
by all the classical writers.

It was probably on the third or fourth day after he
had quitted the Euphrates that Crassus found himself approaching his enemy.   After a hasty and hot
march he had approached the banks of the Belik,
when his scouts brought him word that they had
fallen in with the Parthian army, which was advancing
in force and seemingly full of confidence.   Abgarus

had recently quitted him on the pretence of doing him some undefined service, but in reality to range himself on the side of his true friends, the Parthians. His officers now advised Crassus to encamp upon the river, and defer an engagement till the morrow, but he had no fears ; his son, Publius, a gallant officer formed in the school of Julius Cæsar, was anxious for the fray ; and accordingly the Roman commander gave the order to his troops to take some refreshment as they stood, and then to push forward rapidly. Surenas, on his side, had taken up a position on wooded and hilly ground, which concealed his num-bers, and had even, we are told, made his troops cover their arms with cloths and skins, that the glitter might not betray them. But, as the Romans drew near, all concealment was cast aside ; the signal for battle was given ; the clang of the kettledrums sounded on every side ; the squadrons came forward in their brilliant array ; and it seemed at first as if the heavy cavalry was about to charge the Roman host, which was formed in a hollow square, with the light-armed in the middle, and with supports of horse along the whole line, as well as upon the flanks. But, if this intention was ever entertained, it was altered almost as soon as formed, and the better plan was adopted of halting at a convenient distance, and assailing the legionaries with flight after flight of arrows, delivered without pause, and with extraordi-nary force. The Roman endeavoured to meet this attack by throwing forward his own skirmishers, but they were quite unable to cope with the numbers and superior weapons of the enemy, who forced them almost immediately to retreat, and take shelter behind the line of the legionaries. These were once more exposed to the deadly missiles, which pierced alike through shield and breastplate and greaves, and inflicted the most fearful wounds. More than once the legionaries dashed forward and sought to close with their assailants, but in vain. The Parthian squadrons retired as the Roman infantry advanced, maintaining the distance which they thought best between themselves and their foe, whom they plied with their shafts as incessantly while they fell back as when they rode forward. For a while the Romans maintained the hope that the missiles would at last be all spent, but when they found that each archer constantly obtained a fresh supply of arrows from the rear, this expectation deserted them. It became evident to Crassus under these circumstances that some new movement must be attempted, and, as a last resource, he commanded his son, Publius, whom the Parthians were threatening to outflank, to take such troops as he thought proper and charge. The brave youth was only too glad to receive the order. Selecting the Celtic cavalry which Cæsar had sent with him from Gaul, who numbered a thousand, and adding to them three hundred other horsemen, five hundred archers, and about four thousand legionaries, he advanced at speed against the nearest squadrons of the enemy. The Parthians pretended to be afraid, and beat a hasty retreat. Publius followed with all the impetuosity of youth, and was soon out of sight of his friends, pressing the flying foe, whom he believed to be panic-stricken. But when they had drawn him on sufficiently, they suddenly made a stand, brought their heavy cavalry up against his line, and completely enveloped him and his detachment with their light-armed. Publius made a desperate resistance. His Gauls seized the Parthian pikes with their hands, and dragged the encumbered horsemen to the ground; or, dismounting, slipped beneath the horses of their opponents, and stabbing them in the belly brought steed and rider down upon themselves. His legionaries occupied a slight hillock, and endeavoured to make a wall of their shields, but the Parthian archers closed around them, and slew them almost to a man. Of the whole detachment, nearly six thousand strong, no more than five hundred were taken prisoners, and scarcely a man escaped. The young Crassus might possibly, had he chosen to make the attempt, have forced his way through the enemy to Iehnæ, a Greek town not far distant, but he preferred to share the fate of his men. Rather than fall alive into the hands of the enemy, he caused his shield-bearer to despatch him; and his example was followed by his principal officers. The victors struck off his head, and, elevating it on a pike, returned to resume their attack on the main body of the Roman army.

The main army, much relieved by the diminution of the pressure upon them, had waited patiently for Publius to return in triumph, regarding the battle as well-nigh over, and success as certain. After a time the prolonged absence of the young captain aroused suspicions, which grew into alarm when messengers arrived telling of his extreme danger. Crassus, almost beside himself with anxiety, had given the word to advance, and the army had moved forward a short distance when the shouts of the returning enemy were heard, and the head of the unfortunate Publius was seen displayed aloft, while the Parthian squadrons, closing in once more, renewed the assault on their remaining foes with increased vigour. The mailed horsemen approached close to the legionaries and thrust at them with their long pikes, which sometimes transfixed two men at once ; while the light-armed, galloping across the Roman front, discharged their unerring arrows over the heads of their own men. The Romans could neither successfully defend themselves nor effectively retaliate ; they could neither break the ranks of the lancers, nor reach the archers. Still time brought some relief. Bowstrings broke, spears were blunted or splintered, arrows began to fail, thews and sinews to relax ; and when night closed in both parties were almost equally glad of the cessation of arms which the darkness rendered compulsory.

It was the custom of the Parthians, as of the Persians, to bivouac at a considerable distance from an enemy for fear of a night surprise. Accordingly, as evening closed in, they drew off, having first shouted jeeringly to the Romans that they would grant the general one night in which to bewail his son ; on the morrow they would return and take him prisoner unless he should prefer the better course of surrendering himself to the mercy of Arsaces. A short breathing-space was thus allowed the Romans, who took advantage of it to retire towards Carrhæ, leaving

behind them the greater part of their wounded, to
the number of four thousand.   A small body of horse
under the command· of Egnatius reached Carrhæ
about midnight, and gave the commandant such
information as led him to put his men under arms
and issue forth to the succour of the proconsul.   The
Parthians, though the cries of the forsaken wounded
made them well aware of the Roman retreat, adhered
to their system of avoiding night combats, and
attempted no pursuit till daybreak.   Even then they
allowed themselves to be delayed by comparatively
trivial matters—the capture of the Roman camp, the
massacre of the wounded, and the slaughter of the
numerous stragglers scattered along the line of march
—and made no haste to overtake the retreating army.
The bulk of the troops were thus enabled to effect
their retreat in safety to Carrhæ, where, having the
protection of walls, they were, at any rate for a time,
secure.

It might have been expected that the Romans
would here have made a stand.   The siege of a
fortified place by cavalry is ridiculous, if we understand by siege anything more than a very incomplete
blockade.   And the Parthians were notoriously
inefficient against walls.   There was a chance, moreover, that Artavasdes might have been more successful than his ally, and, having repulsed the Parthian
monarch, might be on his way to bring relief to the
Romans.   But the soldiers were thoroughly dispirited,
and would not listen to these suggestions.   Provisions, no doubt, ran short, since, as there had been
no expectation of a disaster, no preparations had been

made for standing a siege. The Greek inhabitants of the place could not be trusted to exhibit fidelity to a falling cause. Moreover, Armenia was near, and the Parthian system of abstaining from action during the night seemed to render escape tolerably easy. It was resolved, therefore, instead of clinging to the protection of the walls, to issue forth once more, and to endeavour by a rapid night march to reach the Armenian hills. The various officers seem to have been allowed to arrange matters each for himself. Cassius took his way towards the Euphrates, and succeeded in escaping with five hundred horse. Octavius, with a division which is estimated at five thousand men, reached the outskirts of the hills at a place called Sinnaca, and found himself in comparative security. Crassus, misled by his guides, made but poor progress during the night; he had, however, arrived within little more than a mile of Octavius before the enemy, who would not stir till daybreak, overtook him. Pressed upon by their advancing squadrons, he, with his small band of two thousand legionaries and a few horsemen, occupied a low hillock connected by a ridge of rising ground with the position of Sinnaca. Here the Parthian host beset him, and he would infallibly have been slain or captured at once had not Octavius, deserting his place of safety, descended to the aid of his commander. The united seven thousand held their own against the enemy, having the advantage of the ground, and having, perhaps, by the experience of some days, learnt the weak points of Parthian warfare.

Surenas was anxious, above all things, to secure the person of the Roman commander. In the East an excessive importance is attached to this proof of success; and there were reasons which made Crassus particularly obnoxious to his antagonists. He was believed to have originated, and not merely conducted, the war, incited thereto by simple greed of gold. He had refused with the utmost haughtiness all discussion of terms, and had insulted the majesty of the Parthians by the declaration that he would treat with them nowhere but at their capital. If he escaped, he would be bound at some future time to repeat his attempt; if he were made a prisoner his fate would be a terrible warning to others. But now, as evening approached, it seemed to the Parthian that the prize which he so much desired was about to elude his grasp. The highlands of Armenia would be gained by the fugitives during the night, and further pursuit of them would be futile. It remained that he should effect by craft what he could no longer hope to obtain by the employment of force; and to this point all his efforts were henceforth directed. He drew off his troops and left the Romans without further molestation. He allowed some of his prisoners to escape and rejoin their friends, having first contrived that they should overhear a conversation among his men, of which the theme was the Parthian clemency, and the wish of Orodes to come to terms with the Romans. He then, having allowed time for the report of his pacific intentions to spread, rode with a few chiefs towards the Roman camp, carrying his bow unstrung, and his right hand stretched out, in token of amity. "Let the Roman general," he said, "come forward with an equal number of attendants, and confer with me in the open space between the armies on terms of peace." The aged proconsul was disinclined to trust these overtures, but the Roman soldiery, demoralised as it was, clamoured and threatened ; upon which Crassus yielded, and went down into the plain, accompanied by Octavius and a few others. Surenas received the proconsul and his staff with apparent honour, and terms were arranged ; only, with just bitterness, the Parthian chief required that they should be at once reduced to writing, "since," he said, with pointed allusion to the bad faith of Pompey, "you Romans are not very apt to remember your engagements." A movement being requisite for the purpose of drawing up the formal instruments, Crassus and his officers were induced to mount upon horses furnished by the Parthians, who had no sooner seated the proconsul on his steed than they proceeded to hurry him forward, with the evident intention of carrying him off to their camp. The Roman officers took the alarm and resisted. Octavius snatched a sword from a Parthian, and killed one of the grooms who were hurrying Crassus away. A blow from behind stretched him on the ground lifeless. A general *mêlée* followed, and in the confusion Crassus was killed, whether by one of his own side and with his own consent, or by the hand of a Parthian, is uncertain. The army, learning the fate of their commander, with but few exceptions, surrendered. Such as sought to escape under cover of the approaching night were hunted down by the Bedouins, who served under the Parthian standard, and killed almost to a man. Of the entire force which had crossed the Euphrates, consisting of above forty thousand men, not more than a fourth returned. One half of the whole number perished. Nearly ten thousand prisoners were settled by the victors near the extreme east of their empire in the fertile oasis of Margiana (Merv) as bondsmen, compelled after the Parthian fashion to render military service. Here they intermarried with native wives, and became submissive Parthian subjects.

Such was the result of this great expedition, the first attempt of the grasping and ambitious Romans, not so much to conquer Parthia, as to strike terror into the heart of her people, and to degrade them to the condition of obsequious dependants on the will and pleasure of the "world's lords." The expedition failed so utterly, not from any want of bravery on the part of the soldiers employed in it, nor from any absolute superiority of the Parthian over the Roman tactics, but partly from the incompetence of the commander, partly from the inexperience of the Romans up to this date, in the nature of the Parthian warfare, and from their consequent ignorance of the best manner of meeting it. To attack an enemy whose main arm is the cavalry with a body of foot soldiers, supported by an insignificant number of horse, must be at all times rash and dangerous. To direct such an attack on the more open part of the country, where cavalry could operate freely, was wantonly to aggravate the peril. After the first disaster, to quit the protection of walls, when it had once been obtained, was a piece of reckless folly. Had Crassus taken care to get the support of some of the desert tribes, if Armenia could not or would not help him, and had he then advanced, either by the way of the Mons. Masius and the Tigris, or along the line of the Euphrates, the issue of his attack might have been different. He might have fought his way to Seleucia and Ctesiphon, as did Trajan, Avidius Cassius, and Septimius Severus, and might have taken and plundered those cities. He would, no doubt, have experienced difficulties in his retreat; but he might have come off no worse than Trajan, whose Parthian expedition has been generally regarded as rather a feather in his cap, and as augmenting rather than detracting from his reputation. But an ignorant and inexperienced commander, venturing on a trial of arms with an enemy of whom he knew little or nothing, in their own country, without supports or allies, and then neglecting every precaution suggested by his officers, allowing himself to be deceived by a pretended friend, and marching straight into a net prepared for him, naturally suffered defeat. The credit of the Roman arms does not greatly suffer by the disaster, nor is that of the Parthians greatly enhanced. The latter showed, as they had shown in their wars against the Syro-Macedonians, that their somewhat loose and irregular army was capable of acting with effect against the solid masses and well-ordered movements of the best disciplined troops. They acquired by their use of the bow a fame like that which the English bowmen obtained at Crecy and Agincourt. They forced the arrogant Romans to respect them, and to allow that there was at least one nation in the world which could meet them on equal terms and not be worsted in the encounter. They henceforth obtained recognition from the Greco-Roman writers—albeit a grudging and covert recognition—as the Second Power in the world, the admitted rival of Rome, the only real counterpoise upon the earth to the mighty empire which ruled from the banks of the Euphrates to the shores of the Atlantic Ocean.

While the general of King Orodes was thus completely successful against the Romans in Mesopotamia, the king himself had in Armenia obtained advantages of almost equal importance, though of a different kind. Instead of waging an internecine war with Artavasdes, he had come to terms with him, and, having concluded a close alliance, had set himself to confirm and cement it by uniting his· son, Pacorus, in marriage with the sister of the royal Armenian. A series of festivities was in course of being held, to celebrate the auspicious event, when news arrived of the triumph of Surenas and the fate of Crassus. According to the barbarous customs at all times prevalent in the East, the head and hand of the slain proconsul accompanied the intelligence. We are told that, at the moment of the messengers' arrival the two sovereigns, with their attendants, were being amused by a dramatic entertainment. Strolling companies of Greek players were at this time frequent in the East, where they were sure of patronage in the many Greek cities, and might sometimes find an appreciative audience among the natives. Artavasdes, as the master of the revels, had engaged such a company, since both he and Orodes had a good knowledge of the Greek literature and language, in which he had himself composed both historical works and tragedies. The performance had begun, and it happened, that, when the messengers arrived, the actors were engaged in the representation of the famous scene in the " Bacchæ " of Euripides, where Agavé and the Bacchanals come upon the stage with the mutilated remains of the murdered Pentheus. The head of Crassus was thrown to them ; and instantly the player who personated Agavé seized the bloody trophy, and placing it on his thyrsus in lieu of the one that he was carrying, paraded it before the delighted spectators, while he chanted the well-known lines—

> " From the mountain to the hall
> New-cut tendril, see, we bring —
> Blessed prey ! "

The horrible spectacle was one well suited to please an Eastern audience ; loud and prolonged plaudits, we may be sure, rang out ; and the entire assemblage felt a keen satisfaction in the performance. It was followed by a proceeding of equal barbarity, and still more thoroughly Oriental. The Parthians, in derision of the motive which was supposed to have led Crassus to make his attack, had a quantity of gold melted and poured it into his mouth.

Meanwhile Surenas was amusing his victorious troops, and seeking to annoy the disaffected Seleucians by the exhibition of a farcical ceremony. He

spread the report that Crassus was not killed but
captured; and selecting from among the prisoners
the Roman most like him in appearance, he dressed
the man in woman's clothes, mounted him upon a
horse, and requiring him to answer to the names of
"Crassus" and "Imperator," conducted him in triumph
to the Grecian city. Before him went, mounted on
camels, a band arrayed as trumpeters and lictors,
the lictors' rods having purses suspended to them, and
the axes in their midst being crowned with the bleed-
ing heads of Romans. In the rear followed a train of
Seleucian music-girls, who sang songs derisive of the
effeminacy and cowardice of the proconsul. After
this pretended parade of his prisoner through the
streets of the town, Surenas called a meeting of the
Seleucian senate, and indignantly denounced to them
the indecency of the literature which he had found in
the Roman tents. The charge, it is said, was true;
but the Seleucians were not greatly impressed by the
moral lesson read to them, when they remarked the
train of concubines that had accompanied Surenas
himself to the field, and thought further of the loose
crowd of dancers, singers, and prostitutes, that was
commonly to be seen in the rear of a Parthian army.

It might have been expected that the terrible
disaster which had befallen the Roman arms, and the
vast triumph which the Parthians had achieved for
themselves, would have had extraordinary and far-
reaching consequences. No one could have been
surprised if the result had been to shake the very
foundations of the Roman power in the East, or even
to restore to Asia that aggressive attitude towards the

rest of the world, which she had held four hundred and fifty years earlier. But the commotion and change produced was far less than might have been anticipated. Mesopotamia was, of course, recovered by the Parthians to its extremest limit, the Euphrates ; and Armenia was lost to the Roman alliance, and thrown for the time into complete dependence upon Parthia. The whole East was, to some extent, excited ; and the Jews, always impatient of a foreign yoke, and recently aggrieved by the unprovoked spoliation of their Temple by Crassus, flew to arms. But no general movement of the Oriental races took place. It might have been supposed that the Syrians, Phœnicians, Cilicians, Cappadocians, Phrygians, and other Asiatic peoples whose proclivities were altogether Oriental, would have seized the opportunity of rising against their Western lords and driving the Romans back upon Europe. It might have been thought that Parthia at least would have immediately assumed the offensive in force, and have made a determined effort to rid herself of neighbours who had proved so troublesome. But though the conjuncture of circumstances was most favourable—though not only was Rome paralysed in the East, but was also on the point of civil war in the West—yet the man was wanting. Had Mithridates of Pontus or Tigranes of Armenia been living, or had Surenas been king of Parthia instead of a mere general, advantage would probably have been taken of the occasion, and Rome might have suffered seriously. But Orodes seems to have been neither ambitious as a prince nor skilful as a commander ; he lacked at any rate the keen and

all-embracing glance which could sweep the political
horizon, and, comprehending the exact character of the
situation, see at the same time how to make the most
of it.   He allowed the opportunity to slip by without
hastening to put forth his full strength, or indeed
making any considerable effort ; and the occasion
once lost was sure never to return.

If there was a man living at the time who might
possibly have taken full advantage of the situation,
and forced Rome to pay the deserved penalty of her
rashness and aggressiveness, it was Surenas.   But
that chief had lost the favour of his sovereign.
There are services which, in the East, it is not safe
for a subject to render to the head of the state, and
Surenas had exceeded the proper measure.   The
jealousy of Orodes was aroused by the success and
reputation of his general ; and it was not long before
he found an excuse for handing him over to the
executioner.   Parthia was thus left without any commander of approved merit, for Sillaces, the second
in command during the war with Crassus, had in no
way distinguished himself in the course of it.   This
condition of things may account for the feebleness of
the efforts made, in the years B.C. 53 and 52, to
retaliate on the Romans the damage done by their
invasion.   A few weak flying bands only crossed the
Euphrates, and began the work of plunder and
ravage, in which they were speedily disturbed by
Cassius, who easily drove them back across the river.
Rome should have taken advantage of the interval
to strengthen her forces.in these parts, and secure the
inviolability of her frontier ; but those who were at

the head of the Roman State, knowing civil war to
be imminent, declined to detach troops from their
own party standards for the advantage of the
national cause.

Hence, when, in B.C. 51, Orodes had made up his
mind to attempt a blow, and a great Parthian army
under the young prince, Pacorus, and an officer of
ripe age and experience, by name Osaces, appeared
on the eastern bank of the Euphrates, there were no
means of resisting them. Cassius had done his best
to unite and re-organise the broken remnants of the
army of Crassus, which he had formed into two weak

COIN OF PACORUS I.

legions ; but no reinforcements had reached him, and
he did not feel justified in taking the open field with
his small force, much less in giving battle to the
enemy. The Parthians therefore crossed the Euphrates
unopposed, and swarmed into the rich Syrian territory.
The walled towns shut their gates, and maintained
themselves ; but the open country was everywhere
overrun : and a thrill of mingled alarm and excitement passed through all the Roman provinces in
Asia. These provinces were at the time most
inadequately supplied with Roman troops, owing to
the impending civil war in Italy. The natives were
for the most part disaffected, and inclined to hail the

Parthians as brethren and deliverers. Excepting Deiotarus of Galatia, and Ariobarzanes of Cappadocia, Rome had, as Cicero (then proconsul of Cilicia) plaintively declared, not a friend on the Asiatic continent. And Cappadocia was miserably weak, and open to attack on the side of Armenia. Had Orodes and Artavasdes acted in concert, and had the latter, while Orodes sent his armies into Syria, poured the Armenian forces into Cappadocia and then into Cilicia (as it was expected that he would do), there would have been the greatest danger to the Roman possessions. As it was, the excitement in Asia Minor was extreme. Cicero marched into Cappadocia with the bulk of his Roman troops, and summoned to his aid Deiotarus with his Galatians, at the same time writing to the Roman Senate to implore reinforcements. Cassius shut himself up in Antioch, and allowed the Parthian cavalry to pass him by, and even to proceed beyond the bounds of Syria into Cilicia. But the Parthians seem scarcely to have understood the straits of their adversaries or to have been aware of their own advantages. Probably their "information department" was ill organised. Instead of spreading themselves wide, raising the natives, and leaving them to blockade the towns, while with their as yet unconquered squadrons they defied the enemy in the open country, we find them engaging in the siege and blockade of cities, for which they were totally unfit, and confining themselves almost entirely to the narrow valley of the Orontes. Under these circumstances we are not surprised to learn that Cassius, having first beaten

them back from Antioch, contrived to lead them into
an ambush on the banks of the river, and severely
handled their troops, even killing the general, Osaces.
The Parthians withdrew from the neighbourhood
of the Syrian capital after this defeat, which must
have taken place about the end of September, and
soon after went into winter quarters in Cyrrhestica, or
the part of Syria immediately east of Amanus.
Here they remained quietly during the winter months
under Prince Pacorus, and it was expected that the
war would break out again with fresh fury in the
spring ; but Bibulus, the new proconsul of Syria—
" as wretched a general as he was an incapable
statesman "—conscious of his military deficiencies,
contrived to sow dissensions among the Parthians
themselves and to turn the thoughts of Pacorus in
another direction. He suggested to Ornodapantes,
a Parthian noble, with whom he had managed to
open a correspondence, that Pacorus would be a more
worthy occupant of the throne of the Arsacidæ than
his father, and that he would consult well for his own
interests, if he were to proclaim the young prince as
king, and lead the army of Syria against Orodes.
Pacorus had already been associated in the government by his father, and his name appears on some of
his father's later coins ; but this, while stimulating,
did not satisfy his ambition. He appears to have
lent a ready ear to the whispers of Ornodapantes, and
to have been on the verge, if he did not even over-
step the verge, of rebellion. There are Parthian
coins bearing the head of a beardless youth, and
the exact set of titles that had become fashionable

under Orodes, which are with ample reason assigned to this prince, and which must have been struck to be put in circulation when his revolt was declared. But the plot was nipped in the bud. Orodes, learning the designs cherished by Pacorus, summoned him to his Court ; and, the plans laid down not being yet ripe for execution, he felt that there was no other course open to him but to obey. The Parthian squadrons seem to have recrossed the Euphrates in July, B.C. 50. The danger to Rome was past; but the stain was not wiped out from the shield of Roman honour, nor was the reputation of Rome restored in the East. The " First Roman War " ended, after a period of a little more than four years, with the advantage wholly on the side of Parthia, both in respect of glory and of material gain. The laurels lost by Rome at Carrhæ had never been recovered, and the acquisition of Armenia by Parthia was a substantial increase of strength.

XI.

SECOND WAR OF PARTHIA WITH ROME—PARTHIAN INVASION OF SYRIA, PALESTINE, AND ASIA MINOR.

THE end of the first war of Parthia with Rome synchronised nearly with the breaking out of the civil contest between Cæsar and Pompey. In this struggle the sympathies of Parthia were on the Pompeian side. Though Pompey had certainly not given the Parthians much reason for regarding him with favour, since he had openly and flagrantly broken the terms of his treaty of alliance with them, yet on the whole they seem certainly to have preferred his cause to that of his great adversary. Perhaps they viewed Cæsar as more bound in honour than Pompey to seek revenge for the death of Crassus, since he had sent a favourite officer, with a contingent of troops, to his aid, or possibly they may simply have felt more fear of his military capacity. Communications certainly took place between Orodes and Pompey in the course of the year B.C. 49 or 48, and the terms of an alliance were discussed between them. Pompey, who was not very scrupulous, or really patriotic, made the overtures, and desired to know on what terms the Parthian monarch would lend him effective aid in the war which was on the point of breaking out. The reply of Orodes was to the following effect : " If the Roman leader would deliver into his hands the province of Syria, and make it wholly over to the Parthians, Orodes was willing to conclude an alliance with him and send him help ; but not otherwise." It is to the credit of Pompey that he rejected these terms, and, while not above contemplating a foreign alliance against a domestic foe, was unwilling to purchase the assistance to himself at a cost that would have inflicted a serious injury on his country. The rupture of the negotiations produced an estrangement between the negotiators, and Orodes went so far as to throw Hirrus, the envoy of Pompey, into prison, as a means of giving vent to his disappointment. Still, however, Pompey looked upon Orodes as a friend ; and when, a few months later, he had fought his great fight, and suffered his great defeat, at Pharsalus (August 9, B.C. 48), his thoughts reverted to the powerful Parthian king, and he entertained for some time the idea of taking refuge at the Court of Ctesiphon. It is even said that he only relinquished the design, and made his disastrous choice of Egypt as a refuge, when, on the receipt of intelligence that Antioch had declared for his rival, he understood that the route to the Parthian capital was no longer open to him. Otherwise, notwithstanding the persuasions of his friends, who thought the risk too great, both for himself and his wife, Cornelia, to be run with prudence, the world might have have seen the spectacle of a second Coriolanus, thundering at the gates of Rome and demanding recall and reinstatement, at the head of legions recruited in a foreign land and furnished by a foreign enemy. As it was, Roman history was spared this scandal; and at the same time Orodes was spared the awkwardness and difficulty of having to elect between repulsing a suppliant, and provoking the hostility of the most powerful chieftain and the greatest general of the age.

The year B.C. 47 saw Cæsar in Syria and Asia Minor, whither he was drawn by the necessity of crushing the mad schemes of Pharnaces, son of Mithridates of Pontus, who thought he saw in the internal quarrels of the Romans an opportunity of re-establishing his father's empire. After the facile victory of Zela, the Great Roman can scarcely have avoided debating with himself the question, whether he should at once turn his arms against his only other Asiatic enemy, and by a movement as rapid as that which had crushed Pharnaces, strike a blow against Orodes, and so avenge the defeat of Carrhæ. But, if the idea crossed his mind, he dismissed it. The time was not suitable. Too much remained to be done in Africa, in Spain, and at home, for so large a matter as a Parthian War to be, for the moment, taken in hand. Cæsar resolutely averted his gaze from the far East, and deferring the "revenge" to a comparatively remote date, kept whatever projects he may have entertained on the subject to himself, and was careful, while he remained in Asia, to avoid provoking or exasperating by threats or hostile movements, the Power on which the peace of the

East principally depended.   It was not until he had brought the African and Spanish wars to an end that he allowed his intention of leading an expedition against Parthia to be openly talked about.   In B.C. 44, four years after Pharsalus, having put down all his domestic enemies, and arranged matters, as he thought, satisfactorily at Rome, he let a decree be passed, formally assigning to him the Parthian War, and sent the legions across the Adriatic on their way to Asia.   What plan of campaign he may have contemplated is uncertain.   One writer represents him as intending to enter Parthia by way of the Lesser Armenia, and to proceed cautiously to try the strength of the Parthians before engaging them in a battle.   Another credits him with a plan for rapidly overrunning Parthia, and then proceeding by the way of the Caspian into Scythia, from Scythia invading Germany, and after conquering Germany returning into Italy by the way of Gaul!   But neither author is likely to have had any trustworthy authority for his statement.   The Great Dictator would not be likely to have formed any definite scheme ; he would have felt the need of being guided by circumstances. Still, there can be no doubt that an expedition under his auspices would have constituted a most serious danger to Parthia, and might have terminated in her subjection to Rome.   The military talents of Julius were of the most splendid description ; his powers of organisation and consolidation enormous ; his prudence and caution equal to his ambition and courage. Once launched on a career of conquest in the East, it is impossible to say whither he might not have carried the Roman eagles, or what countries he might not have added to the empire. But Parthia was saved from the imminent peril without any effort of her own. The daggers of the "Liberators" struck down on the 15th of March, B.C. 44, the only man whom she had seriously to fear; and with the removal of Julius passed away even from Roman thought for many a year the design which he had entertained, and which he alone could have accomplished.

In the civil war which followed on the murder of Julius, the Parthians appear to have actually taken a part. The East fell into confusion on the withdrawal of Julius after Zela, and in the course of the troubles a Parthian contingent was sent to the aid of a certain Cæcilius Bassus, a Pompeian adherent, who was seeking to obtain for himself something like an independent principality in Syria. The soldiers of Bassus, after a while (B.C. 43), went over in a body to Cassius, who was in the East collecting troops for his great struggle with Antony and Octavian; and thus a handful of Parthians came into the power of the second among the "Liberators." Of this accidental circumstance he determined to take advantage, in order to obtain, if possible, a considerable body of troops from Orodes. He therefore presented each of the Parthian soldiers with a sum of money for their immediate wants, and dismissed them graciously to their homes, at the same time seizing the opportunity to send some of his own officers as ambassadors to Orodes, with a request for substantial aid. On receiving this application, the Parthian monarch seems to have come to the conclusion that it would be a

wise policy to comply with it.   It was for the interest
of Parthia that the Roman arms, instead of being
directed to Asiatic conquests, should be engaged for
as long a time as possible in intestine strife ; and
Orodes might well conceive that he was promoting
his own advantage by fomenting and encouraging
the quarrels which, at any rate for the time, secured
his own empire from attack.   He may have hoped
also to obtain some equivalent in territory from the
gratitude of Cassius at some future period, since
Cassius was at the time Proconsul of Syria, and, if
successful against Octavian and Antony, might be
expected to choose the East for his province and to
make a fresh arrangement of it.   At any rate, he
complied with Cassius's request, and sent him a body
of Parthian horse, which were among the troops
engaged at Philippi.

The crushing defeat suffered by the " Liberators "
(November, B.C. 42) was an immediate disappointment
to Orodes, but, as instead of producing a pacification
of the Roman world, it only intensified the strife and
general confusion, it cannot be said to have worked
disadvantageously for his interests.   He himself, at
any rate, judged otherwise.   The Roman world
seemed to him more divided against itself than ever ;
and the " self-wrought ruin," which Horace prophesied,
seemed absolutely impending.   Three rivals held
divided sway in the corrupted State, each of them
jealous of the other two, and anxious for his own
aggrandisement.   The two chief pretenders to the
first place were bitterly hostile ; and while the one
was detained in Italy by insurrection against his

authority, the other was plunged in luxury and dissipation, enjoying the first transports of a lawless passion, at the Egyptian capital. The nations of the East were, moreover, alienated by the exactions of the profligate Triumvir, who, to reward his parasites and favourites, had laid upon them a burden that it was scarcely possible for them to bear. The condition of things generally seemed to invite a foreign power to step in, and, taking the opportunity offered by Rome's weakness, seriously to cripple her power.

Parthia enjoyed also at the time the rare good fortune of having at her disposal the services of a Roman general. Quintus Labienus, the son of Titus, Cæsar's legate in Gaul, who had gone over to the Pompeians, having been sent as envoy to Orodes by Brutus and Cassius a little before Philippi, had, on learning the severities of the Triumvirs, elected to make Parthia his home, and had taken service under the Parthian banner. Though not an officer of much distinction among his countrymen, he had the advantage of knowing the weak points of their military system ; and it might well seem to Orodes, that the occasion which thus offered itself ought to be utilised.

Under these circumstances, the Parthian monarch, who had never accepted the failure of Pacorus in B.C. 52–50 as final, made preparations during the winter of B.C. 41–40, for a fresh attack upon the Roman territory. Having collected an imposing force from all parts of his dominions, he placed it under the joint command of his son, Pacorus, and the Roman refugee, Q. Labienus, and sent it across the Euphrates with the first blush of spring, while Antony was still occupied

with his Egyptian dalliance, and Octavius, having at
last captured Perusia, was applying himself to the
pacification of Italy.   Antony might perhaps have
exchanged the soft delights of Cleopatra's Court
for the perils of a Parthian campaign, since when
roused to action by what seemed to him a sufficient
motive, he had all the instincts of a soldier ; but it
happened that, just at the time, messengers reached
him from his brother Lucius, imploring him to hasten
to the West, and arrest before it was too late the
victorious progress of Octavius.   With one regretful
glance in the direction of Syria, the self-seeking
Triumvir sailed away from Alexandria to Italy,
leaving the care of Roman interests in the East to the
incompetent hands of his lieutenant, Decidius Saxa,
who had already alienated the affections of the
provincials by his exactions, and was about to lose
their respect by his incapacity.   The Parthian hordes,
thus weakly opposed, burst into Syria with irresistible
force, rapidly overran the open country between the
Euphrates and Antioch, and entering the rich valley
of the Orontes, threatened the great seats of Hellenic
civilisation in these parts, Antioch, Apameia, and
Epiphaneia.   From Apameia, situated (like Durham)
on a rocky peninsula almost surrounded by the river,
they were at first repulsed ; but, having shortly
afterwards defeated Decidius Saxa and his legions
in the open fields, they received the submission of
Apameia and Antioch, which latter city Saxa
abandoned at their approach, flying precipitately
into Cilicia.

Encouraged by these successes, Labienus and

Pacorus agreed to divide their troops, and to engage simultaneously in two great expeditions. Pacorus undertook to carry the Parthian standard throughout the entire extent of Syria, Phœnicia, and Palestine, while Labienus took upon himself to invade Asia Minor, and see if he could not wrest some of its more fertile regions from the Romans. Both expeditions were crowned with extraordinary success. Pacorus reduced all Syria, and all Phœnicia, except the single city of Tyre, which he was unable to capture for want of a naval force. He then advanced into Palestine, which he found in its normal condition of intestine commotion. Hyrcanus and Antigonus, two princes of the Asmonæan house, uncle and nephew, were rivals for the Jewish crown ; and the latter, whom Hyrcanus had driven into exile, was content to make common cause with the invader, and to be indebted to a rude foreigner for the possession of the kingdom whereto he aspired. He offered Pacorus a thousand talents—nearly a quarter of a million of our money—and five hundred Jewish women, if he would espouse his cause, and seat him upon his uncle's throne. The offer was readily embraced, and by the irresistible help of the Parthians a revolution was effected at Jerusalem. Hyrcanus was deposed and mutilated. A new priest-king was set up in the person of Antigonus, the last Asmonæan prince, who reigned at Jerusalem for three years—B.C. 40–37—as a Parthian satrap or *vitaxa*, the creature and dependant of the great monarchy on the further side of the Euphrates.

Meanwhile, in Asia Minor, Labienus carried all

14

before him. Decidius Saxa, having once more (in Cicilia) ventured upon a battle, was not only defeated, but slain. Pamphylia, Lycia, and Caria—the whole south coast—were overrun. Stratonicea was besieged ; Mylasa and Alabanda were taken. According to some writers, the Parthians even pillaged Lydia and Ionia,.and were in possession of Asia Minor to the shores of the Hellespont. It may be said that for a full year Western Asia changed masters : the rule and authority of Rome disappeared ; and the Parthians were recognised as the dominant power. Under these circumstances, it is perhaps not surprising that Labienus lost his head ; that he affected the style and title of " Imperator ; " struck coins, and placed his own head and name on them, and even added the ridiculous title " Parthicus," which to a Roman ear meant " Conqueror of the Parthians "— a title of honour whereto he had no possible claim.

But the fortune of war now began to turn. In the autumn of B.C. 39, Antony, having patched up his quarrel with Octavius and set out from Italy to resume his command in the East, sent his lieutenant, Publius Ventidius, into Asia, with orders to act against Labienus, and the triumphant Parthians. Ventidius landed unexpectedly on the coast of Asia Minor, and so alarmed Labienus, who happened to have no Parthian troops with him, that the latter fell back hurriedly towards Cilicia, evacuating all the more western provinces, and at the same time sending urgent messages to Pacorus to implore succour. Pacorus despatched a strong body of cavalry to his aid ; but these troops, instead of putting themselves under his command, had the folly to act independently, and the result was, that, in a rash attempt to surprise the Roman camp, they were defeated by Ventidius, whereupon they fled hastily into Cilicia, leaving Labienus to his fate. The self-styled "Imperator," upon this, deserted his men and sought safety in flight; but his retreat was soon discovered; and he was pursued, captured, and put to death.

Meanwhile, the Parthians under Pacorus, alarmed at the turn which affairs had taken in Asia Minor, left Antigonus, the Asmonæan prince, to manage their interests in Palestine, and concentrated themselves in Northern Syria and Commagêné, where they awaited the approach of the Romans. A strong detachment, under a general named Pharnapates, was appointed to guard the "Syrian Gates," a narrow pass over Mount Amanus, leading from Cilicia into Syria. Here Ventidius gained another victory. He had sent forward an officer called Pompædius Silo with some cavalry to endeavour to seize this post, and Pompædius had found himself compelled to an engagement with Pharnapates, in which he was on the point of suffering defeat, when Ventidius himself, who had probably feared for his subordinate's safety, appeared on the scene, and turned the scale in favour of the Romans. The detachment under Pharnapates was overpowered, and Pharnapates himself was among the slain. When news of this defeat reached Pacorus, he thought it prudent to retreat, and accordingly withdrew his troops across the Euphrates. This movement he appears to have executed without being molested by Ventidius, who thus recovered

Syria to the Romans towards the close of B.C. 39, or early in B.C. 38.

But Pacorus was far from intending to relinquish the contest. He had made himself popular among the Syrians by his mild and just administration, and knew that they preferred his government to that of the Romans. He had many allies among the petty princes and dynasts, who occupied a semi-independent position on the borders of the Parthian and Roman empires, as, for example, Antiochus, King of Commagêné ; Lysanias, tetrarch of Ituræa ; Malchus, sheikh of the Nabatæan Arabs, and others. Moreover, Antigonus, whom he had established as king of the Jews, still maintained himself in Judæa against the efforts of Herod, to whom Octavius and Antony had assigned the throne. Pacorus therefore arranged during the remainder of the winter for a fresh invasion of Syria in the spring, and, taking the field earlier than his adversary expected, made ready to recross the Euphrates. We are told that, if he had crossed at the usual point, he would have come upon the Romans quite unprepared, the legions being still in their winter quarters, some of them north and some south of the great mountain range of Taurus. Ventidius, however, contrived by a stratagem to induce him to effect his passage at a different point, considerably lower down the stream, and in this way to waste some valuable time, which he himself employed in collecting his scattered forces. Thus, when the Parthians appeared on the right bank of the Euphrates, the Roman general was prepared to engage them, and was not even loth to decide the fate of the war by a single battle. He had taken care to provide himself with a strong force of slingers, and had entrenched himself in a position on high ground at some distance from the river. The Parthians, finding their passage of the Euphrates unopposed, and, when they fell in with the enemy, seeing him entrenched, as though resolved · to act only on the defensive, became over bold ; they thought the force opposed to them must distrust its own strength, or its own fighting capacity, and would be likely to yield its position without a blow, if suddenly and vigorously attacked. Accordingly, as on a former occasion, they charged up the hill on which the Roman camp was placed, hoping, like the Boers at Majuba, to take it by mere audacity. But the troops in the camp were held ready, and at the proper moment issued forth ; the assailants found themselves in their turn assailed, and, fighting at a disadvantage on the slope, were soon driven down the declivity. The battle was continued in the plain below, where the mail-clad horse of the Asiatics made a brave and prolonged resistance ; but the slingers galled them severely, and in the midst of the struggle it happened by ill fortune that Pacorus was slain. The result followed which is almost invariable in the case of an Oriental army : having lost their leader, the soldiers almost everywhere gave way ; flight became universal, and the Romans gained a complete victory. The Parthian army fled in two directions. Part made for the bridge of boats by which it had crossed the Euphrates, but was intercepted by the enemy and destroyed. Part turned northwards into Commagêné, and there took refuge with the king, Antiochus, who refused to surrender them to the demand of Ventidius, and no doubt allowed them to return to their own country. It was said that this final encounter took place on the anniversary of the great disaster of Carrhæ, and Rome flattered herself that she had at last retrieved that disgrace, having compensated for the loss of her own legions by the destruction of a Royal Parthian army, and having by the death of the associated monarch, Pacorus, more than avenged the slaughter of Crassus.

Thus terminated the great Parthian invasion of Syria under Labienus and Pacorus; and with it terminated the prospect of any further spread of the Arsacid dominion towards the West. When the two great world-powers, Rome and Parthia, first came into collision, when the hard blow struck by the latter in the annihilation of the army of Crassus was followed up by the advance of their clouds of horse into Syria, Palestine, and Asia Minor—when Apameia, Antioch, and Jerusalem fell into their hands, when Decidius Saxa was defeated and slain—Cilicia, Pamphylia, Lycia, and Caria occupied, Lydia and Ionia ravaged —it seemed as if Rome had met, not so much an equal, as a superior; it looked as if the power hitherto predominant would be compelled to draw back and retreat, while the new power, Parthia, would make a long step in advance, and push her frontier to the Ægean and the Mediterranean. The history of the contest between the East and West, between Asia and Europe, is a history of re-actions. At one time one of the two continents, at another time the other, is in the ascendant. The time appeared to have come when the Asiatics were once more to recover their own, and to beat back the European aggressor to his proper shores and islands. The triumphs achieved by the Seljukian Turks between the eleventh and the fifteenth centuries would in that case have been anticipated by above a thousand years through the efforts of a kindred and not dissimilar people. But it turned out that the effort now made was premature. While the Parthian warfare was admirably adapted for the national defence on the broad plains of inner Asia, it was ill suited for conquest, and, comparatively speaking, ineffective in more contracted and difficult regions. The Parthian military system had not the elasticity of the Roman—it did not in the same way adapt itself to circumstances, or admit of the addition of new arms, or the indefinite expansion of an old one. However loose and seemingly flexible, it was rigid in its uniformity ; it never altered ; it remained under the thirtieth Arsaces such as it had been under the first, improved in details perhaps, but essentially the same system. The Romans, on the contrary, were always modifying and improving their system, always learning new combinations, or new manœuvres, or new modes of warfare, from their enemies. They met the Parthian tactics of loose array, continuous distant missiles, and almost exclusive employment of cavalry, with an increase in the number of their own horse, a larger employment of auxiliary irregulars, and a greater use of the sling. At the same time they learnt to take full advantage of the Parthian inefficiency against walls, and to practise against them the arts of pretended retreat and ambush. The result was that Parthia found she could make no serious impression upon the dominions of Rome, and having become persuaded of this by the experience of a decade of years, thenceforth laid aside for ever the dream of Western conquest. She took up, in fact, from this time a new attitude. Hitherto she had been consistently aggressive. She had laboured constantly to extend herself at the expense of the Bactrians, the Scythians, the Syro-Macedonians, and the Armenians. She had proceeded, like Rome, from one aggression to another, leaving only short intervals between her wars, and had always been looking out for some fresh enemy. Henceforth she became, comparatively speaking, pacific. She was content, for the most part, to maintain her limits. She sought no new foe. Her contest with Rome degenerated, in the main, into a struggle for influence over the border kingdom of Armenia ; and her hopes were limited to the reduction of that kingdom to a subject position.

The grief of Orodes at the death of Pacorus was something extreme and abnormal, even in the emotional East. For many days he would neither eat, nor speak, nor sleep ; then his sorrow took another turn. He imagined that his son had returned ; he thought continually that he heard or saw him ; he could do nothing but repeat his name. Every now and then, however, he awoke to a sense of the actual fact, and mourned the death of his favourite with tears. After a while this excessive grief wore itself out; and the aged king began to direct his attention once more to public affairs, and to concern him-

self about the succession. Of the thirty sons who
still remained to him there was not one who had
made himself a name, or was in any way distinguished
above the remainder. In the absence, therefore, of
any personal ground of preference, Orodes — who
seems to have regarded himself as possessing a right
to nominate the son who should succeed him—thought
that the claims of primogeniture were entitled to be
considered, and selected as his successor, Phraates, the
eldest of the thirty. Not content, however, with
nominating him, or perhaps doubtful whether the
nomination would be accepted by the Megistanes, he
proceeded further to abdicate in his favour, whereupon
Phraates became actual king. The transaction proved
a most unhappy one. Phraates, jealous of some of
his brothers, who were the sons of a princess married
to Orodes, whereas his own mother was only a concubine, removed them by assassination, and when the
ex-monarch ventured to express disapproval of the
act, added the crime of parricide to that of fratricide
by putting to death his aged father. Thus perished
Orodes, son of Phraates, the thirteenth Arsacid, after
a reign of eighteen or twenty years — the most
memorable in the Parthian annals. Though scarcely
a great king, he carried Parthia to the highest pitch
of her glory, less however by his own personal merits,
than by his judicious selection of able officers for the
command of his armies. Exceedingly ambitious, he
allowed no scruples to interfere with his personal
aggrandisement, but, having waded to power through
the blood of a father and a brother, maintained himself in power by the sacrifice of his foremost subject,

His affection for his son Pacorus is the most amiable trait in his character, and redeems it from the charge, to which it would otherwise be liable, of a complete defect of humanity. Even here, however, he showed a want of balance and moderation; and, by allowing his mind to become unhinged, brought disaster on himself, and on those dearest to him. It may have been a just Nemesis, that he should die at the hands of one of his sons, but it seems hard that affection for one son should have put him altogether in the power of another.

XII.

EXPEDITION OF MARK ANTONY AGAINST PARTHIA —ITS FAILURE—WAR BETWEEN PARTHIA AND MEDIA.

PHRAATES, the son of Orodes, who is generally known as Phraates the Fourth, ascended the Parthian throne in the year B.C. 37. The Roman world was still in the throes of revolution. A mock peace had indeed been patched up between the irreconcilable rivals, Octavian and Antony, in the year B.C. 40, by the sacrifice of " the fair, the modest, and the discreet Octavia "—" that marvel of a woman," as Plutarch calls her—to the short-lived passion of the coarse Triumvir ; but dissension had quickly broken out— the bride and bridegroom had quarrelled—and, before the year B.C. 37 was over, had parted, never to come together again. Antony and Octavian were once more acknowledged enemies, and felt it necessary to place half the world between them in order that they might not at once come to blows. Antony betook himself to the eastern portion of the Roman Empire, and renewed his dalliance with his Egyptian mistress. Octavian remained in Italy, launching recriminations against his rival, and preparing for the deadly struggle which, he well knew, impended. Phraates probably thought himself safe from attack under the circumstances, and felt himself free to indulge his natural temperament, which was cruel, jealous, and bloodthirsty. Not content with having brushed from his path the brothers whose title to the throne was better than his,[1] he proceeded to make a clean sweep, and killed the remainder of the thirty. Nor was this all. From the massacre of his own relations, he passed to executions of Parthian nobles who had provoked his jealousy, and at last created such a panic among them, that numbers of them fled the

COIN OF PHRAATES IV.

country, and taking refuge in the territory west of the Euphrates, filled the camps and cities of the Roman provinces. Among these fugitives was a certain Monæses, a nobleman of high distinction, who appears to have gained more than one military success in the Syrian war of Pacorus.[2] This officer represented to Antony that Phraates had by his tyrannical and sanguinary conduct made himself detested by his subjects, and that a revolt on the part of large numbers could easily be effected. " If the Romans would support him," he said, " he was quite willing to

[1] See above, p. 201.　　　　[2] Hor. " Od.," iii. 6 ; l. 10.

invade Parthia, and he made no doubt of wresting
the greater portion of it from the hands of the tyrant,
and of being himself accepted as king. In that case, he
would consent to hold his crown of the Romans, as their
dependant and feudatory; and they might count on
his fidelity and gratitude." Antony received Monæses
with ostentatious generosity, and, affecting the munifi-
ence of an Artaxerxes towards a Themistocles, made
him a present of three cities of Asia, Larissa, Arethusa,
and Bambycé, or Hierapolis. The Parthian monarch,
alarmed at the prospect, sought to withdraw his
traitorous subject from the enemy's blandishments
by the offer of pardon and renewed favour; and
Monæses, after duly balancing the proposals made to
him one against the other, came to the conclusion
that his home prospects were the more promising.
He therefore represented to Antony that he might
probably do him better service as a friend at the
Court of Phraates than as a pretender to his crown,
and asked permission to accept the overtures which
he had received, and to return to his native country.
It is probable that the Triumvir was clever enough to
see through his motives, and to understand that no
dependence was to be placed on his protestations;
but it fitted in with his own interests to amuse
Phraates for a short time longer with pacific pro-
fessions, and he saw in the request of Monæses an
opportunity for throwing dust in the eyes of a not very
keen-sighted barbarian. Monæses thus obtained permission to rejoin his sovereign, and was instructed to
assure him that the Roman commander desired
nothing so much as peace, and asked only that the

standards captured by the Parthians in the war with
Crassus and Ventidius, and such of the prisoners
taken as still survived, should be handed over to the
Romans.

But while thus playing with his adversary, and de-
luding him with fond expectations, the Triumvir had
fully made up his own mind to plunge into war, and
was leaving no stone unturned to perfect his preparations. It is very unlikely that it had required the
overtures of a Monæses to put a Parthian expedition
into his thoughts. The successes of his own lieutenants
must have been stimulants of far greater efficacy. C.
Sosius, as governor of Syria, had performed several
martial exploits on the frontiers of that province.
Canidius Crassus had defeated the Armenians, with
their Albanian and Iberian allies, and had once more
planted the Roman standards at the foot of the
Caucasus. Above all, the great glory of Ventidius,
who had been allowed the much-coveted honour of a
"triumph" at Rome on account of his defeats of the
Parthians in Cilicia and Syria, must have rankled in
his mind, and have moved him to emulation, and caused
him to cast about for some means of outshining his
lieutenants and exalting his own military reputation
above that of his subordinates. Nothing, he well
knew, could be so effectual for this purpose as a
successful Parthian expedition—the infliction upon
this hated foe of an unmistakable humiliation, and
the dictating to them of terms of peace on their own
soil after some great and decisive victory. Nor did
this now appear so very difficult. After the successes
of Ventidius and Canidius Crassus the prestige of the

Parthian name was gone. The legionaries could be trusted to meet them without any undue alarm, and to contend with them in the usual Roman fashion, without excitement or flurry. Time had shown the weakness, as well as the strength, of the Parthian military system, and the Roman tacticians had succeeded in devising expedients by which its strong points might be met and triumphed over. With the forces at his command Antony might well expect to attack Parthia successfully, and not merely to avoid the fate of Crassus, but to obtain important advantages.

At the same time he had his eyes open to all the possibilities of the military situation, and was making his preparations with the greatest prudence and secrecy. He collected Roman troops from every available quarter, and gradually raised his legions to the number of sixteen, or (according to some) of eighteen. These he disposed in the different cities of Asia, and did not begin to mass them until he had no further need for concealment. He had brought with him from Europe Gallic and Iberian horse to the number of ten thousand; his Roman infantry is reckoned at sixty thousand; and the cavalry and infantry of the Asiatic allies amounted to thirty thousand. The Armenian monarch, Artavasdes, was secretly won over in the course of the winter, and promised a contingent of seven thousand foot and six thousand horse. Thus the entire number of all arms on which he could count to begin the campaign was 113,000.

Antony was in no hurry to begin. More lover than soldier, he was glad to defer the hour for parting

with the siren by whose charms he was fascinated,
and exchanging the delights of voluptuous dalliance
for the hardships of life in the field.   Thus it was not
until the midsummer of B.C. 36 had arrived that he
could bring himself to dismiss his mistress to her
Egyptian home, and place himself at the head of his
legions.   It was his original intention to cross the
Euphrates into Mesopotamia, and to advance against
Parthia by the direct route, as Crassus had done ; but,
on reaching the banks of the Euphrates, possibly
at Zeugma, he found the attitude of defence assumed
by the enemy on his own frontier so imposing, that
he abandoned his first design, and, turning northwards, entered Armenia, resolved to attack Parthia,
in conjunction with his Armenian ally, from that
quarter.   Artavasdes gladly welcomed him, and
recommended that he should begin the war, not by
invading Parthia itself but by an attack on the
dominions of a Parthian feudatory, the King of
Media Atropatênê, whose territories adjoined Armenia on the south-east.   The king, he said, was
absent, having been summoned to join his suzerain
on the banks of the Euphrates, and having marched
away with his best troops to the rendezvous.   His
territory, therefore, would be ill-defended, and open to
ravage ; it was even possible that Praaspa, his capital,
might be an easy prey.   The prospect excited Antony,
and he put himself at the disposition of Artavasdes.
Dividing his army into two portions, and ordering
Oppius Statianus, one of his best officers, to follow
him leisurely with the more unwieldly portion of the
troops, the siege-batteries, and the baggage-train, he

himself proceeded by forced marches to Praaspa, under the guidance of Artavasdes, accompanied by all the cavalry and infantry of the better sort. This town was situated at the distance of nearly three hundred miles from the Armenian frontier ; but the way to it lay through well-cultivated plains, where food and water were abundant. Antony accomplished the march without any difficulty, and sat himself down before the place. But the want of his siege-engines and battering-train caused him to make little impression ; and he was compelled to have recourse to the long and tedious process of raising up a mound against the walls. For some time he cherished the hope that Statianus would arrive to his relief ; but this illusion was ere long dispelled. News arrived that the Parthian monarch, having been made acquainted with his plans and proceedings, had followed on the footsteps of his army, had come up with Statianus, and made a successful onslaught on his detachment. Ten thousand Romans were killed in the engagement; many prisoners were taken ; all the baggage-waggons and engines of war fell into the enemy's hands ; and Statianus himself was among the slain. A further and still worse result followed. The Armenian monarch was so disheartened by the defeat, that, regarding the Roman cause as desperate, he retired from the contest, drew off his troops, and left Antony to his own resources.

The situation became now one of great difficulty. Autumn was approaching ; supplies were falling short ; the siege works which Antony had attempted made no progress ; and it was impossible to construct a fresh battering-train to replace that which had been taken. If Antony could only capture the town before the winter set in, he would feel himself in safety, and, having a breathing-space during which he might repair his losses, would be able to recruit himself for another campaign. He therefore made desperate efforts to overcome the resistance offered by the besieged, and to obtain possession of the city. But all was in vain. The walls were too strong and too high. His mound was never brought to a level with their summit. From time to time the defenders made sallies, drove off his workmen, and inflicted serious damage on his construction. The Parthian monarch, hovering about in the neighbourhood, looked with scorn on his unavailing endeavours, and contented himself with hindering his supplies and interfering with his foraging parties. Efforts made by Antony to bring on a general engagement by means of a foraging expedition on a large scale failed, the Parthians retreating as soon as attacked, and exhibiting their marvellous power of getting out of an enemy's reach almost without suffering any losses. The Roman commander, as the equinox drew near, came to the conclusion that he must withdraw from the siege and retire into Armenia, but before making this confession of failure, as a last resource, he sought to persuade his adversary to terms of accommodation. He would at once relinquish the siege, and recross the frontier, he said, if Phraates would only yield up to him the Crassian captives and standards. The demand was preposterous, and the Parthians simply laughed at it, feeling

that it was for Antony rather to purchase an unmolested retreat, than for themselves to pay him for
retiring. Each day that he lingered placed him in
a worse position, and made it more certain that he
could not escape serious disaster.

At last the equinox arrived, and retreat became
imperative. There were two roads by which it would
be possible to reach the Araxes at the usual point of
passage. One lay to the left, through a plain and
open country, probably along the course of the Jag-
hetu and the eastern shores of Lake Urumiyeh, which
is the route that an army would ordinarily take; the
other, which was shorter but more difficult, lay to the
right, leading across a mountain tract, but one fairly
supplied with water, and in which there were a number
of inhabited villages. The Triumvir was informed by
his scouts that the Parthians had occupied the easier
route in the expectation that he would select it, and
were hopeful of overwhelming his entire force with
their cavalry in the plains. He therefore took the
road to the right, through a rugged and inclement
country—probably that between Takht-i-Suleïman
and Tabriz—and, guided by a Mardian who was well
acquainted with the district, set out to make his way
back to the Araxes. His decision took the Parthians
by surprise, and for two whole days he was unmolested. By the third day, however, they had thrown
themselves across his path. Antony, expecting no
interference, was pursuing his march in a somewhat
disorderly manner, when the Mardian guide, perceiving signs of recent injury to the route, gave him warning that the enemy could not be far off, and the

Roman general had just time to make his troops form in battle array, and bring his light armed and slingers to the front, when the Parthian horsemen made their appearance on all sides, and began a fierce assault. But the Roman light troops, especially those armed with slings and darts, made a vigorous resistance, the leaden missiles of the slingers being found particularly effective; and, after a short combat, the Parthians, following their usual tactics, drew off, only, however, to return again and again, until at last Antony's Gallic cavalry found an opportunity of charging them, when they broke and fled hastily, having received a serious check, from which they did not recover during the remainder of the day.

However, on the day following, they reappeared; and thenceforth for nineteen consecutive days they disputed with Antony every inch of his road, and inflicted on him the most grievous losses. " The sufferings of the Roman army during this time," says a modern historian of Rome, " were unparalleled in their military annals. The intense cold, the blinding snow and driving sleet, the want sometimes of provisions, sometimes of water, the use of poisonous herbs, and the harassing attacks of the enemy's cavalry and bowmen, which could only be repelled by maintaining the dense array of the phalanx or the tortoise, reduced the retreating army by one-third of its numbers." Much gallantry was shown, especially by some of the officers, as Flavius Gallus; and Antony himself displayed all the finest qualities of a commander, except judgment; but every effort was in vain : as the Roman army dwindled in numbers, that

of the Parthians increased ; as the strength of the
individual soldiers failed through scantiness or un-
wholesomeness of food, the courage and audacity of
their adversaries were augmented ; the Roman losses
grew greater from day to day, and at last culminated
in one occasion of extreme disaster, when eight thousand men were placed *hors de combat*, three thousand
of them, including Gallus, being slain. At length,
after a march of 300 Roman, or 277 British, miles,
the survivors reached the river Araxes, probably at
the Julfa ferry, and, crossing it, found themselves in
Armenia. But the calamities of the return were not
yet ended. Although it had been arranged with
Artavasdes that the bulk of the Roman army should
winter in Armenia, yet, before the various detachments could reach the quarters assigned them in
different parts of the country, eight thousand more
had perished, through the effect of past privations or
the severity of the Armenian winter. Altogether,
out of the hundred thousand men whom Antony had
taken with him into Media Atropatênê in the midsummer of B.C. 36, less than seventy thousand remained to commence the campaign of the ensuing
year. Well may the unfortunate commander have
exclaimed during the later portion of his march, as
he compared his own heavy losses with the light ones
suffered by Xenophon and his Greeks in these same
regions : " Oh, those Ten Thousand ! those Ten Thousand ! "

On the withdrawal of Antony into Armenia, a
quarrel broke out between Phraates and his Median
vassal. The latter complained that he was wronged

in the division made of the Roman spoils, and expressed himself with so much freedom as seriously to
offend his suzerain.   Perceiving this, he became
alarmed lest Phraates should punish his boldness
by deposing him from his office and setting up
another *vitaxa* in his place.   He thought it necessary
therefore to look out for some powerful support, and
on carefully considering the political situation, came
to the conclusion that his best hope lay in making a
friend of his late foe Antony, and placing himself
under Roman protection.   Antony was known to
have been deeply offended by the conduct of his
Armenian ally in the late campaign, and to be
desirous of taking vengeance on him.   He had
already made an attempt to get possession of his
person, which had failed through the suspiciousness
and caution of the wily Oriental.   Hostilities between
Armenia and Rome were evidently impending, and
might break out at any moment.   It would be clearly
for Antony's interest, when war broke out, to have a
friend on the Armenian frontier, and especially one
who was strong in cavalry and bowmen.   The Median
monarch therefore sent an ambassador of rank to
Alexandria, where Antony was passing the winter,
and boldly proposed an alliance.   Antony readily
accepted the offer.   He was intensely angered by the
conduct of his late confederate, and resolved on
punishing his disaffection and desertion ; he viewed
the Median alliance as of the utmost importance, not
only as against Armenia, but still more in connection
with the design, which he still entertained, of invading
Parthia itself ; and he saw in the Atropatenian ruler

a prince whom it would be well worth his while to bind to his cause indissolubly. He therefore embraced the overtures made to him with joy, and even rewarded the messenger who had brought them with a principality. After sundry efforts to entice Artavasdes into his power, which occupied him during the greater part of B.C. 35, but which were unsuccessful, in the spring of B.C. 34 he suddenly made his appearance in Armenia. His army, which had remained there from the previous campaign, held all the most important positions, and, as he professed the most friendly feelings towards Artavasdes, even proposing an alliance between their families, that prince, after some hesitation, at length ventured into his presence. He was immediately seized and put in chains. Armenia was rapidly overrun. Artaxias, the eldest son of Artavasdes, whom the Armenians made king in the room of his father, was defeated, and forced to take refuge with the Parthians. Antony then arranged a marriage between a daughter of the Median monarch and his own son by Cleopatra, Alexander ; and leaving garrisons in Armenia to hold it as a conquered province, carried off Artavasdes, together with a rich booty, into Egypt.

Phraates, during these transactions, had remained wholly upon the defensive. He was not a man of much enterprise, and probably thought that a waiting policy was, under the circumstances, the best one. It cannot have been displeasing to him to see Artavasdes punished ; and doubtless he must have been gratified to observe how Antony was injuring his own cause by exasperating the Armenians, and teaching

them to detest Rome even more than they detested
Parthia. But while the Roman troops held possession
both of Syria and of Armenia, and the alliance between Rome and Media Atropatênê continued, he
could not venture to take any aggressive step, or think
of doing more than protecting his own frontier.
Almost any other Roman commander than Antony
would, after crushing Armenia, have at once carried
the war, in conjunction with his Median ally, into
Parthia, and have endeavoured to strike a blow that
might avenge the defeat of Carrhæ. Phraates naturally expected an invasion of his territories both in
B.C. 34, after Antony's occupation of Armenia, and in
the following year, when he again appeared in these
parts, and advanced to the Araxes. But Antony's
attention was so much engrossed by the proceedings
of his rival, Octavian, in the West, and it was so clear
to him that the great contest for the mastership of
the Roman world could not be delayed much longer,
that Eastern affairs had almost ceased to interest him,
and his chief desire was to be quit of them. The
object of his advance to the Araxes in B.C. 33 was to
place things in such a position that his presence might
be no longer necessary. It seemed to him that the
interests of Rome would be sufficiently safeguarded,
if the Median alliance were assured, and he therefore
sought an interview with the Atropatenian king, and
concluded a treaty with him. The terms were very
favourable to the Median. He received a body of
Roman heavy infantry in exchange for a detachment
of his own light horsemen ; his dominions were considerably enlarged on the side of Armenia ; and the

marriage previously arranged between his daughter, Jotapa, and Antony's son, Alexander, was accomplished. Antony then marched away to meet his Roman rival, flattering himself that he had secured, at any rate for some years, the tranquillity of the Asiatic continent.

But Phraates now saw his opportunity. In conjunction with Artaxias, he attacked the Median king, and, though at first repulsed by the valour of the Roman troops in the Median service, succeeded, after Antony had required them to rejoin his standard, in inflicting on him a severe defeat, and even making him a prisoner. This success led to another. Artaxias, having now only the Roman garrisons to contend with, re-entered and recovered Armenia. The Roman garrisons were put to the sword. Armenia became once more wholly independent of Rome ; and it is probable that Media Atropatêné returned to the Parthian allegiance.

The result of the expedition of Antony was thus rather to elevate Parthia than to depress her. Antony, notwithstanding his undoubted courage, let it be clearly seen that he shrank from a direct encounter with the full force of the Parthian kingdom. Hence his avoidance of any invasion of actual Parthian territory, and the limitation of his efforts to the injuring of his enemy by striking at her through her dependencies, Media and Armenia. Nor was the timidity thus exhibited compensated for by success in the comparatively small enterprises to which he confined himself. The expedition against Media Atropatêné was a complete failure, and resulted in the loss of thirty thousand men.   The Armenian campaign succeeded at the time, but it alienated a nation which it was of the utmost importance to conciliate, and it was followed almost immediately by a revolt in which Rome suffered fresh disasters, and which drew Armenia closer to Parthia than she had ever been drawn previously.   On the retirement of Antony from the East, Parthia occupied as grand a position as had ever before been hers, excepting during the brief space of her successes under Pacorus and Labienus.

XIII.

INTERNAL TROUBLES IN PARTHIA—HER RELATIONS
WITH ROME UNDER AUGUSTUS AND TIBERIUS.

PHRAATES, justly proud of his successes against
Antony, and of the re-establishment of his authority
over Media Atropatêné, regarding, moreover, his position in Parthia as thereby absolutely secured, proceeded to indulge the natural cruelty of his disposition, and resumed the harsh and tyrannical treatment
of his subjects, by which he had made himself odious
in the early years of his reign.[1]   So far did he push
his oppression, that ere long the patience of the people
gave way, and an insurrection broke out against his
authority, which compelled him to fly the country (B.C.
33).   The revolt was headed by a certain Tiridates, a
Parthian noble, who, upon its success, was made king
by the insurgents.   Phraates fled into Scythia, and
appealed to the nomads to embrace his cause.   Ever
ready for war and plunder, the hordes were nothing
loth ; and, crossing the frontier in force, they succeeded without much difficulty in restoring the exiled
monarch to the throne from which his subjects had
deposed him.   Tiridates fled at their approach, and,

---

[1] See above, p. 204.

having contrived to carry off in his flight the youngest
son of Phraates, presented himself before Octavian,
who was in Syria at the time (B.C. 30) on his return
from Egypt, surrendered the young prince into his
hands, and requested his aid against the tyrant.
Octavian accepted the valuable hostage, but, with his
usual caution, declined to pledge himself to furnish
any help to the pretender ; he might remain, he said,
in Syria, if he so wished, and while he continued
under Roman protection a suitable provision should
be made for his support, but he must not expect to be

COIN OF TIRIDATES II.

replaced upon the Parthian throne by the Roman
arms.   Some years later (B.C. 23), Phraates in his turn
made application to the Imperator for the surrender
of the person of Tiridates and the restoration of his
kidnapped son ; but the application was only partially
successful.   Octavian said he willingly restored to him
his son, and would not even ask a ransom ; but the
surrender of a fugitive was a different matter, and one
that he could not possibly consent to.   Where would
be the honour of Rome, if such a thing were done ?
Phraates would, no doubt, feel that some return was
due on account of his son.   An acceptable return

would be the delivery to the Romans of the standards and captives taken from Crassus and Antony. The Parthian monarch made no direct reply to this suggestion. He gladly received his son, but ignored the rest of the message. It was not until three years later, when Octavian (now become Augustus) visited the East, and war seemed the probable alternative if he continued obdurate, that the Parthian monarch brought himself to relinquish the trophies, which were as much prized by the victors as by the vanquished. The act was one so unpatriotic as to be scarcely pardonable ; but we must remember that Phraates held his crown by a very insecure tenure—he was extremely unpopular with his subjects, and Augustus had it in his power at any moment to produce a pretender, who had once occupied, and with Roman help might easily have ascended for a second time, the throne of the Arsacids.

The remaining years of Phraates—and he reigned for nearly twenty years after restoring the standards —were almost unbroken by any event of importance. The result of the twenty years' struggle between Rome and Parthia had been to impress either nation with a wholesome fear of the other. Both had triumphed on their own ground ; both had failed when they ventured on sending expeditions into their enemy's territory. Each now stood on its guard, watching the movements of its adversary across the Euphrates. Both had become pacific. It is a well-known fact that Augustus left it as a principle of policy to his successors that the Roman territory had reached its proper limits, and could not with any ad-

vantage be extended further. This principle, followed
with the utmost strictness by Tiberius, was accepted
as a rule by all the earlier Cæsars, and only regarded
by them as admitting of rare and slight exceptions.
Trajan was the first who, a hundred and thirty years
after the accession of Augustus, made light of it, and
set it at defiance. With him re-awoke the spirit of
conquest, the aspiration after universal dominion.
But in the meantime there was peace—peace not
indeed absolutely unbroken, for border wars occurred,
and Rome was sometimes tempted to interfere by
arms in the internal quarrels of her neighbour ; but a
general state of peace and amity prevailed ; neither
state made any grand attack on the other's dominions ;
no change occurred in the frontier ; no great battle
tested the relative strength of the two peoples. Such
rivalry as still continued was exhibited less in arms
than in diplomacy, and showed itself mainly in endeavours on either side to obtain a predominant influence in Armenia. There alone during the century
and a half that intervened between Antony and Trajan
did the interests of Rome and Parthia come into collision, and in connection with this kingdom alone was
there during these years any struggle between the two
empires.

After Phraates had yielded to Augustus in the important matter of the standards and the prisoners, he
appears for many years to have studiously cultivated
his good graces. In the interval between B.C. 11 and
B.C. 7, having reason to distrust the intentions of his
subjects towards him, and to suspect that they might
not improbably depose him and place one of his sons

upon the Parthian throne, he resolved to send these possible rivals out of the country ; and on this occasion he paid Augustus the compliment of selecting Rome for his children's residence. The youths were four in number—Vonones, who was the eldest, Seraspadanes, Rhodaspes, and Phraates ; two of them were married and had children. They resided at Rome during the remainder of their father's lifetime, and were treated as became their rank, being supported at the public charge, and in a magnificent manner. The Roman writers speak of them as " hostages " given by Phraates to the Roman Emperor ;[1] but this was certainly not the intention of the Parthian monarch, and it was scarcely possible that the idea could be entertained by the Romans at the time of their residence.

The friendly relations thus established between Phraates and Augustus would probably have continued undisturbed until the death of the one or the other had not a revolution broken out in Armenia, which tempted the Parthian king beyond his powers of resistance. On the death of Artaxias, in the year B.C. 20, Augustus, who was then in the East, had sent Tiberius into Armenia, to arrange the affairs of the nation ; and Tiberius had thought it best to place upon the throne a brother of Artaxias, named Tigranes. Parthia had made no objection to this arrangement, but had tacitly admitted the Roman suzerainty over the Armenian nation. Fourteen years afterwards, in B.C. 6, Tigranes died ; and the Armenians, without

[1] Vell. Paterculus, Suetonius, Tacitus, Justin, Eutropius, Orosius, &c.

waiting to know the pleasure of the Roman Emperor,
conferred the sovereignty on his three sons, whom
their father had previously designated for the royal
office by associating them with him in the government.   But this was a liberty which Augustus could
not possibly allow.   He therefore, in B.C. 5, sent an
expedition into Armenia, deposed the three sons of
Tigranes, and established in the kingdom a certain
Artavasdes, whose birth, rank, and claims to the royal
position are unknown.   But the Armenians were dissatisfied and recalcitrant.   After enduring the rule of
Rome's nominee for the short space of three years,
they rose in revolt against him, defeated the Romans
who endeavoured to support his authority, and drove
him out of the kingdom.   Another Tigranes was
placed upon the throne; and, at the same time, Parthia
was called in to give the Armenians their protection,
in case Rome should again interfere with the choice
of the nation.   Phraates could not bring himself to
reject the Armenian overtures.   Ever since the time
of the second Mithridates, it had been a settled principle of Parthia's policy that Armenia should be dependent on herself; and, even at the cost of a rupture
with Rome, it seemed to Phraates that he must respond to the appeal made to him.   The rupture might
not come.   Augustus was now advanced in years, and
might submit to the indignity offered him without
resenting it.   He had lately lost the services of his
best general—his stepson, Tiberius—who, in consequence of the slights put upon him, had gone into
retirement at Rhodes.   He had no one that he could
entrust with an army but his grandsons, youths who

had not yet fleshed their maiden swords. Phraates probably hoped that, under such circumstances, Augustus would draw back before the terrors of a Parthian war, and would allow without remonstrance —or, at any rate, without resistance—the passing of Armenia into the position of a Parthian subject-ally.

But, if such were his expectations, he had greatly miscalculated. Augustus had as keen a sense of what the honour of Rome required now that he was an old man of sixty as when he was a youth of twenty. From the time that he first heard of the Armenian outbreak, and of the support lent it by Parthia, he appears never to have wavered in his determination to re-assert the Roman claim to a pre-ponderating influence over Armenia, but only to have hesitated for a time as to the individual whose services it would be best to employ in the business. Tiberius naturally presented himself to his mind as by far the fittest person for such a work—a work in which diplomatic and military ability might be, both of them, almost equally required ; but Tiberius had recently taken offence at certain slights which he supposed himself to have received, and had withdrawn from the public service and from official life altogether. In default of his brave and astute stepson, Augustus could only fall back upon his grandsons ; but the eldest of these, Caius, was now, in the year B.C. 2, no more than eighteen years of age, and the policy of employing so young a man in so difficult and important a business could not but appear to him extremely questionable. Augustus therefore hesitated, and it was not until late in the year B.C. 1 that he despatched

Caius to the East, with authority to settle the Parthian and Armenian troubles as it should seem best to him.

Meanwhile, however, a change had occurred in Parthia. Phraates, when somewhat advanced in life, had married an Italian slave-girl, called Musa, who had been sent to him as a present by Augustus, and had had a son born to him from this marriage, who, as he grew up, came to hold an important position in the Parthian state. It was perhaps through the influence of this youth's mother, Musa, that Phraates was induced to send his four elder boys to Rome, there to receive their education. At any rate, their absence left an opening for her son, Phraataces, of which she took care that he should have the full advantage ; and the youth, becoming his father's sole support in his declining years, came to look upon himself, and to be looked upon by others, as his natural successor. Conscious, however, of the weakness of his claim to the throne, and doubtful of his father's intentions with regard to him, if he allowed events to take their natural course, the ambitious youth resolved to become the shaper of his own future, and, in conjunction with his mother, administered poison to the aged monarch, from the effects of which he died. Phraataces then seized the throne, and reigned as joint sovereign with his mother, to whom he allowed the titles of " Queen " and " Goddess," and whose image he placed upon the reverse of most of his coins.

Among the first acts of Phraataces as king was the sending of an embassy to Augustus, whom he professed to regard as still friendly to Parthia, though he must have known that the Parthian attitude towards

Armenia had alienated him. He informed Augustus of his accession to the throne of the Arsacidæ, apologised for the circumstances under which it had taken place, and proposed a renewal of the treaty of peace which had subsisted between Augustus and his father, adding a request that the Roman Emperor would, in consideration of the peace, kindly surrender to him his four brothers, whose proper place of residence was not Rome, but Parthia. With respect to Armenia he observed a discreet silence, leaving it to Augustus to initiate negotiations on the subject or to accept the *status quo.* Augustus replied to this message in terms of extreme severity. Addressing Phraataces by his

COIN OF PHRAATACES AND MUSA.

bare name, without adding the title of king, he required him to lay aside the royal appellation, which he had so arrogantly and unwarrantably assumed, and at the same time to evacuate all the portions of Armenia which his troops wrongfully occupied. With respect to the surrender of the Parthian princes, the brothers of Phraataces, and their families, he said nothing. Nor did he respond to the appeal concerning the formal renewal of a treaty of peace. He left Phraataces to infer that his brothers would be retained at Rome, as pretenders to the throne of Parthia, whom it might be convenient at some future time to bring forward ; and he not obscurely intimated that no treaty of peace would be concluded until the Parthian troops were withdrawn across the Armenian frontier. Phraataces, however, was not to be cowed by mere words. He repaid Augustus in his own coin, sending him a contemptuous message, in which, while assuming to himself the high-sounding Oriental designation of " King of Kings," he curtly addressed the Roman Emperor as " Cæsar."

It is probable that this attitude of defiance would have been maintained, and that the Parthian troops would have continued to garrison Armenia, had Augustus refrained from active measures, and been content with menaces. But when, in B.C. 1, the Emperor proceeded from words to acts, and despatched his grandson, Caius, to the East at the head of a large force, with orders to re-establish the Roman influence in Armenia, even at the cost of a Parthian war, and when Caius showed himself in Syria with all the magnificent surroundings of the Imperial dignity, Phraataces became alarmed. It was arranged during the winter that an interview should be held between the two princes in the spring of A.D. 1, on an island in the Euphrates, where the terms of an arrangement between the two empires should be discussed and settled. For the first and almost the last time a Parthian monarch and a scion of the Roman Imperial House met amicably for the purpose of negotiation, and discussed the terms on which the two empires could be friends. On either bank of the " great river " were drawn up the mighty hosts, which, within a few days, if no agreement were come to, would be loosed at each other's throats. The two chiefs, accompanied by an equal number of attendants, passed from their respective banks to the island, and there, in the full sight of both armies, proceeded to hold the conference. An arrangement satisfactory to both sides was made, the chief proviso of which was the evacuation of Armenia by the Parthians. Feasting and banqueting followed. The Parthian king was first entertained by Caius on the Roman side of the river, after which Caius was in his turn feasted by the Parthian on the opposite bank. Cordial relations were established. For once in the course of the long struggle with Rome, Parthia seems to have actually made up her mind to relinquish Armenia to her adversary. She gave up her claims, withdrew her troops, and, during the serious troubles which followed—troubles wherein Caius lost his life—honourably abstained from all interference, either by intrigue or arms, in Armenian affairs, and allowed Rome to settle them at her pleasure.

The willingness of Phraataces thus to efface himself, and concede to Rome the foremost position in Asia, arose probably from the unsettled state of the kingdom, and the internal difficulties which threatened him. To be a parricide was not in Parthia an absolute bar to popularity and a quiet reign, as had been proved by the prosperous reign of Phraates IV., but there were circumstances connected with the recent palace revolution, which threw special discredit upon the principal agent in it, and grievously offended the pride or the Parthian nobles. Private and selfish motives had alone actuated the young prince, who could not even pretend any public ground for the extreme step that he had taken.   His subjection to female influence, especially when the female was a foreign slave-girl, enraged the nobles and drew down their contempt. The exalted honours which he heaped on her offended their pride.   Rumours, which may have had no foundation in fact, increased his unpopularity, and covered his companion on the throne with even a deeper shade of disgrace.   The Megistanes consulted together, and within a few years of his establishment as king raised a revolt against his authority, which terminated in his deposition or death.   An Arsacid,

COIN OF ORODES II.

named Orodes, was chosen in his place ; but he too, in a short time, displeased his subjects, and was murdered by them, either at a banquet or during a hunting expedition.   It then occurred to the Megistanes to fall back on the legitimate heir to the throne, who was still at Rome, whither he had been sent by his father some fifteen years previously.   Accordingly, they despatched an embassy to Augustus (A.D. 5), and asked to have Vonones, the eldest son of Phraates IV., sent back to Parthia, that he might receive his father's kingdom.   Augustus readily complied, since he regarded it as for the honour of Rome to give a king to Parthia, and Vonones was sent out to Asia with much pomp and many presents, to occupy a position which was the second highest that the world had to offer.

It is said that princes are always popular on their coronation day ; and certainly Vonones was no exception to the general rule. His subjects received him with every demonstration of joy, pleased like children with a new plaything. But this state of feeling did not continue very long. The foreign training of the young monarch soon showed itself. Bred up at Rome, amid the luxuries and refinements of Western civilisation, the rough sports and coarse manners of his countrymen displeased and disgusted him. He took no pleasure in horses, seldom appeared in the hunting-field, absented himself from the rude feastings which formed a marked feature of the national manners, and, when he showed himself in public, was usually seen reclining in a litter. He had brought with him, moreover, from the place of his exile, a number of Greek companions, whom the Parthians despised and ridiculed. The favour which he showed these interlopers excited their jealousy and rage. It was to no purpose that he sought to conciliate his angry subjects by the openness and affability of his demeanour, or by the readiness with which he allowed access to his person. Virtues and graces, unknown to the nation hitherto, were, in the eyes of the courtiers, not merits but defects. Dislike of the monarch led them to look back with dissatisfaction on the part which they had taken in placing him upon the throne. " Parthia had indeed degenerated," they said, " in asking for a king who belonged to another world, and into whom there had been engrained a foreign and hostile civilisation. All the glory gained by destroying Crassus and repulsing Antony was utterly lost and gone, if the country was to be ruled by Cæsar's bond-slave, and the throne of the Arsacidæ to be treated as if it were a Roman province. It would have been bad enough to have had a prince imposed upon them by the will of a superior, if they had been conquered ; it was worse, in all respects worse, to suffer such an insult, when they had not even had war made upon them." Under

COIN OF VONONES I.

the influence of these feelings, the Parthians, after they had tolerated Vonones for a few years, rose in revolt against him (about A.D. 10), and summoned Artabanus, an Arsacid, who had grown to manhood among the Dahæ of the Caspian region, but was at this time subject-king of Media Atropatênê, to rule over them.

A crown, when it is offered, is not often declined, though a few crowns may have gone begging in the modern world, now that kingship has lost its glamour ; and Artabanus, on receiving the overture from the Parthian nobles, at once expressed his willingness to

accept the proffered dignity. He invaded Parthia at
the head of an army consisting of his own subjects,
and engaged Vonones, to whom in his difficulties
the bulk of the Parthian people had rallied. This
engagement resulted in the defeat of the Median
monarch ; and Vonones was so proud of his victory
that he immediately had a coin struck to commemo-
rate it, bearing on the obverse his own head, with the
legend of, ΒΑΣΙΛΕΥΣ ΟΝΩΝΗΣ, and on the reverse a
Victory with the legend—ΒΑΣΙΛΕΥΣ ΟΝΩΝΗΣ ΝΕΙ-
ΚΗΣΑΣ ΑΡΤΑΒΑΝΟΝ—"King Onones on his defeat

COIN OF ARTABANUS III.

of Artabanus." But the self-gratulation was premature. Artabanus had made good his retreat into his
own country, and, having there collected a larger army
than before, returned to the attack. This time he
was successful. The forces of Vonones were defeated,
and he himself, escaping from the battle with a few
followers, fled on horseback to Seleucia, while his
vanquished army, following more slowly in his track,
was pressed upon by the victorious Mede, and suffered
great losses. Artabanus, entering Ctesiphon in
triumph, was immediately acclaimed king. Vonones
took refuge in Armenia, and, the throne happening to

be vacant, was not only given an asylum, but appointed to the kingly office. Artabanus naturally remonstrated, and threatened war unless Vonones were surrendered to him. Armenia was alarmed, and began to waver ; whereupon Vonones withdrew himself from the country, and sought the protection of Creticus Silanus, the Roman governor of Syria, who received him with favour, gave him a guard, and allowed him the state and title of king, but at the same time kept him in a sort of honourable captivity.

It was under these circumstances that the Roman Emperor, Tiberius, who had recently succeeded Augustus, determined to entrust the administration and pacification of the East to a personage of importance—one who should combine the highest rank with considerable experience, and should strike the imagination of the Orientals, and command their attention, at once by the dignity of his office, and by the pomp and splendour of his surroundings. It may be that, in his selection of the individual, he was actuated by motives of jealousy, and by the wish to separate one, whom he could not but regard as a rival, from an army which had grown too much attached to him. But it seems scarcely fair to attribute these motives to him upon mere suspicion, and it is difficult to see what better choice than the one he made was open to him under the circumstances of the period. Germanicus was, at the time, the second man in the State. He had knowledge of affairs ; he was a good soldier and general ; his manners were courteous and agreeable ; and he was popular with all classes. At once the nephew and the adopted son of the sove-

reign, he would scarcely seem to the Orientals to
shine with a reflected radiance ; they would see
in him the *alter ego* of the great Western autocrat,
and would be awed by the grandeur of his position, while fascinated by the charm of his personality. The more to affect their minds, Tiberius
conferred on his representative none of the ordinary
and well-worn titles of Roman administrative employment, but coined for him a phrase unknown
in official language previously, investing him with
an extraordinary command over all the Roman
dominions east of the Hellespont. Full powers were
granted him for making peace or war, for levying
troops, annexing provinces, appointing subject kings,
concluding treaties, and performing other sovereign
acts without referring back to Rome for instructions.
A train of unusual magnificence accompanied him to
his charge, calculated to impress the Orientals with
the conviction that this was no common negotiator.
Germanicus arrived in Asia in the spring of A.D. 18,
and within the space of a single year completed the
task, which he had undertaken, satisfactorily. Having
visited Artaxata in person, and ascertained the feelings and disposition of the Armenians, he made up
his mind not to demand the re-instatement of Vonones,
which would have been throwing down the gauntlet
to Parthia, nor yet to allow the establishment of an
Arsacid on the Armenian throne, which would have
been exalting Parthia to the shame and dishonour of
Rome, but to pursue a middle course, at which neither
the Armenians nor the Parthians could take offence,
while Roman dignity would be upheld, Roman tradi-

tions maintained, and something done to soothe the
feelings and gratify the wishes of both the irritated
Asiatic nations.   There was in Armenia, where he had
grown up, a foreign prince, named Zeno, the son of
Polemo, once king of the curtailed Pontus, and afterwards of the Lesser Armenia, who was in very good
odour among the Armenians, since he had, during a
long residence, conformed himself in all respects to
their habits and usages.   Finding that it would please
the Armenians, Germanicus determined on giving
them this man for ruler, and at the seat of government, Artaxata, in the presence of a vast multitude
of the people, and with the consent and approval of
the principal nobles, he placed with his own hand
the diadem on the brow of the favoured prince, and
saluted him as king under the Armenian name, which
he had never hitherto borne, of "Artaxias."   For the
satisfaction of the Parthian monarch, who required
that Vonones should either be delivered into his hands
or removed to a greater distance from the Parthian
frontier, he "interned" the unhappy prince in the
Cilician city of Pompeiopolis—a change of residence
so much disliked by the prince himself that the next
year he endeavoured to escape from it, but, his
attempt being discovered, he was pursued, overtaken,
and slain in a skirmish on the banks of the river
Pyramus.   The pacification of the East was thus,
with some difficulty, effected ; and Germanicus, quitting Asia, indulged himself in the luxury of a pleasure
trip to Egypt.

The dispositions which Germanicus had made
sufficed to preserve the tranquillity of the East for the

space of fifteen years. Artabanus, at peace with
Rome and with Armenia, employed the time in the
chastisement of border-tribes, and in petty wars,
which however increased his reputation. Success
followed on success ; and by degrees his opinion of
his own military capacity was so much raised that he
began to look upon a rupture with Rome as rather to
be desired than dreaded. He knew that Germanicus
was dead ; that Tiberius was advanced in years, and
not likely to engage in a distant military expedition ;
and that the East was under the rule of an official
who had never yet distinguished himself as a commander. When, therefore, in A.D. 34, the Armenian
throne was made vacant by the death of Artaxias
III., the nominee of Germanicus, he boldly occupied
the country, and claiming the disposal of the vacant
dignity, bestowed it upon his own eldest son, a prince
who bore the name of Arsaces. Nor did he rest
content with this. Insult must be added to injury.
Ambassadors were despatched to Rome with a
demand for the restoration of the treasure which
Vonones had carried off from Parthia and taken with
him into Roman territory ; and a threat was held
out that Artabanus was about to reoccupy all the
territory which, having been once Macedonian or
Persian, was now properly his, since he was the
natural successor and representative of Cyrus and
Alexander. According to one writer,[1] the Parthian
monarch actually commenced military operations
against Rome by the invasion of Cappadocia, which
had been for some time a Roman province.

[1] Dio Cassius.

It is uncertain what response Tiberius would have made to these demands and proceedings had the internal condition of Parthia been sound and satisfactory. He was certainly averse to war at this period of his life, and had actually sent instructions to Vitellius, the governor of Syria, *after* the seizure of Armenia by Artabanus, that he was to cultivate friendly relations with Parthia. But the Parthian kingdom was internally in a state of extreme disquiet ; insurrection was threatened ; and the nobles were in active correspondence with the Imperial court on the subject of bringing forward a pretender. "Artabanus," they said, "had, among his other cruelties, put to death all the adult members of the royal family who were in his power, and there was not an Arsacid in Asia of age to reign ; but for a successful revolt an Arsacid leader was absolutely necessary : would not Rome supply the defect ? Would she not send them one of the surviving sons of Phraates IV., to head the intended insurrection, which would then be sure to succeed ? One son, named Phraates, like his father, was still living, and was, they understood, at Rome ; if Tiberius would only send him, and he were once seen on the banks of the Euphrates, they guaranteed a successful outbreak—Artabanus would be driven from his throne without difficulty. Tiberius was prevailed upon to do as they desired. He furnished Phraates with all things necessary for his journey, and sent him into Asia, to lay claim to his father's kingdom.

Phraates, however, was unequal to the task assigned him. The sudden change in his life and habits, which his new position necessitated, broke

down his health, and he was but just arrived in Syria
when he sickened and died. Tiberius replaced him
by a nephew, named Tiridates, probably a son either
of Rhodaspes or of Seraspadanes, and proceeded to
devote to the affairs of the East all the energies of a
mind eminently sagacious and fertile in resources.
At his instigation, Pharasmanes, king of Iberia, a
portion of the modern Georgia, was induced to take
the field, and invade Armenia ; where, after removing
the reigning Parthian prince, Arsaces, by poison, he
occupied the capital, and established his own brother,
Mithridates, as king. Artabanus met this movement
by giving the direction of affairs in Armenia to
another son, Orodes, and sending him with all speed
to maintain the Parthian cause in the disputed
province ; but Orodes proved no match for his adversary, who was superior in numbers, in the variety of
his troops, and in familiarity with the localities.
Pharasmanes had obtained the assistance of his
neighbours, the Albanians, and opening the passes of
the Caucasus, had admitted through them a number
of the Scythic or Sarmatian hordes, who were
always ready, when their services were well paid, to
take a part in the quarrels of the south. Orodes
failed to secure either mercenaries or allies, and had
to contend unassisted against the three enemies who
had joined their forces to oppose him. For some time
he prudently declined an engagement ; but it was
impossible to restrain the ardour of his troops, whom
the enemy exasperated by their reproaches. After a
while he was compelled to accept the battle which
Pharasmanes incessantly offered. The troops at his

disposal consisted entirely of cavalry, while Pharasmanes had, besides his horse, a powerful body of
infantry. The conflict was nevertheless long and
furious ; the Parthians and Sarmatians were very
equally matched ; and the victory might have been
doubtful, if it had not happened that in a hand-to-
hand combat between the two commanders, Orodes
was struck to the ground by his antagonist, and
thought by most of his own side to be killed. As
usual under such circumstances in the East, a rout followed. If we are to believe Josephus, " many tens
of thousands " were slain. Armenia was wholly lost
to Parthia ; and Artabanus found himself left with
diminished resources and tarnished reputation to
meet the intrigues of his domestic foes.

Still, he would not succumb without an effort. In
the spring of A.D. 36, having levied the whole force of
the empire, he took the field in person, and marched
northwards, with the intention of avenging himself
on the Iberians and recovering his lost province. But
his first efforts were unsuccessful ; and before he
could renew them the Roman general, Vitellius, put
himself at the head of his legions, and, moving
towards the Euphrates, threatened Mesopotamia with
invasion. Placed thus between two dangers, the
Parthian monarch felt that he had no choice but to
abandon Armenia and return to the defence of his
own proper territories, which in his absence must
have lain temptingly open to an invader. His return
caused Vitellius to change his tactics. Instead of
challenging Artabanus to an engagement, and letting
the quarrel be decided by a trial of strength in the

open field, he fell back on the weapon of intrigue so
dear to his master, and proceeded by a lavish expenditure of money to excite disaffection once more
among the Parthian grandees. This time the conspiracy was successful. The military disasters of the
last two years had alienated from Artabanus the
affections of those whom his previous cruelties had
failed to disgust or alarm ; and he found himself
without any armed force whereon he could rely,
beyond a small number of the foreign guards whom
he maintained about his person. It seemed to him
that his only safety was in flight ; and accordingly
he quitted his capital, and removed himself hastily to
Hyrcania, in the immediate vicinity of the Scythian
Dahæ, among whom he had been brought up. Here
the population was friendly to him, and he lived a
retired life, waiting (as he said) until the Parthians,
who could judge an absent prince with fairness,
although they could not long continue faithful to a
present one, should repent of their behaviour to him.

When the flight of Artabanus became known to
the Romans, Vitellius immediately advanced to the
banks of the Euphrates, and introduced Tiridates
into his kingdom. Fortunate omens were said to
have accompanied the passage of the river, and these
were followed by adhesions, the importance of which
was undoubted. Ornospades, satrap of Mesopotamia,
and a former comrade of Tiberius in the Dalmatic
war, was the first to join the standard of the pretender
with a large body of horse. Next came Sinnaces,
who had long been in correspondence with the
Romans, with a contingent ; then his father, Abda-

geses—"the pillar of the party," as Tacitus calls him—and the keeper of the royal treasures, together with other persons of high position. Vitellius, on seeing the pretender thus warmly welcomed by his countrymen, regarded his mission as accomplished, and returned with his troops into Syria. Tiridates proceeded through Mesopotamia and Assyria, receiving on his way the submission of many Greek and some Parthian cities, as Halus and Artemita. The Greeks saw in his Roman breeding a guarantee of the politeness and refinement which had been wholly wanting in Artabanus, brought up among the uncivilised Scyths. In the great city of Seleucia he was received with an obsequiousness that bordered on adulation. Besides paying him all the customary royal honours, both old and new, they flatteringly compared him with his predecessor, who, they said, had been no true Arsacid. Tiridates was pleased to reward these unseemly compliments by a modification of the Seleucian constitution in a democratic sense. From Seleucia he crossed the Tigris to Ctesiphon, where, after a short delay, caused by the absence of some important governors of provinces, he was crowned King of Parthia according to the established forms by the Surena, or Commander-in-chief of the period.

Tiridates thought that now all was secure. Artabanus was in hiding in Hyrcania, leading a miserable existence. The whole of the western provinces had declared for him, and no signs of hostility appeared in the East. He deemed his rule acquiesced in generally, and there is reason to suppose that his anticipations would have proved correct, had not discontent shown itself at the Court and among the higher officials. There had been many who had hoped for the office of Grand Vizier, and in nominating one to it Tiridates had displeased all the rest. There were also many, who through accident or hesitation in making up their minds had been absent from the coronation ceremonial, and who believed themselves to be on that account suspected of disaffection, or at any rate of lukewarmness. It is also more than probable that the "Roman breeding" of the new monarch, which delighted his Grecian, offended his Parthian subjects. At any rate, however we may account for it, disaffection certainly broke out. Emissaries from the nobles sought the dethroned monarch in his obscure retirement, and placed before him the prospect of a restoration, which they declared themselves anxious to bring about. Distrustful at first of what seemed to him mere levity and fickleness, Artabanus was ultimately persuaded that the overtures made to him were sincere, and that if he himself were not the object of any very devoted affection on the part of the malcontents, Tiridates at any rate was the object of a very real and pronounced hostility. He therefore placed himself in the hands of the conspirators, and, having first secured the services of a body of Dahæ and other Scyths, marched westward with all speed, anxious at once to cut short the preparations which were being made to resist him by his enemies, and to forestall the desertions, which he could not but anticipate, on the part of his friends. The good policy of this rapid movement is unquestionable. It startled and greatly discomposed Tiridates and his counsellors. Of these, some recommended an immediate attack on the troops of Artabanus before they were recovered from the fatigues of their long march; while others, and among them Abdageses, the chief vizier, advised a retreat into Mesopotamia, and a junction with the Armenian levies, and with the Roman troops, which Vitellius, on the first news of the insurrection, had thrown across the Euphrates. The more timid counsel prevailed, and a retreat was determined on. But *reculer pour mieux sauter* is a maxim only suited to the West. In the East the first step in retreat is the first step towards ruin. No sooner was the Tigris crossed and the march through Mesopotamia begun than the host of Tiridates melted away like an iceberg in the Gulf Stream. The Arabs of the Mesopotamian desert were the first to break up and disband themselves, the nearness of their homes offering an irresistible attraction; but their example was soon followed by the rest of the army, which had no such excuse. Some directed their steps homewards; others joined the enemy; Tiridates was at last left with a mere handful of adherents, and, hastening into Syria, put himself once more under Roman protection.

The attempt to establish the influence of Rome over the Parthian kingdom, by fixing a Roman puppet on the throne of the Arsacidæ, thus proved altogether a failure. But the general effect of the struggle was advantageous to Rome, and reflects credit on the prince who, at the age of seventy-seven, at once vindicated the Roman honour and baffled the schemes of one of the ablest of the Parthian monarchs. Artabanus, when after his various vicissitudes he recovered his throne, had no longer any stomach for great enterprises. He took no further steps to disturb Mithridates in his possession of Armenia, and he left Vitellius unmolested on the Euphrates. When, towards the close of A.D. 36, or very early in A.D. 37, he had an interview with the Roman proconsul half-way between the two banks of the river, he distinctly renounced all claims to the Armenian kingdom ; at the same time agreeing to send one of his sons, Darius, to Rome in a position which Rome regarded as that of a hostage, and further consenting to offer incense to the emblems of Roman sovereignty—an act, as the Romans understood it, of submission and homage. Artabanus, by these concessions, the meaning of which he did not perhaps fully understand, decidedly lowered the prestige of his nation, and yielded to Rome a pre-eminence which was scarcely admitted by any other monarch, or at any other period. We cannot be surprised that the credit of concluding such a peace, though belonging really to Tiberius, was falsely claimed by his flatterers for Caligula, the new emperor, soon after whose accession in March, A.D. 37, the news of the successful negotiations reached Rome.

XIV.

ASINAI AND ANILAI—AN EPISODE OF PARTHIAN HISTORY.

IT was during the troubled reign of Artabanus the Third, when the state was distracted between foreign war and domestic feud, that disturbances broke out in Mesopotamia, which have been graphically described by the Jewish writer Josephus, and which serve to throw considerable light on the internal condition of the Parthian Empire at this period. There was a large Jewish element in the population of the more western provinces of the empire, an element which dated from a time anterior to the rise, not only of the Parthian, but even of the Persian monarchy. That system of "transplantation of nations," which was pursued on so large a scale by the Assyrian and Babylonian sovereigns of the eighth, seventh, and sixth centuries before Christ, had introduced into the heart of Asia a number of strange nationalities, and among these there was none more remarkable than that of the Hebrews. Whatever had become of the descendants of the Ten Tribes—whether in any places they still constituted distinct communities, or had long ere this been absorbed into the general population of the country —at any rate, colonies of Jews, dating from the time of Nebuchadnezzar's Captivity, maintained themselves, often in a flourishing condition, in various parts of Babylonia, Armenia, Media, Mesopotamia, Susiana, and probably in other Parthian provinces. These colonies exhibited very generally the curious but well-known tendency of the Jewish race to a rate of increase quite disproportionate to that of the population among which they are settled. The Hebrew element became continually larger and more important in Babylonia, Mesopotamia, and the the adjacent countries, notwithstanding the large draughts which from time to time were made upon it by Seleucus Nicator, and others of the Syrian princes. And this alien element in the population, for the most part prospered. The Jewish settlers seem to have enjoyed under the Parthians the same sort of toleration, and the same permission to exercise a species of self-government, which both Jews and Christians enjoy now in several parts of Turkey. In many cities they formed a recognised community under their own magistrates; some towns they had wholly to themselves; those who dwelt in Mesopotamia possessed a common treasury; and it was customary for them to send up to Jerusalem from time to time the offerings of the faithful, escorted by a convoy of thirty thousand or forty thousand armed men. The Parthian kings treated them well, and probably regarded them as a valuable counterpoise to the disaffected Greeks and Syrians of this part of the empire. They laboured under no disabilities ; suffered no oppression ; had no grievances of which to complain ; and it would have seemed beforehand very improbable that they would ever become the cause of trouble or disturbance to the state ; but circumstances seemingly trivial threw the whole community into commotion, and led on to disasters of an unusual and lamentable character.

There were two young Jews, named respectively Asinai and Anilai, brothers, natives of Nearda, the city in which the general treasury of the community was established, who, on suffering some ill-usage at the hands of the manufacturer in whose service they were, threw up their employment, and, retiring to a marshy district enclosed between two arms of the Euphrates, made up their minds to exchange the dull career of honest labour for the more exciting one of robbery. The vagabonds of the neighbourhood, by the attraction which draws like to like, soon gathered about them, and a band was formed which in a little time became the terror of the entire vicinity. They exacted a black mail from the peaceable population of shepherds and others who lived near them, occasionally made plundering raids to a distance, and required a contribution from all travellers and merchants who passed through their district. Their proceedings having become notorious and intolerable, the satrap of Babylonia thought it his duty to put them down, and marched against them with the troops at his disposal, intending to take them by surprise on the Sabbath day, when it was supposed that their religious scruples would prevent them from making any resistance. But his intentions got wind, and the robber band, having agreed among themselves to disregard the obligation of the Sabbatical rest, turned the tables upon their assailant, and, instead of allowing themselves to be surprised, surprised him, and inflicted on him a severe defeat. Tidings of the affair having reached Artabanus, who had his hands already sufficiently occupied, he thought it best to make pacific overtures to the victors, and having induced them to pay him a visit at his Court, instead of inflicting any punishment, assigned to Asinai, the elder of the two brothers, the entire government of the Babylonian satrapy. At first the experiment appeared to be a success. Raised from the condition of an outlaw to that of a *vitaxa*, or Persian provincial governor, Asinai was perfectly content, and administered his province with zeal, diligence, and ability. For the space of fifteen years all things went smoothly in Babylonia, and no complaint was raised against the administration. At the end of that time, however, the lawless temper which from the first had characterised the two brothers, reasserted itself, not, however, in Asinai, but in Anilai. Having fallen in love with the wife of a Parthian nobleman, who seems to have been the commander of the Parthian troops stationed in Babylonia, and not knowing how otherwise to accomplish his purpose, he made an open attack upon the chieftain and killed him. Having thus removed the obstacle to a marriage, he, within a short space, made the object of his affections his wife, and having established her as the mistress of his house, allowed her to introduce into it the heathen rites whereto she had always been accustomed. But this gave great offence to the entire Jewish community, who were shocked that idolatrous practices should be permitted in a Hebrew household, and laid their complaint before Asinai, calling upon him to interfere in the matter, and compel Anilai to divorce his Parthian wife. Asinai came into their views, and would probably have enforced them upon his brother, had not the lady, alarmed at her impending disgrace, and, it may be, sincerely attached to her Jewish husband, anticipated the accomplishment of the project by secretly poisoning her brother-in-law. On the death of Asinai the authority which he had wielded with so much satisfaction to all concerned, passed, apparently without any fresh appointment by the crown, into Anilai's hands, who thus became satrap of the extensive province of Babylonia, at this time the most important in the empire.

Anilai, however, possessed unfortunately none of his brother's capacity for administration and government. His instincts were those of a mere ordinary freebooter, and he was no sooner settled in his province than he proceeded to give them free vent by invading, without so much as a pretext, the territory of a neighbouring satrap, named Mithridates, who was not only a Parthian noble of the highest rank, but was connected with the Royal house, being married to a daughter of Artabanus. Mithridates flew to arms in defence of his province, but Anilai, who had military if he had no other talent, fell suddenly upon his encampment in the night, completely routed his troops, and took Mithridates himself prisoner. The unhappy captive was subjected to extreme indignity; by the orders of Anilai, he was stripped naked, set upon an ass, and in this guise conducted from the battlefield to the camp of the victors, where he was paraded before the eyes of the soldiery. Not daring, however, to put to death a connection of the Great King, of whose vengeance he had a wholesome dread, Anilai felt compelled after a time to release his captive and allow him to return to his satrapy. There the account which he gave of his sufferings so exasperated his wife, that she set herself to make his life a burden to him, and never rested until he consented to collect a second army and continue the war. His forces advanced against Anilai's stronghold, but the Jewish captain was too proud to remain within it. Quitting the marshes, he led his troops a distance of ten miles through a hot and arid plain to meet the enemy, thus foolishly and quite unnecessarily exhausting them, and exposing them to the attack of the enemy under circumstances of the greatest disadvantage. The natural consequence followed. Anilai was defeated with great loss, but he himself escaped, and having enrolled fresh troops of a worthless character, proceeded to revenge himself by carrying fire and sword over the lands of his own Babylonian subjects, whom he must have looked upon as on the point of escaping from his jurisdiction. The unfortunate natives sent to Nearda and required that Anilai should be given up to them; but the Jews of Nearda, even supposing them to have had the will, had not the power to comply. Negotiations werè then tried, but with no better

result, except that, in the course of them, the Babylonians contrived to obtain an exact knowledge of
the position which Anilai and his troops occupied,
together with a general notion of their habits.
Taking advantage of the knowledge thus acquired,
they one night fell suddenly upon them, when they
were all either drunk or asleep, and at one stroke
exterminated the whole band.   Such was the end of
Anilai.

Up to this point, though the occurrences had been
strange and abnormal, indicative of extreme disorganisation and weakness on the part of the Parthian government, yet no very great harm had been
done.   Two Jewish bandits had been elevated into
the position of Parthian satraps, and had borne
rule over an important province, with the result, in
the first place, of fifteen years of peace and prosperity,
and subsequently of a short civil war, terminating in
the destruction of the surviving robber chief and the
annihilation of the entire band of marauders.   But
worse consequences were to follow.   The bonds of
civil order cannot be relaxed or disturbed without
extreme danger to the whole social edifice.   There
had long been a smouldering feud between the native
Babylonian population and the Jewish colonists in
Babylon, which from time to time had broken out
into actual riot and commotion.   Diverse in race, in
manners, and in religion, the two nationalities were
always ready to fly at each other's throats when a
fitting occasion offered.   The present seemed an occasion not to be missed ; authority was relaxed ; the
Jewish element in the population of Mesopotamia

was at once disgraced and weakened. It had made itself obnoxious to the dominant power in the state, and was not likely to receive government support or protection. Moved by these considerations, the native Babylonian population, very shortly after the destruction of Anilai, rose up against the Hebrews settled in their midst and threatened them with extermination. Finding themselves unable to make an effectual resistance, and receiving no assistance from the government, the Hebrews came to a determination to withdraw from the conflict by retiring altogether from a city where they provoked such hostility and were subjected to such ill-usage. Notwithstanding the enormous pecuniary loss which such a migration necessarily entails, and the vast difficulty of finding new homes for a population of many scores of thousands, they quitted Babylon in a body and transferred themselves to Seleucia. Seleucia, originally a Hellenic city, had at this time a tripartite population, consisting of Greeks, Syrians, and Jews. The Greeks and Syrians were opposed to each other, but hitherto the Hebrew element had managed to live on tolerably friendly terms with both the other nationalities. Now, however, the new-comers felt themselves drawn to the Syrians, who were a kindred race, and, uniting with them against the Greeks, forced these last to succumb, and to accept a subordinate position. But such a condition of things could not last ; the Greeks found it insupportable ; and before many months were past they succeeded in gaining over the Syrians to their side, and persuading them to join in an organised attack upon the Hebrews.

Too weak to make head against so powerful a combination, the Hebrews were utterly overpowered, and in the massacre that ensued they lost, it is said, above fifty thousand men.   Those who escaped crossed the Tigris, and transferred their abode to Ctesiphon, but the malice of their enemies was still unsatisfied.   The persecution continued, and did not come to an end until the entire Jewish population, deserting the metropolitan cities, withdrew to the smaller provincial towns, which had no other inhabitants.

The series of events here related derives its interest, partly from its connection with the Jewish people, whose history will always, more or less, command our sympathies, but partly also, and indeed mainly, from the light which it throws on the character of the Parthian rule, and the condition of the countries under Parthian government.   Once more the resemblance between the Parthian and the Turkish systems is brought vividly to our notice, and the scenes enacted in Syria and the Lebanon before our own eyes—the mutual animosities of Christian and Druse and Maronite, the terrible conflicts, and the bloody massacres that have been an indelible disgrace to Turkish administration, present themselves to our thoughts and memories.   The picture has the same features of antipathies of race, unsoftened by time and contact, of perpetual feud bursting out into occasional conflict, of undying religious hatreds, of strange combinations, of massacres, of fearful outrages, and of a government looking tamely on, and allowing things for the most part to take their course. It is clear that the Parthian system failed utterly to blend together or amalgamate the conquered races ; and not only so, but that it rubbed off none of their angles, rendered them after the lapse of centuries not one whit more friendly, or better disposed one towards another than they had been at the first, did absolutely nothing towards producing the "unity, peace, and concord," which ought to knit together the subjects of a single government, the constituent elements of a single kingdom. Moreover, the Parthian system, as set before us in the events which we are considering, was impotent even to effect the first object of civil government, the securing of quiet and tranquillity within its borders. If we were bound to regard the events of the Asinai and Anilai episode as representing to us truthfully the *normal* condition of the peoples and countries with which it is concerned, and to take the picture as a fair sample of the general condition of the empire, we should be forced to conclude that Parthian government was merely a euphemistic name for anarchy, and that it was a rare good fortune which prevented the State from falling to pieces at this early period, within three centuries of its establishment. But, on the whole, there is reason to believe that the reign of Artabanus III. puts before us, not the normal, but an exceptional state of things—a state of things which could only arise in Parthia when the machinery of government was deranged in consequence of rebellion and civil war. We have to bear in mind that Artabanus III. was actually twice driven from his kingdom, and that during the greater part of his reign he lived in perpetual fear of revolt and insurrection. It is not at all improbable that the culminating atrocities of the struggle which we have described, synchronised with the second expulsion of the Parthian monarch, and are thus not so much a sign of the ordinary weakness of the Parthian rule, as an indication of the terrible strength of the forces which that rule for the most part restrained and held under control

XV.

END OF THE REIGN OF ARTABANUS III.—GOTARZES AND HIS RIVALS.

ARTABANUS did not continue on the throne very long after his undignified submission to Vitellius.[1] His proceedings probably disgusted his subjects, who vented their indignation in murmurs and threats of revolt. These threats coming to the knowledge of the king, provoked him to adopt severe measures against the malcontents; who thereupon banded themselves together, and from malcontents became open conspirators. Artabanus felt himself unequal to the task of coping with the movement, and, quitting his capital, fled to the Court of Izates, tributary king of Adiabênê, who received him hospitably, and undertook to replace him upon the throne from which he had been driven. It lends an interest to this portion of Parthian history to learn from Josephus, who relates it, that Izates, and his mother, Helena, were converts to Judaism, and entertained so much affection for the Jewish people as to send supplies of corn to Jerusalem, when (about A.D. 44) that city was threatened with famine.[2] Meanwhile,

---

[1] See above, p. 245.   [1] Compare Acts xi. 28-30.

however, the Parthian Megistanes had deposed
Artabanus, and elected in his place a certain
Kinnamus, or Cinnamus, a distant relation of the
cashiered monarch, brought up by him in his house.
War would probably have broken out had not
Cinnamus, who was of a gentle disposition, waived his
claim in favour of his benefactor, and written to him,
inviting him to return. Artabanus upon this remounted
his throne, while Cinnamus carried his magnanimity
so far as to take the diadem from his own head, and,
replacing it on that of the old monarch, to salute
him as king. It was a condition of the restoration,
guaranteed both by Artabanus and Izates, that the
transaction should be accompanied by a complete
amnesty for all political offences. Such mildness,
very unusual among the Parthians, may perhaps be
ascribed to the gentle councils of the Judæan Izates.

It seems that Artabanus died very shortly after his
restoration to the throne. His last days were
clouded by the calamity of the revolt of Seleucia,
far the most important of the Hellenic cities of the
empire. We may assume that the disturbed condition of the Parthian kingdom, the frequent revolts,
the occasional civil wars, the manifest tendency to
disruption which the empire about this time showed,
had raised among the Hellenic subjects of the
Parthian crown, always disaffected, a belief, or at
any rate a hope, that they might succeed in shaking
off the yoke of their barbaric lords. Seleucia, naturally, took the lead. Had she succeeded in establishing her independence, other lesser towns, as
Apollonia, Nicephorium, Edessa, Carrhæ, might

have followed her example. Rome might have been called in as a protector, and might perhaps have undertaken the charge. An *imperium in imperio* might conceivably have been established. But, as the event proved, the attempt now made was ill-judged. Though Artabanus himself failed to recover the revolted city, which maintained a precarious independence for the space of over six years (A.D. 40–46), yet there was at no time any reasonable prospect of a prosperous issue. Rome held aloof. The unhappy Greeks were overmatched. Though Parthia was thought to have incurred some disgrace [1] by her inability to reduce a single rebel city to subjection for the space of nearly seven years, yet ultimately she prevailed. Seleucia succumbed to a son of Artabanus in A.D. 46, and resumed a subject position under her old masters.

On the death of Artabanus, the succession was disputed between two of his sons, Vardanes and Gotarzes. According to Josephus, the crown was left by his father to the former, who was probably the elder of the two ; but, as he happened to be at a distance, while Gotarzes was present in the capital, or close at hand, the last named had the opportunity of occupying the throne, and, being an ambitious prince, availed himself of it. He reigned, however, at this time only for a few weeks. Having put to death a brother, named Artabanus, together with his wife and son, and otherwise shown a tyrannical disposition, he so alarmed his subjects, that they sent hurriedly for Vardanes, and offered him the post of

---

[1] Tacit. ".Ann.," xi. 9 : " Non sine dedecore Parthorum."

king.   Vardanes, a man of prompt action, instantly complied, and, having accomplished a journey of 350 miles in two days, drove Gotarzes from the kingdom ; after which he received the submission of the provinces and cities generally, the only exception being Seleucia, which maintained its revolt, and resisted all his efforts to reduce it.   Meantime Gotarzes had fled to the Dahæ of the Caspian region, and thrown himself upon their support and protection.   The Dahæ, who were not Parthian subjects, willingly gave him an asylum ; and from this secure retreat he proceeded to seduce the neighbouring Hyrcanians from their

COIN OF VARDANES I.

allegiance to his brother, and drew together so large a power, that Vardanes felt himself under the necessity of raising the siege of Seleucia, and marching in person to the distant East.   The two armies confronted each other in the plain country of Bactria, but before they came to an engagement, the commanders on either side thought it expedient to hold a conference, and arrange, if possible, terms of peace.   It had come to the knowledge of Gotarzes, that there was a design afloat among the chief nobles in either army to get rid of both the brothers, and elect to the throne a wholly new king. Having informed his brother of this alarming discovery, he succeeded in arranging a secret meeting with him, where pledges were interchanged, and an understanding come to with respect to the future. Gotarzes agreed to relinquish his claims to the Parthian crown, and was assigned a residence in Hyrcania, which was probably made over to his government. Vardanes returned to the West, and resuming his siege operations, finally compelled Seleucia to a surrender in the year A.D. 46, the seventh year of the insurrection.

Regarding himself now as firmly settled in his kingdom, and as having nothing more to fear from his brother, Vardanes thought that the time was come for taking in hand a new and important enterprise. This was no less than the recovery of Armenia from the Roman influence. That country, relinquished to Tiberius by Artabanus III. in A.D. 37, and placed by Rome under the government of Mithridates, an Iberian, had suffered various vicissitudes, and was now (A.D. 46) extremely discontented with its ruler, as well as with his Roman patrons and upholders. Vardanes thought that there would be no great difficulty in driving out Mithridates from the kingdom upon which he had so weak a hold, and replacing Armenia within the sphere of the Parthian rule and influence. But for success in such an enterprise he required the hearty concurrence and support of his principal feudatories, and especially of the great Izates, whose services to Artabanus had been rewarded by an important enlargement of his dominions, and who was now king both of Adiabênê and of Gordyênê or

Upper Mesopotamia. Accordingly, he took this prince into his councils, and requested his opinion as to the prudence of the course which he was contemplating. Izates gave the project his most strenuous opposition. He was profoundly convinced of the military strength and greatness of Rome, and on that account wholly disinclined to quarrel with her, while further he had a private and personal motive for desiring to maintain amicable relations with the great Western power from the fact that five of his sons were residing in Rome, whither he had sent them in order that they might receive a polite education. He refused, therefore, to abet Vardanes in his design, and the latter, indignant at a refusal, which he regarded as an act of rebellion, proceeded to engage in hostilities against his feudatory.

It was probably this condition of things which induced Gotarzes suddenly to come forth from his retirement, and again assert his claim to the Parthian throne—a claim which he had only withdrawn under the pressure of necessity. The quarrel of Vardanes with Izates had weakened his power, and inclined even the nobles who had hitherto supported his cause to desert him, and go over to his adversary. Many of them invited Gotarzes to resume the struggle ; and Vardanes found himself compelled for the second time to march eastward. Several battles were fought between the two pretenders to the throne in the country between the Caspian and Herat, in which the advantage mostly rested with Vardanes ; but his successes in the field failed to overcome the aversion in which he was held by his

subjects ; and on his return from the war a number
of them, in spite of the glory which he had acquired,
conspired against him, and treacherously slew him in
the hunting-field.

Gotarzes was then unanimously accepted as king,
and reigned for some years in peace. But he had
the common Parthian defect of a cruel and suspicious
temper, while he added to this defect the comparatively unusual faults of indolence and addiction to
luxury. In a short time he alienated the affections
of his subjects from him, partly by his severities,

COIN OF GOTARZES.

partly by his luxurious living, and to some extent by
his ill-success in some small military expeditions.
In the year A.D. 49, steps were taken by those especially opposed to him, for relieving their country from
the incubus of a thoroughly bad king. Claudius, the
Roman Emperor, was approached, and entreated to
come to the aid of his Parthian "friends and allies."
"The rule of Gotarzes," they said, "had become intolerable, alike to the nobility and the common
people. He had murdered all his male relations, or
at least all those who were within his reach—first his

brothers, then his near kinsmen, finally even those whose relationship was more remote; nor had he stopped there; he had proceeded to put to death their young children and their pregnant wives. He was sluggish in his habits, unfortunate in his wars, and had betaken himself to cruelty, that men might not utterly despise him for his want of manliness. They knew that Rome and Parthia were bound together by the terms of a treaty, and they wanted no infringement of it. Let Rome send them an Arsacid worthy of reigning in the place of the unworthy scion of the house under whose tyranny they groaned. They asked for Meherdates, the son of Vonones, and grandson of Phraates IV., who was resident at Rome, and, having been so long accustomed to Roman manners, might be expected to rule justly and moderately." This speech was delivered in the Roman Senate, Claudius being present, and also Meherdates, the candidate for the Parthian throne. The Emperor made a favourable response—. " He would follow the example of the Divine Augustus, and allow the Parthians to receive from Rome the monarch whom they requested. That prince, bred up in the City, had always been remarkable for his moderation. He would (it was to be hoped) regard himself in his new position, not as a master of slaves, but as a ruler of citizens. He would find that clemency and justice were the more appreciated by a barbarous people, the less they had experience of them. Meherdates might accompany the Parthian envoys; and a Roman of rank, Caius Cassius, the prefect of Syria, should be instructed to receive them on their arrival in Asia, and to see them safely across the Euphrates."

Meherdates thus set out for his proposed kingdom under the fairest auspices. He had a large party devoted to his cause in Parthia itself ; he was backed by the great name of Rome ; and he had the active support of a Roman of distinction, well acquainted with the East, and of good antecedents. Moreover, when he arrived at Zeugma on the Euphrates, he found himself welcomed, not only by a number of the Parthian nobles, but by a personage of great importance in those parts, no other than Abgarus, the Osrhoënian king, who commanded the passages of the Euphrates, and held the country to the east of the river, probably as far as the Khabour, or at any rate of the Ras-el-Ain, its western tributary. The parting advice of Cassius to his young *protégé* was, that he should lose no time in pressing forward against his rival, Gotarzes, since the barbarians were always impetuous at the commencement, but lost their energy, or even grew perfidious, if there was delay. Meherdates, however, fell entirely under the influence of the Osrhoënian monarch, who seems to have been a traitor, like his predecessor in the time of Crassus,[1] and to have determined from the first to lure the young prince to his destruction. By the persuasions of Abgarus, Meherdates was induced, first of all, to waste precious time while he indulged in a series of feasts and banquets at Edessa, the Osrhoënian capital, and then to proceed against his antagonist by the difficult and circuitous Armenian

[1] See p. 164.

route, which followed the course of the Tigris by Diarbekr, Til, and Jezireh, instead of striking directly across Mesopotamia to Ctesiphon. The rough mountain passes and the snow-drifts of Armenia harassed his troops and seriously delayed his progress, ample time being thus given to Gotarzes for collecting a strong force and disposing it in the most convenient situations. Fortune, however, still continued to smile on the pretender. When he reached Adiabênê, Izates, the powerful monarch of that tract, openly embraced his cause, and brought a body of troops to his assistance. Pressing forward towards Ctesiphon, Meherdates possessed himself of the fort which occupied the ancient site of Nineveh, as well as of the strong post of Arbela, and there found himself in the near vicinity of his adversary. But Gotarzes was unwilling to risk all on the fate of a battle. He stood on the defensive, with the river Corma in his front, and would not suffer himself to be provoked, or tempted, to an engagement. Reinforcements were still reaching him, and he had a good hope of drawing to his own side, or at any rate persuading to neutrality, a portion of his adversary's adherents, if he could set his emissaries at work among them. These tactics were crowned with success. After a brief hesitation, Izates, the Adiabenian, and Abgarus, the Osrhoënian monarch, proved faithless to the cause which they had professedly espoused, and drew off their troops. Meherdates feared that other desertions might follow, and resolved, before losing more of his army, to precipitate a fight. Gotarzes being also willing to engage, since he was no longer outnumbered, the battle took place. It was stoutly contested. For a long time neither side could boast any decided advantage ; but at last Carrhenes, the chief general on the side of Meherdates, having repulsed the troops opposed to him, was tempted to pursue them too far, and being intercepted by the enemy on his return was either killed or made prisoner. His misfortune decided the engagement. The loss of their principal commander caused a general panic among the soldiers of Meherdates, who dispersed in all directions. The pretender might perhaps have escaped ; but having entrusted his person to a certain Parrhaces, a dependent of his father's, who promised to conduct him to a place of safety, he was seized, bound, and delivered up to Gotarzes. Gotarzes seems to have been touched with compassion by his rival's youth and helplessness. Instead of awarding him the usual punishment of rebels and pretenders who fall into their enemies' hands, he contented himself with inflicting on him a slight mutilation, sufficient, according to Oriental ideas, to incapacitate him from ever exercising sovereignty.

This victory which brought the troubles of Gotarzes with his rivals to an end, was regarded by him as worthy of commemoration in an unusual way. The Parthians had but little taste for mimetic art, and seldom indulged in artistic representations of any of the events of their history. But Gotarzes on this occasion took the exceptional course of commemorating his achievement by a rock tablet. On the great and sacred mountain of Behistun (originally, Baghistan, " The Place of the Gods "), which was already adorned by a sculptured tablet representing the Achæmenian monarch, Darius, the son of Hystaspes, with two attendants, receiving a number of conquered rebels, he caused to be engraved a second, though much smaller tablet, representative of his own exploit. In this he appeared seated on horseback, with a heavy spear in his right hand, while a Victory flying in the air crowned him with a wreath or diadem, and behind him his army galloped over the plain in pursuit of the flying foe. Some of the figures formed, apparently, a walking procession ; while an inscription in the Greek character and language explained the intention of the monument. This inscription is now almost illegible, but, when first found, contained in two places the name " Gotarzes," and in one the name " Mithrates," an undoubted equivalent of " Meherdates."

It appears that the successful monarch did not long survive his victory. His death, which is assigned by the best authorities to the year A.D. 50, is variously related by the historians. According to Tacitus, it was natural, the result of disease ; but according to Josephus it was violent, and effected by a conspiracy. There would be nothing surprising in this, since through his whole reign he was unpopular, and must have had many bitter enemies. But Tacitus is an authority who cannot be lightly set aside ; and his emphatic words — " morbo obiit " — have generally been accepted as closing controversy on the subject. The reign of Gotarzes must be considered to have helped forward in no small degree the disorganisation of the Parthian state. It showed Rome how easy it was to interfere in the internal affairs of her eastern neighbour, and to paralyse her action beyond her frontier, by raising troubles within it. It accustomed the Parthians themselves to intrigue, civil war, and confusion. It must have tended, moreover, to exhaust the resources of the empire. At any rate the downward course of the state from this time, though not rapid, is marked and continuous ; and, though the tenacity of the race enables it to prolong its independent existence for nearly two centuries longer, yet the student of the history clearly sees that a decline has set in from which any real recovery is impossible.

XVI.

PARTHIA IN THE TIME OF NERO—VOLOGASES I. AND CORBULO.

GOTARZES was succeeded by a distant relative, an Arsacid called Vonones, and known in Parthian history as "Vonones the Second." This prince did not occupy the throne more than about two months, and is chiefly remarkable as the father of three kings much more celebrated than himself—Vologases I., King of Parthia, Tiridates, King of Armenia, and Pacorus, dependent King of Media. Tiridates appears to have been the eldest, Pacorus the second, and Vologases the third son; but, on the death of their father, the two elder princes agreed to cede the Parthian throne to their younger brother. This was the more remarkable as Vologases was the son of Vonones by a Greek concubine, whereas his two brothers were legitimate. Probably he had given indications of an ability, which they did not recognise in themselves, and for which he may have been indebted to the foreign blood that flowed in his veins. At any rate he found himself, in A.D. 50 or 51, established upon the throne, and able to reward Pacorus for his complaisance by bestowing on him

the quasi-royal government of Media. For Tiridates
something more was needed, and Vologases may be
presumed to have been anxiously on the watch,
during the earlier portion of his reign, for an opportunity of conferring on his other brother a dignity
worthy of his acceptance. The opportunity came
in A.D. 51, through circumstances which had lighted
up the flames of war in the neighbouring territory of
Armenia.

The origin of the strife was the following. Rhadamistus, the eldest son of Pharasmanes, King of

COIN OF VOLOGASES I.

Iberia, was a youth of such recklessness, and
possessed with such a lust for power, that, for the
security of his own crown, his father thought it
necessary to divert his son's thoughts to the acquisition of another. He therefore pointed out to him
that his uncle, Mithridates, King of Armenia under
the Romans, was a most unpopular ruler, and that
it might not be difficult to supplant him, if he took
up his residence at his court and gave his mind to
ingratiating himself with the Armenian people. The
ambitious youth followed the advice offered him, and

ere long succeeded in making himself a general
favourite, after which, having contrived to get
Mithridates into his power, he ruthlessly put him to
death, together with his wife and children. This was
a challenge to the Romans, who had established
Mithridates in his kingdom ; but the Roman officer,
Ummidius Quadratus, president of Syria, whose
business it was to take up the challenge, neglected
to do so, and another official, Julius Pelignus, pro-
curator of Cappadocia, even went further, and
authorised Rhadamistus to assume the title and
insignia of king. A large party in Armenia was,
however, adverse to the new rule, distrusted Rhadamistus, and condemned the course which he had
pursued. The country was accordingly thrown into
a ferment ; and Vologases, having recently ascended
the Parthian throne, and needing a principality for
his brother Tiridates, thought he saw in the situation
of Armenia an excellent opportunity of at once
gratifying his brother and advancing his own reputation. To detach Armenia once more from the
dominion of Rome and re-attach it to Parthia would
be a happy inauguration of his reign, and one that
would draw down upon him the open applause and
secret envy of his neighbours.

Accordingly, Vologases, in A.D. 51, the year of his
accession, having collected a large force, led an
expedition into Armenia. At first it seemed as if
he would effect an easy conquest. The Iberian
garrison, on whose support Rhadamistus principally
relied, quitted the field without risking a battle ; his
Armenian troops made but a poor resistance ;

Artaxata and Tigrano-certa, his two principal cities, opened their gates to the foe ; Vologases took possession of Armenia, and established Tiridates at Artaxata, the capital. But this fair beginning was soon clouded over. A severe winter, and some defect in the commissariat arrangements, caused the outburst of a pestilence, which so thinned the Parthian garrisons that Vologases was compelled to withdraw them. Rhadamistus returned, and, though ill-received by his subjects, and occasionally in danger of losing his life, on the whole contrived to maintain himself during the three years extending from A.D. 51 to 54, and was still in possession when Vologases, in the last-named year, having brought some other wars to an end, found himself in a position to resume his designs upon Armenia.

The delay in grappling with the Armenian difficulty had had a double origin. In A.D. 52 a dispute had arisen between Vologases and one of his principal feudatories, Izates, *vitaxa* of Adiabênê, whose pretensions to exclusive privileges appeared to his feudal lord excessive and even dangerous. After fruitless negotiations, Izates appealed to arms, and took up a position on the Lower Zab, which was the southern limit of his territory. Vologases had advanced to the opposite bank of the river, and was on the point of crossing, and attacking his adversary when tidings reached him of the invasion of his own dominions by a foreign enemy. The Dahæ, and the Scythians in their neighbourhood, had passed into Parthia Proper from the Caspian region, and were threatening to carry fire and sword through the entire province.

Domestic revolt could be chastised at any time, but a foreign foe must be met as soon as he showed himself. Vologases, accordingly, marched away from Adiabêné to the Parthian and Hyrcanian frontier, east of the Caspian sea, where he met and repulsed the band of marauders, who had probably only ventured to invade his territory because they knew him to be engaged in a serious quarrel at a considerable distance, and imagined that they would therefore be unresisted. Successful in this quarter, he was about to resume his operations in Adiabêné, when information reached him of the death of Izates, which brought his domestic difficulties to an end. The pretensions of the deceased monarch had been personal, being grounded upon special privileges granted him by Artabanus III., which would not pass to a successor, and Vologases had consequently no quarrel with Monobazus, Izates' brother, who had inherited his throne. He thus found himself, at the close of A.D. 53, wholly his own master, and free to engage in whatever enterprise might seem to him most promising.

Under these circumstances, it is not surprising that, in A.D. 54, he turned his attention once more to Armenian affairs, and resumed his project of establishing his brother, Tiridates, upon the throne of that ancient, and still semi-independent, kingdom. Rhadamistus, though he continued in possession of the nominal sovereignty, had failed to establish his power, or to obtain any firm hold on the affections of his subjects, and might be attacked with a good prospect of success, unless he received external assistance. The real question was, would Rome interfere? Would she come to the aid of a monarch, who had not received his throne from herself, but had obtained it by supplanting, and finally murdering, her *protégé*? Vologases was probably aware that a new sovereign had recently ascended the Imperial throne, a youth not yet eighteen years of age, one wholly destitute of military tastes or training, devoted to music and the arts, who could not be credited with very keen patriotic feelings, or with a very full comprehension of the niceties of the political situation. Would this raw youth grasp the meaning of a diminution of Roman influence in the far East, or rush to arms because a border kingdom—not a Roman province—wavered in its allegiance? Vologases, it would seem, answered three questions in the negative : or perhaps, while recognising the risk, he may have thought the immediate advantage so great as to make it worth his while to encounter the hazard. At any rate, early in A.D. 54, he made his invasion, drove Rhadamistus out of Armenia, reduced the whole country to subjection, and established his brother, Tiridates, as king in the capital city of Artaxata.

The boldness of this stroke took the Romans by surprise, and produced something like a panic in the Imperial city. But the traditions of Imperial policy were too firmly fixed in the minds of the official class for any doubt to be entertained as to the necessity of meeting and resisting the aggression. Orders went forth at once for recruiting the Oriental legions up to their full strength, and for moving them

nearer to the Armenian frontier ; preparations were
made for bridging the Euphrates ; Agrippa II.,
King of Chalcis, and Antiochus, King of Commagêné,
were ordered to raise troops and make ready for an
invasion of Parthia ; new governors were appointed
over Sophêné and the Lesser Armenia ; above and
beyond all, the brave and experienced Corbulo,
universally allowed to be the best general of the
time, was summoned from his command in Germany,
and given the general superintendence of the war in
Armenia, with Cappadocia and Galatia as his provinces. Ummidius Quadratus was maintained in
the proconsulship of Syria, but required to co-operate
with Corbulo, and made practically his second in
command. Four legions, together with numerous
auxiliaries were concentrated on the Armenian
frontier ; and it seemed as if the next year would
see the contest between Rome and Parthia renewed
on a scale which would recall the times of Antony
and Phraates IV.

But to ardent spirits the new year brought nothing
but disappointment. Instead of rushing to arms,
and pouring their combined legions into Armenia or
Parthia, the two Roman commanders suddenly
showed a disposition for peace. Emissaries from
both sought the Court of Vologases with offers of
peace—offers which implied an acceptance of the
status quo, provided that the Parthian monarch would
take no further steps in opposition to Rome, and
would place some Parthians of importance in the
hands of the Romans as hostages. This he was
quite willing to do, as he knew many of the nobles

to be disaffected, and their absence from his Court would relieve him of the necessity of watching them. Internal troubles, probably fomented by Rome had commenced by the open revolt of his son, Vardanes, whose defection from his father Tacitus places in A.D. 54,[1] and whose coins show that he had assumed the royal title, and set himself up as a rival to Vologases, certainly before the end of the next year. A truce with Rome was, consequently, what the Parthian monarch must earnestly have desired ; and we can only feel surprised that the Roman

COIN OF VARDANES II.

commanders should have consented to play into his hands, and have left him wholly unmolested in the time of his greatest difficulties. Probably they were already jealous of each other, and disinclined to press forward a war in which each felt that mere accident might give the chief laurels to the other.

Vologases was thus able to give his whole attention, during the three years from A.D. 55 to A.D. 58, to the contest with his son. Its details have not come down to us ; but it appears to be certain that by the spring of A.D. 58 he had succeeded in crushing the revolt,

---

[1] Tacit., " Ann.," xiii. 7, *ad fin.*

and re-establishing his authority over the whole kingdom.   As Vardanes is no more heard of, we may presume that he either perished in battle, or was executed.   His coins, which are numerous, belong to the years A.D. 55–58, and show a strong, masculine, type of face, with an expression that is fierce and determined.

The Great King, being now at liberty to resume the projects and plans, which his son's rebellion had compelled him to drop, took up once more the Armenian question, which was still unsettled between his own Court and that of Rome, and by his envoys pressed for a final arrangement.   He claimed that of right, and by ancient possession, Armenia was a Parthian province, or at least a Parthian dependency, and required that not only should Tiridates be left in undisturbed possession of it, but that there should be a distinct understanding that he held it, not as a Roman, but as a Parthian, feudatory.   To this the Romans, and especially Corbulo, demurred.   Armenia, they said, had been added to the Roman Empire by Lucullus, or at any rate by Pompey, and it was not consistent with the greatness of Rome to surrender territory which she had once acquired.   Let Tiridates remain quiet, and the matter be settled by negotiation; otherwise Rome would be compelled to use force.   Corbulo had utilised the three years of waiting by recruiting his legions from Cappadocia and Galatia, by tightening their discipline, and by accustoming them to the hardships of winter marches and movements; he had also obtained an additional legion from Germany; and he now felt ready for a campaign.

Tiridates soon gave him the opportunity which he seems to have desired. Having received a contingent of troops from Vologases, he commenced proceedings against the Roman partisans in Armenia, harrying them with fire and sword; whereupon Corbulo crossed the frontier to their relief. A number of partial engagements were fought in which Rome had the advantage, and at last, after three years' fighting, Tiridates, having lost his capital city, Artaxata, in A.D. 58, and Tigrano-certa, the second city of his kingdom, in A.D. 60, withdrew from the contest, and yielded the entire possession of Armenia to the Romans. By the favour of Nero, Tigranes, grandson of Archelaus, a former monarch of Cappadocia, was made king; but, as his ability to administer so large a territory was doubted, portions of it were detached from his rule, and made over to the neighbouring princes. Pharasmanes of Iberia, Polemo of Pontus, Aristobulus of the Lesser Armenia, and Antiochus of Commagênê, profited by the new arrangement, which could not, however, but be distasteful to the Armenians, who saw the country of which they were so proud, not merely conquered, but broken into fragments.

Corbulo's success must be attributed in a great measure to the absence of Vologases from the scene of contest. The Armenian monarch had been called away in A.D. 58 to his north-eastern frontier by a revolt, perhaps fomented by Rome,[1] of the distant province of Hyrcania, and had found full occupation there for his utmost energies, so that he was wholly

[1] So Dean Merivale, "Roman Empire," vol. vii. p. 23.

unable to lend effectual aid to his brother. But, about the year A.D. 62, the Hyrcanian troubles came to an end, and, the hands of Vologases being once more free, he had to consider and determine whether he should accept the state of things established in Armenia by Corbulo, or interfere by force of arms to modify it. To what conclusion he would have come, had his own dominions been left unmolested, it is impossible to say : as it was, the intolerable aggressions of Tigranes upon his rich province of Adiabênê, and the bitter complaints of his subjects, who threatened to transfer their allegiance to Rome, left him no choice. His own interests and the honour of his country alike required him to assert his cause in arms ; and Vologases, having made up his mind to declare war, announced his intention to a council of his nobles in a speech which is reported as follows : " Parthians, when I obtained the sovereignty of Parthia by the cession of my brothers' claims, my intention was to substitute for the old system of fraternal hatred and strife, a new one of domestic affection and agreement ; my brother Pacorus, accordingly, received Media from my hands at once ; and Tiridates, whom you see now present before you, I shortly afterwards inducted into the royal appanage of Armenia, a dignity reckoned the third in the Parthian kingdom. Thus I put my family matters on a peaceful and satisfactory footing. But these arrangements are now disturbed by the Romans, who have never hitherto gained anything by breaking faith with us, and will scarcely do so on the present occasion. I shall not deny that up to this time I have proposed to maintain my right to the dominions left me by my ancestors by fair dealing rather than by shedding of blood, by negotiation rather than by arms; if however I have erred in this, and have been weak to delay so long, I will now amend my fault by showing the more vigour. You at any rate have lost nothing by my holding back; your strength is intact, your glory undiminished. Nay, you have added to your other well-known merits, the credit of moderation—a virtue which not even the highest among men can afford to despise, and which the gods view with special favour?" His speech ended, Vologases placed a diadem on the brow of Tiridates, in token of his determination to restore him to the Armenian throne, at the same time commanding Moneses, a Parthian noble, and Monobazus, the Adiabenian king, to take the field and invade Armenia, while he himself collected the whole strength of the empire, and marched to attack the Roman legions on the Euphrates.

The campaign which followed was of less importance than might have been anticipated from these preparations for it. Vologases, instead of invading Syria, marched no further than Nisibis, which was well within the limits of his own dominions. Moneses and Monobazus, on the other hand, carried out the concerted programme, and having invaded Armenia, and advanced to Tigrano-certa, which had now become the capital of the kingdom, besieged Tigranes in that city (A.D. 62). But the Parthian attack on walled places was always ineffective, and Tigrano-certa happened to be exceptionally strong. The walls are said

to have been seventy-five feet in height, the river
Nicephorius, a broad stream, washed a portion of
them ; a huge moat protected the remainder ; the
town was strongly garrisoned ; and the besieging
force, though not wanting in gallantry, proved unable
to make any serious impression upon the place.
Vologases, as time went on, began to despair of
effecting very much under existing circumstances by
force of arms, and leant towards negotiation, which
Corbulo invited.   His army, which consisted almost
entirely of cavalry, was reduced to inaction by want
of forage, Mesopotamia having recently suffered from
a plague of locusts.   Hence he consented to conclude a truce with his antagonist, and to send a fresh
embassy to Rome for the purpose of making a satisfactory arrangement.   The truce was to last until the
ambassadors returned ; and, meanwhile, Armenia was
to be evacuated by both parties, and care was to be
taken that no collision should occur between the
soldiers of the two nations.

But this well-meant effort at pacification was
entirely without result. Nero gave the envoys no
answer ; and, indeed, he had made arrangements before their arrival, from which he anticipated a triumphant issue to the contest instead of a mere patched-up
and unstable convention.   At the request of Corbulo,
who was anxious not to arouse his jealousy, he had
sent out a second commander to the East, a special
favourite of his own, and from the conduct of the war
by this new leader he looked for immediate results of
the most important character.   L. Cæsennius Pætus
was a man of energy and boldness, confident in him-

self, and contemptuous of the prudence and caution of his colleague. He held a separate command, with forces equal to those led by Corbulo, and soon let it be known that he was about to carry on the war in a new fashion. "Corbulo," he said, "had shown no dash or vigour ; he had neither plundered nor massacred ; if he had besieged cities, it had been in name rather than in reality. His own method would be different. Instead of setting up shadowy kings he would bring Armenia under Roman law, and reduce it to the condition of a province." These brave words were followed up by a show of brave deeds. Crossing the Euphrates, Pætus invaded Armenia with two legions, and spreading his troops over a wide extent of country, burnt the strongholds, ravaged the territory, and carried off a considerable booty. But he neither fought a single battle, nor ventured to besiege a single town. As winter approached, he withdrew his troops into Cappadocia, but, intent on pleasing his Imperial master, he gave in his despatches an exaggerated account of what he had achieved in his short campaign, and spoke as if the war was well-nigh over.

Corbulo, on his part, maintained the prudent attitude habitual to him. He bridged the Euphrates in the face of a large opposing force by anchoring vessels laden with military engines in mid-stream. He then passed his troops across, and occupied a strong position in the hills at a little distance from the river, where he caused his legions to construct an entrenched camp, and remained on the defensive. He greatly distrusted Pætus, and would not allow himself to be so entangled in military operations as not to be able at any moment to march to his colleague's assistance if he should hear that he was in any danger.

The prudence of this course soon became evident. Pætus, regarding the season for war as over, sent one of his legions to winter in Pontus, while he himself with the other two took up his quarters in the country between the Taurus and the Euphrates, and allowed free furloughs to all the soldiers who applied for them. While his legions were in this way much weakened, he suddenly heard that Vologases, braving the inclemency of the season, was advancing against him at the head of a strong force. The crisis revealed his incapacity. He was uncertain whether to await the enemy in quarters or to take the field against him, whether to concentrate his troops or to disperse them. Now he adopted one course, now another. The only consistency that he showed was in imploring aid from Corbulo, to whom he sent messenger after messenger. That general, however, was in no hurry to render help, since he did not wish to appear upon the scene as deliverer until it was clear that the danger threatening Pætus was imminent. Vologases, meanwhile, steadily pursued his way. Without attempting any rapid movements, he closed in upon Pætus, his adversary, swept away the small force that Pætus had detached to guard the passes of Taurus, and blocked up the remainder of his army in a position from which extrication, unless his colleague came to his aid, was almost impossible. Corbulo was now on his march, and pressing forward with all speed, but a panic had seized on Pætus and his soldiers. Though he had abundant provisions, and might have prolonged the defence

for weeks, or even for months, yet in his cowardly
alarm he preferred to precipitate matters, and having
entered into negotiations with Vologases, he practically
capitulated to him. The terms granted were, that the
blockaded army should be allowed to quit its entrench-
ments, and be free to march away, but that it must
at once quit Armenia ; its stores and its fortified posts
must be surrendered ; no further hostilities must be
engaged in ; and Pætus should obtain from Nero the
exact conditions on which he would now be willing to
make peace. These terms were carried out, not however without the addition of some further insults and
indignities. The Parthians entered the Roman en-
trenchments before the legionaries had quitted them,
claiming and seizing whatever they professed to
recognise as Armenian spoil ; they even took possession of the soldiers' arms and clothes, which were
tamely relinquished to them with the object of avoiding a conflict. Armenia was then quitted hastily, and
not without disorder, Pætus setting the example of
unseemly hurry. Corbulo was reached after a three
days' march, and received the fugitives without reproaches, and with every demonstration of sympathy.

Vologases followed up his success against Pætus by
at once re-establishing his brother, Tiridates, in the
Armenian kingdom. At the same time he devised a
plan whereby, he thought, the interminable quarrel
between the two empires of Rome and Parthia might
be made up, and a *modus vivendi* arrived at. Rome,
under Nero at any rate, was not really bent upon further conquests. It was rather her honour for which she
was jealous than her power which she desired to see

augmented. Vologases therefore sent an embassy to the Court of Nero, and explained that, so long as his brother was accepted and acknowledged by Rome as Armenian king, he would offer no objection to his going in person to Rome and receiving investiture from the Imperial hands.   Nero and his counsellors in reality approved this compromise, but they felt that it would be too palpable a surrender of former claims, and too manifestly a concession extorted by recent disaster, if they closed with the suggestion of the Parthian monarch *at once*. No ; Rome must not make an open confession of defeat ; her recession from a claim must be glossed over, cloaked.   Dust must be thrown in the eyes of the nations, and they must be induced to think that, whatever change Rome made in her political arrangements was made of her own free will, and because she regarded it as for her advantage.   Accordingly, the envoys of Vologases were dismissed with an ambiguous answer.   Pætus was recalled from the East, and Corbulo reinstated in sole command, and invested with a new and almost unlimited authority. The number of his troops was augmented, and their quality improved by draughts from Egypt and Illyricum.   He was bidden once more to take the offensive, and, in the spring of A.D. 63, he crossed the frontier, and penetrated to the heart of Armenia by the road formerly opened by Lucullus.   Tiridates met him, not however in arms, but for negotiation.   On the site of the camp of Pætus, an interview was held between the Roman general and the Armenian monarch, where the terms suggested by the envoys of Vologases at Rome were accepted.   It was agreed that Rome should withdraw her support from Tigranes, and acknowledge Tiridates as rightful monarch, while Tiridates should perform an act of homage to Rome for his kingdom, and be nominally Rome's feudatory. To indicate his acceptance of these terms, Tiridates, in the presence of Corbulo and his suite, divested himself of the regal ensigns, and placed them at the foot of the statue of Nero, undertaking not to resume them except at Nero's hands. For actual investiture he undertook to journey to Rome as soon as circumstances permitted, and meanwhile he placed in the hands of Corbulo one of his daughters as a hostage. Corbulo, on his part, undertook that Tiridates should be treated with the utmost honour and respect, both during his stay at Rome and on his journey to and from Italy, should be entitled to wear his sword, and have free access to all the provincial authorities upon the route. Peace was made upon these terms to the satisfaction of both parties, and it only remained that the terms should be faithfully executed.

The execution was delayed for the space of above two years; but in the spring of A.D. 66, Tiridates, having set the affairs of Armenia in order, started upon his promised journey, accompanied by his wife, by a number of the Parthian princes and nobles, including sons of Vologases, Pacorus, and Monobazus, and by an escort of three thousand Parthian cavalry in all the glittering array of their gold ornaments and bright-gleaming panoplies. The long cavalcade passed, like a magnificent triumphal procession, through two-thirds of the Roman Empire, and was everywhere received with warmth, and

entertained with profuse hospitality.   The provincial
cities which lay upon the line of route selected were
gaily decorated to receive their unwonted visitors,
and the loud acclamations of the assembled multitudes showed that they fully appreciated the novel
spectacle. The whole journey, except the passage of the
Hellespont, was made by land, the cavalcade proceeding through Thrace and Illyricum to the head of the
Adriatic Gulf, and then descending the peninsula.
The Roman Treasury defrayed the entire expenses of
the travellers, which are said to have amounted to
an average daily cost of 800,000 sesterces, or about
£6250 of English money.   As this outlay was
continued for nine months, the entire sum expended
by the Treasury must have exceeded a million and
a half pounds sterling.   Audience was given to the
Parthian prince at Naples, where Nero happened to
be residing, and passed off without serious difficulty.
At first, indeed, an obstacle presented itself; it was
the etiquette of the Roman Court that those introduced to the Emperor were to be unarmed, and
consequently the usher, when Tiridates approached
the Hall of Audience, requested him to lay aside his
sword.   This he refused to do, since he was entitled
to wear it by the terms of his agreement with
Corbulo.   The affair might have ended in a dead-
lock, had not it been ingeniously suggested, that the
Emperor's safety might be assured and the Parthian
prince's honour saved, by the simple expedient of
fastening the obnoxious weapon to its scabbard with
half a dozen nails.   This done, Tiridates was introduced into the Imperial presence, where he made

obeisance, bending one knee to the ground, interlacing his hands, and at the same time saluting the Emperor as his " lord."

The investiture was reserved for a subsequent occasion, and was made a spectacle to the Roman populace. On the night preceding, all the streets of the city were illuminated and decorated with garlands; as morning approached, " the Tribes," clothed in long white robes and bearing branches of laurels in their hands, entered the Forum and filled all the middle space, arranged as was customary ; next came the Prætorians, in their splendid arms and with their glittering standards, stationing themselves in two lines which reached from the further extremity of the Forum to the Rostra, to maintain the avenue of approach clear ; all the roofs of the houses which gave upon the Forum were hidden beneath the masses of spectators ; at break of day Nero himself entered, accompanied by the Senate and by his own body-guard, wearing the garb appropriated to Triumphs, and, passing down between the two lines of Prætorians, ascended a raised platform near the Rostra, and took his seat in an archaic curule chair. Tiridates was then introduced ; silence was proclaimed ; and in a short speech of a sufficiently abject character, the Parthian prince placed himself at the Roman Emperor's disposal. Nero responded haughtily, but executed the covenanted investiture. Saluting Tiridates as king of Armenia, he handed him to a seat prepared for the purpose at his own feet, gave him the kiss which sovereigns only gave to sovereigns, and with his own hand placed upon his brow the coveted diadem, the symbol of Oriental sovereignty. Magnificent entertainments followed, with shows and games of various kinds, in which the emperor himself took part; but this condescension astonished, more than it pleased, the Asiatic. However, he doubtless appreciated better the closing act of the entire drama, which was a parting gift from his nominal suzerain of not much less than a million sterling !

Tiridates returned to Asia across the Adriatic, and by the ordinary route through Greece, no doubt well pleased with his visit. At the cost of a formal sub-mission, and a certain amount of personal humiliation, he had obtained a sum which not even a king could despise, and an assured title to the throne of a con-siderable kingdom. Vologases, who must be regarded as the moving spirit throughout the whole transaction, may also well have been satisfied. He had firmly established his brother upon the Armenian throne, and if he had conceded to Roman vanity the honour and glory of the arrangement, yet he had secured for himself the substantial advantage. As Dean Merivale well observes, "While Tiridates did homage for his kingdom to Nero, he was allowed to place himself really under the protection of Vologases." [1]

[1] " Roman Empire," vol. vii. p. 26.

XVII.

VOLOGASES I. AND VESPASIAN—PACORUS II. AND DECEBALUS OF DACIA.

THE establishment of peace between Rome and Parthia, while no doubt a fortunate circumstance for the subjects of the two empires, is one vexatious to the modern historian of the Parthians, since it places him at a considerable disadvantage. Until the conclusion of the peace, he is able to obtain tolerably ample materials for his narrative from the Greek and Roman writers who describe the condition of affairs in the East under the early Roman Emperors, and who have to trace the causes and course of the hostilities in which the two countries were engaged almost continuously. From the date of the pacification he wholly loses the benefit of this consecutive history, and has nothing to rely upon except a few scattered and isolated notices, not always very intelligible, occurring here and there in the pages of the classical authors, together with the series, which now becomes very confused and confusing, of the Parthian coins. The view obtainable of Parthian history is thus, for the space of above half a century, most imperfect and disjointed. Even the succession of the kings is uncertain ; and the attribution of the coins to this or that monarch, rests frequently on conjecture.

The latest authorities seem to be of opinion that Vologases I.—the monarch who ascended the Parthian throne in A.D. 50 or 51—continued to reign until about A.D. 77. If so, he must have been contemporary with six Roman Emperors—Claudius, Nero, Galba, Otho, Vitellius and Vespasian—reigning contemporaneously with the last named of these for about eight years. The relations between the two rulers were, for the most part, friendly. When Vespasian first came forward as a candidate for empire (A.D. 70), Vologases went so far as to offer him the services of forty thousand horse-archers to assist in his establishment upon the throne ; but the successes of his generals in Italy enabled the Emperor to decline this magnificent proposal, and so to escape the odium of employing foreign troops—"barbarians," the Romans would have said—against his own countrymen. In the same spirit, when, a year later, Titus paid a visit to the Roman station of Zeugma on the Euphrates, the Parthian monarch sent to congratulate him on his successful conclusion of the Jewish war, and begged him to accept at his hands a crown of gold. Titus, with his usual amiability, consented ; and, to show his appreciation of the compliment paid him, invited the envoys of Vologases to a banquet and sumptuously entertained them.

Shortly after this, however, by the machinations of Cæsennius Pætus, the unsuccessful general in the last Armenian campaign, who had been recently promoted to the office of Syrian proconsul, these pleasing prospects were overclouded, and a rupture in the amicable relations that had hitherto subsisted between the two monarchs, appeared to be imminent. Cæsennius Pætus—on what grounds it is impossible to say, perhaps on no reasonable grounds at all—sent a report to Vespasian, in A.D. 72, of a most important and alarming character. He had discovered a plot, he said, for the transfer of the Roman dependency of Commagêné, a portion of Upper Syria, from the Roman to the Parthian allegiance—a plot concerted, he declared, between Vologases and the Commagenian king, Antiochus, and about to be almost immediately put into execution. Samosata, the capital of Commagêné, which commanded the passage of the Euphrates, was to be put into the hands of the Parthian monarch by the Commagenians, and a ready access thereby given him to the Roman provinces of Cappadocia, Cilicia, and Syria itself, which could all be easily invaded from the important site. Unless he were authorised at once to take steps to prevent the transfer, it would within a very short space be accomplished, and the East once more thrown into confusion. Vespasian, who had no reason to doubt the correctness of the proconsul's information, replied to him without delay, and gave him full liberty of acting as he thought best. Hereupon, Pætus, who had made every preparation in anticipation of such a response, immediately marched a strong force into Commagêné, and meeting with no resistance, proceeded against Samosata, which he carried by a *coup de main.* It cannot but be suspected that the whole story told to Vespasian was the invention of

Pætus, who desired war as a field for his energies. His sudden invasion only failed to produce the crisis that he sought to bring about, owing to the moderation and prudence of the two sovereigns against whom his charges had been made. Antiochus, the Commagenian monarch, refused altogether to assume the part of rebel which had been assigned him, and, though his sons took arms against Pætus, himself withdrew from the country, and passing into the Roman province of Cilicia, took up his abode at Tarsus. Vologases declined to give the action taken by the sons of Antiochus any support. He folded his arms, and simply looked on while they contended with Pætus ; when, on their father's withdrawal into Cilicia, their troops abandoned them, and they were forced to take to flight, he contented himself with allowing them a temporary refuge in Parthia, and writing a letter to Vespasian on their behalf. It was probably this letter which induced Vespasian so far to pardon the young princes as to allow them to reside in Rome with their father, while at the same time he made the family an ample allowance from his privy purse.

It was not long after he had escaped the danger of a Roman war that Vologases was attacked by a savage enemy from another quarter. The Alani, a Scythic, or more probably a Finnish tribe from the regions east of the Caspian, having made alliance with the important nation of the Hyrcanians, which in later Parthian history gave many signs of being disaffected, burst through the Caspian Gates suddenly in the year A.D. 75, and, pouring into Media, drove

King Pacorus, the brother of Vologases, to take refuge
in the fastnesses of the mountains, while they carried
fire and sword over the open country. From Media
they passed on into Armenia, which was still held by
Tiridates, defeated him in a pitched battle, and very
nearly succeeded in making him prisoner by means
of a lasso. Vologases, in great alarm, sent an embassy
to Vespasian, and relying on his own offer, a few years
previously, to lend the Roman Emperor, if he required
it, a body of forty thousand horse archers, asked
that an efficient contingent of Roman troops might
now be placed at his disposal. He further requested
that their commander might be either Titus or Domitian. The latter prince, jealous of his brother's
military fame, was most anxious to be selected, and
to be placed at the head of a powerful army, so that
he might have an opportunity of rivalling the great
achievements of Titus. But Vespasian, with the
caution of old age, felt averse from embarking the
State in fresh adventures, and bluntly declared that
he saw no reason for making himself a busybody in
affairs that no way concerned him. Had he accepted
the proffered support of Vologases in years previously,
the case would have been different, but, as he had
declined it, his hands were unshackled, and he was
free either to consent or to refuse as he chose. The
best interests of the State seemed to him to require
abstention, and he therefore sent a negative reply to
Vologases. The Parthian prince was not only dis-
appointed, but angered, and vented his spleen by
withholding from the Emperor, in subsequent diplomatic correspondence, his rightful titles. Vespasian,

with a sense of humour rare in persons so highly placed, made no remonstrance beyond the ironic one of adopting in his reply the humble style assigned him by his correspondent. To the salutation— " Arsaces, King of Kings, to Flavius Vespasianus sends greeting," he answered, " Flavius Vespasianus, to Arsaces, King of Kings, sends greeting."

A coolness in the relations between the two powers now set in. Parthia, thrown on her own resources, was forced to submit to considerable loss in the way of. booty at the hands of the Alani and their allies, and was unable to take any revenge upon them for their unprovoked attack ; but she succeeded in main‧taining her western territories intact, and in recover‧ing both Media and Armenia. Hyrcania, it may be suspected, was from this time detached from her rule, and the cause of continual trouble and disturbance, falling under the dominion of pretenders who claimed Arsacid descent, and even took the full titles of Par‧thian sovereignty.

Vologases died about A.D. 78, and was succeeded by a certain Pacorus, not his brother, but probably his son, who appears by his coins to have been, at his accession, a very young man, and seems to have reigned for thirty years, from A.D. 78 to A.D. 108. This prince was thus contemporary with five Roman Emperors—Vespasian, Titus, Domitian, Nerva, and Trajan—but with none of these does he seem to have held any communications. The " coolness " which had set in under his father gradually deepened into hostility ; and, when the warlike Trajan came to the throne, it was soon apparent that an open quarrel could not be long avoided. Rome's pretensions to a predominating influence in Armenia were revived, and Parthia, not knowing how soon she might be attacked, began to look out for allies among the avowed enemies of the Roman Empire. Relations were established between Pacorus and Decebalus,[1] the Dacian monarch, who had been at war with Rome in the reign of Domitian (A.D. 81–90), and was now (A.D. 101) again threatened by Trajan. Pacorus, however, had not the courage to lend his ally any active assistance, either by sending troops to his aid in the

COIN OF PACORUS II.

struggle that went on upon the Danube, or by effecting a diversion in his favour upon the Euphrates. When Decebalus fell, in A.D. 104, and Dacia became a Roman province, Pacorus must have felt that he stood alone, and that, having provoked the hostility of Rome by his relations with her enemy, he might expect at any moment an attack. Trajan, however, was too wise and too cautious to precipitate matters ; an invasion of the East needed careful preparation ; and the invasion which he contemplated was one of

[1] Plin., "Epist.," x. 16 ; Merivale, "Roman Empire," vol. viii. p. 154.

unusual importance and magnitude : he therefore abstained for the present from all offensive measures, and contented himself with paving the way for his intended expedition by intrigues in Armenia and elsewhere, by accumulating warlike stores, and increasing the strictness of military discipline. Pacorus was thus left in peace to the termination of his long reign (A.D. 108), and the storm which had so long threatened did not burst until the time of his successor. A pretender, however, Artabanus IV., who has left coins, falls into this reign.

COIN OF ARTABANUS IV.

XVIII.

CHOSROËS AND TRAJAN—TRAJAN'S ASIATIC CON-
QUESTS—RELINQUISHMENT OF THESE CON-
QUESTS BY HADRIAN.

PACORUS THE SECOND was succeeded upon the
throne by Chosroës, his brother, whom the Parthian
Megistanes preferred over the heads of Exedares and
Parthamasiris, Pacorus's two sons, as more fit to rule
under the difficult circumstances of the period. It

COIN OF CHOSROËS.

was known, or at any rate suspected, that the warlike
and experienced Trajan designed an expedition
against the East, and it therefore seemed necessary
to entrust the government of the Parthian state to a
man of mature age and sound judgment. The sons of
Pacorus were young and rash, certainly incompetent
to cope with so dangerous an antagonist as Trajan.

Chosroës was of ripe age, at any rate, and, though untried, was believed to possess ability, a belief which after events, on the whole, justified.

The ostensible cause of quarrel between Rome and Parthia was, as so frequently before, Armenia. On the death of Tiridates, in or about the year A.D. 100, Pacorus appears, without any consultation with Rome, to have placed his own son, Exedares, upon the Armenian throne. This was certainly throwing out a challenge to Trajan, and was a high-handed proceeding, not justified by the previous relations of the countries. On the last occasion of the throne being vacant, though Parthia had nominated the prince, Rome's right to give investiture had been admitted, and Tiridates had, in fact, received his diadem from the hands of Nero. But Pacorus probably knew that Trajan had his hands fully occupied with the Dacian troubles, and was therefore not likely to engage in another war, while he may perhaps have thought that the right of investiture was too shadowy a matter for Rome greatly to value it. Events so far justified his expectations that Trajan made neither remonstrance nor threat at the time, but seemingly acquiesced in the new departure. When, however, the Dacian War was over, and the country reduced into the form of a Roman province (about A.D. 114), the Emperor, whose appetite for conquest was whetted rather than satisfied by his Danubian successes, considered that the time was come for taking the affairs of the East into his serious consideration, and for placing them on a footing which should give Rome security against the troubles that had now, for about a century and a half, threatened her from this quarter.

Two views might be taken of the Oriental question. It might be regarded in the light in which the greatest of the Roman Emperors—Augustus, Tiberius, Vespasian—had hitherto regarded it, as chronic—a fatal necessity involving continuous trouble, continuous effort, and at the best of times only admitting of a sort of patched-up arrangement. Or it might be viewed in a more heroic light, as Alexander the Great had viewed it in his day, as an evil to be conquered, a difficulty to be overcome, an intolerable state of things, which might be brought to an end, and ought to be brought to an end as soon as possible. Ordinary minds would naturally see it in the former light. There had always been an East, there would necessarily always be an East, set in antagonism to the West, with a perpetual quarrel going on between them. The case would then only admit of palliatives, partial remedies, *modi vivendi*, such expedients as a wise diplomacy might suggest, and carry out, for avoiding collisions or minimising them, and carrying on such intercourse as was necessary with as little friction as possible. The other view opened a wider range both of thought and action. Might it be practicable to crush the East, to get rid of the constant antagonism; and if so, by what means, and at what cost?

That this latter alternative was not an altogether hopeless one had been shown by Alexander himself. Alexander had conquered the East, and for a century and a half there had been no great barbaric

Oriental monarchy standing over against the West, thwarting it and threatening it. The ambition of Trajan seems to have been fired by the thought of what Alexander had achieved, and an idea of rivalry seems to have taken possession of him. Without divulging his intentions even to his intimates, much less, like Crassus,[1] making an open boast of them, he determined on an attempt to bring the Eastern question to an end by the subjugation of Parthia. At first, however, he veiled his designs under a cloak of pretended moderation. He professed that his sole object was the vindication of the Roman honour in respect of Armenia. Both Pacorus and Chosroës, he said, had insulted Rome by dealing with Armenia as if its government were altogether a Parthian, and not a Roman, affair. He maintained, on the contrary, that the authority of Rome was paramount. It was in vain that Chosroës offered to fall back upon the *modus vivendi* which had been accepted by Nero, and to allow Trajan to invest his nephew, Parthamasiris, a son of Pacorus, and younger brother of Exedares, with the diadem. Trajan replied ambiguously that he would see what was fittest to be done when he arrived in Syria, and proceeded to hasten his march, to augment the number of his troops, and to make preparations of an unusual character. The autumn of A.D. 114 saw him at Antioch, and in the spring of the ensuing year, undaunted by the terrible earthquake which had almost destroyed the Syrian capital in the winter of A.D. 114–5, he set out upon his march from Antioch to the Armenian frontier. The satraps

[1] See above, pp. 149, 150.

and petty princes of the region made submission as
he advanced, and sought his favour with gifts of
various kinds, which he was pleased to receive
graciously, while he made his way from Zeugma, the
Roman outpost, to the passages of the Euphrates at
Samosata and Elegia. Here, on the frontier of the
Greater Armenia, he awaited the arrival of Parthamasiris, who, after attempting to negotiate with him
as an equal, and being treated with disdain, had been
encouraged to present himself as a suppliant in the
Roman camp, and to ask his crown of Trajan. There
can be no doubt that the Armenian prince understood
that the scene was to be a repetition of that enacted
at Rome in A.D. 66, when Tiridates received the
diadem from Nero. But Trajan was otherwise
minded. When the young prince, having ridden
into the camp at the head of a small retinue, stript
the diadem from his own brows and laid it at the feet of
the Roman Emperor, then stood in dignified silence,
expecting that his mute submission would be
graciously accepted, and that the emblem of sovereignty would be returned to him, Trajan made no
movement. The army, which stood around, prepared, no doubt, for the occasion, shouted with all
their might, and, saluting Trajan anew as Imperator,
congratulated him on his "bloodless victory." Parthamasiris saw that he had fallen into a trap, and
would fain have fled ; but the troops had closed in
upon him on all sides, and he found his retreat intercepted. Hereupon he once more confronted the
Emperor, and demanded a private audience, which
was granted him. A short conference was held be-

tween the two in the Emperor's tent, but the proposals of Parthamasiris were rejected. He was given
to understand that he must submit to the forfeiture
of his crown, and summoned a second time before the
Imperial tribunal, to show cause, if he desired to do
so, against the proposed forfeiture, and to hear the
Emperor's decision. Parthamasiris, justly indignant,
spoke at some length, and with much boldness.
"He had neither been defeated," he said, "nor made
prisoner by the Romans, but had come of his own
free will to hold a conference with the chief of the
Roman State, in full assurance that he would suffer no
wrong at his hands, but would be invested by him with
the Armenian sovereignty, just as Tiridates had been
invested by Nero. He demanded to be set at liberty,
together with his retinue." Trajan answered curtly
that he did not intend to give the sovereignty of
Armenia to any one. The country belonged to Rome,
and should have a Roman governor. Parthamasiris
might go where he pleased with his Parthians; but
any Armenians that he had brought with him must
remain—they were Roman subjects. Parthamasiris,
upon this, rode off; but Trajan had no intention of
allowing him to escape, and become the leader in an
Armenian war. He ordered some of his troops to
follow and arrest him, and, if he resisted, to put him
to death. These instructions were carried out, and
Parthamasiris was killed, as a recent historian says,
" brutally."

Cruel and brutal acts are frequently successful—at
any rate, for a time. Trajan's "sharp and sudden
blow " was effective, and produced the prompt and

complete submission of Armenia. No resistance was made. It did not, perhaps, much matter to the bulk of the inhabitants whether a Parthian *vitaxa* or a Roman proconsul governed them. Trajan found no difficulty in carrying out his intention of absorbing Armenia into the empire. The two Armenias— the Greater and the Less—were united together, placed under a Roman governor, and reduced into the form of a province.

Attention was then turned to the neighbouring countries. Friendly relations were established with Anchialus, king of the Heniochi and Macheloni, and gifts were sent him in return for those which his envoys had brought to Trajan. A new king was given to the Albanians. Alliances were concluded with the Iberi, Sauromatæ, Colchi, and even with the distant tribes settled on the Cimmerian Bosphorus. These names recalled to the Romans the glorious times of the great Pompey, and made it evident to them that Roman influence was now paramount in the entire region between the Caucasus, the Caspian, and the Araxes.

Still, the Emperor viewed what he had achieved as a mere prelude to what he was bent on achieving. It was Parthia, not Armenia, against which his expedition had been really aimed. Accordingly, having arranged matters in the north-east, and left garrisons in the principal Armenian strongholds, he made a counter-movement towards the south-west, on which side Parthia seemed to him most assailable. Stationing himself at Edessa, the capital of the province of Osrhoëné, which was still administered by a Parthian vassal, bearing the usual name of Abgarus, he partly terrified, partly coaxed, that shifty prince into sub-mission, after which he entered into negotiations with Sporaces, phylarch of Anthemusia, Mannus, an Arabian chieftain, and Manisares, a Parthian satrap, who had a quarrel of his own with Chosroës. Having drawn these chiefs to his side, he commenced his attack on the great Parthian kingdom by a double movement. Part of his troops marched southward, by the route which Crassus had followed, and made themselves masters of the tract known as Anthemusia, or that between the Euphrates and the Khabour ; part proceeded eastward against Batnæ, Nisibis, and Gordyênê, or the country of the Kurds. No serious resistance was offered to the invaders on either route. Chosroës had withdrawn his forces to the further side of the Tigris, and left the defence of the provinces to his vassals, who were for the most part too weak to venture on opposing the march of a well-appointed Roman army. By the end of the year the whole tract between the Euphrates and the Tigris, as far south as the town of Singara and the modern range of Sinjar, had been overrun, and occupied ; Upper Mesopotamia, in the broadest sense of the term, had become Roman ; and the conqueror, pursuing the system which he had resolved on adopting from the first, absorbed the newly won territory into the empire and made Mesopotamia a Roman province. At Rome these successes were greeted with enthusiasm : medals were struck, on which the subjected countries were represented as prostrate under the foot of their conqueror, and the Senate conferred on him the titles, which now appear upon his coins, of " Armeniacus " and " Parthicus."

As winter approached, the Emperor quitted his army, and retired to Edessa or Antioch, leaving his generals to maintain possession of the conquered regions, and giving them very special instructions with respect to the preparations that they were to make for the campaign of the ensuing year. As Trajan had resolved not to attempt the passage through the desert which intervenes between the Sinjar range and Babylonia, the crossing of the Tigris would be the first important operation to be accomplished. But the banks of the Tigris were, as Trajan knew, very deficient in wood, or at any rate in wood suitable for the construction of such boats as were required for the building of a bridge across the river. He therefore gave orders that, during the winter, a large fleet should be prepared at Nisibis, the headquarters of the army, where timber was excellent and abundant, so constructed that the vessels could be readily taken to pieces and put together again. These, when the spring came, were conveyed in waggons to the western bank of the Tigris, probably at the point where it debouches from the mountains upon the low country, a little above Jezireh. Trajan and his army accompanied them, meeting with no resistance until they reached the river and began their preparations for passing it. Then, however, the inhabitants of the opposite bank —not disciplined soldiers, but brave mountaineers —gathered together in force, to dispute the passage. It was only by launching a number of his boats at different points, laden with companies of heavy-armed and archers, which advanced into mid-stream and engaged the enemy, while at the same time they threatened to land at many different points, that Trajan was able, slowly and with difficulty, to complete his construction, and finally bridge the river. His troops then effected their passage, the enemy dispersing ; and the Emperor rapidly overran the whole of the rich country of Adiabênê, between the river and the hills, occupying in succession Nineveh, Arbela, and Gaugamela, and nowhere meeting with any resistance. Chosroës remained aloof, waiting till he had drawn his enemy further away from his base of operations, and nursing his own resources. Mebarsapes, the *vitaxa* or subject-king of Adiabênê, who had hoped to be able to defend the line of the Tigris, finding that forced, appears to have despaired, and withdrew from the struggle. One after another the forts and strongholds of the district were taken and occupied. Adenystræ, a place of great strength, was captured by a small knot of Roman prisoners, who, when they found their friends near, rose upon the garrison, killed the commandant, and opened the gates to their countrymen. In a few weeks all Adiabênê, the heart of the ancient Assyria, was conquered ; and a third province was added to the empire.

It might now have been expected that the Roman army would advance directly upon Ctesiphon. The way was open ; and Trajan might well have anticipated, as Napoleon did in 1812, that the capture of the enemy's main capital would conclude the war.

But for reasons that are not made clear to us, the
Emperor determined otherwise. Having repassed the
Tigris into Mesopotamia, he took Hatra, one of the
most considerable towns of the Middle Mesopotamian
region, and, crossing to the Euphrates, visited the
bitumen pits at Hit, so famous in the world's history,
whence the march was easy to Babylon. As still no
enemy showed himself, Babylon was approached, invested, and taken—so far as appears—without a blow
being struck. Seleucia soon afterwards submitted ;
and it only remained to attack and reduce the capital
in order to have complete possession of the entire
region watered by the two rivers. Here a fleet was
again needful ; and Trajan, accordingly, transported
the flotilla, which he had taken care to have in readiness on the Euphrates, across the narrow tract between the streams in N. lat. 33°, on rollers, and
launched it upon the Tigris. He was prepared for a
vigorous resistance, but once more found himself
unopposed. Ctesiphon opened its gates to him.
Chosroës had some time previously evacuated it, with
his family and his chief treasures, withdrawing further
into the interior of his vast empire, and seeking to
weary out his assailant by means of distance, natural
obstacles, and guerilla warfare. The tactics pursued
resemble those which have not uncommonly been
adopted by a comparatively weak enemy when
attacked by superior force, and remind us of the
method by which Idanthyrsus successfully defended
Scythia against Darius Hystaspis in the sixth century
B.C., and by which the Russian Alexander baffled the
Great Napoleon in the days of our own fathers or grand-

fathers. But Trajan may be excused if he took his enemy's retreat for entire withdrawal from the contest, and the apathy of the Western provinces for the complete submission of the empire. Ctesiphon was his; Babylon was his; Susa, the old capital of the Achæmenidæ, was his; the war might be regarded as over; and so, not troubling himself to pursue his flying foe into the remote and barbarous regions of the far East, he proceeded to enjoy his triumph, embarked on a pleasure voyage down the Tigris, and even launched his bark upon the waters of the Persian Gulf. The career of Alexander the Great presented itself vividly to his imagination; and he sighed to think that, at his age, he could not hope to reach the limits which had been attained by the Macedonian. He instituted inquiries, however, with respect to India, and may have contemplated sending an expedition there, when he had had time to settle and arrange his Parthian conquests, and to place Mesopotamian affairs on a satisfactory footing. No suspicion seems to have crossed his mind that the conquests which he had so rapidly effected were insecure—no prevision of coming trouble appears to have disturbed his self-complacency. In a fool's paradise he dreamed away the closing weeks of the summer of A.D. 116, and was still lazily floating on the waters of the Southern Sea, when intelligence of a startling character was suddenly brought to him.

Revolt had broken out in his rear. At Seleucia, at Hatra, at Nisibis, at Edessa, the natives had flown to arms, had ejected the Roman garrisons from their cities, or in some instances massacred them. His whole line of retreat was beset by foes, and he ran a great risk of having his return cut off, and of perishing in the distant region which he had invaded. The occasion called for the most active exertions and for the greatest energy ; fortunately for the Romans, Trajan was equal to it. Personally, he hastened northwards, while he issued peremptory orders to his generals that they should everywhere take the most active measures against the rebels, and do their utmost to check the spread of insurrection. The chastisement of Seleucia was intrusted to Erucius Clarus and Julius Alexander, who stormed the city, and ruthlessly delivered it to the flames. Lucius Quietus succeeded in recovering Nisibis, and punished its rebellion in the same way. He also plundered and burnt Edessa. Maximus, however, one of Trajan's most trusted officers, on coming to an engagement with the enemy, was defeated and slain. A Roman army with its legate was cut to pieces. Trajan himself, having returned to Ctesiphon, and made himself acquainted with the whole condition of affairs, woke up from his dream of an easy conquest, and saw that a complete change of policy was necessary. Parthia must not be treated like Armenia and Mesopotamia—its people must be humoured and conciliated. A native king and a show of independence must be allowed them. Accordingly, he selected a certain Parthamaspates, a man of Arsacid descent, who had embraced the side of Rome in the recent struggle, and summoning the Parthians of the capital and its neighbourhood to a great meeting in a plain near Ctesiphon, he produced before them the individual whom he favoured, commended him to their loyal affection in a speech of considerable length, and, after magnifying somewhat injudiciously the splendour of his own achievements, placed the diadem with his own hand upon his brow. He then commenced his retreat.   Taking the direct line through Mesopotamia, he marched, in the first instance, upon Hatra, one of the towns which had revolted from him, and had not yet been reduced. The place was small, but strongly fortified.   It lay in the desert between the Tigris and Euphrates, nearer to the former, and was protected, by the scantiness of its water, and the unproductiveness of the region around, from attack except by a small force.   Trajan battered down a portion of the wall, and attempted to enter by the breach ; but his troops met with a decided repulse, and he himself, having rashly approached too near the walls, was in the greatest danger of being wounded. The horseman nearest to him was actually struck by an arrow and slain.   After this the siege did not last long.   As autumn approached the weather broke up, and thunderstorms prevailed, with rain and violent hail.   It was believed that whenever the Romans proceeded to the assault, the fury of the elemental war increased in severity.   Moreover, a plague of insects set in.   Gnats and flies disputed with the soldiers every morsel of their food and every drop of their drink.   Under these circumstances the Emperor felt compelled to relinquish the siege and beat a retreat.   He retired through Mesopotamia upon Syria, and took up his quarters at Antioch, having suffered, it would seem,[1] considerable loss upon the way.   At

---

[1] So Fronto, "Princip. Hist." p. 338.

Antioch the effects of his heavy toils and exertions began to show themselves. He fell sick, and quitting his army, made an attempt to reach Rome, but succumbed to his malady before he had proceeded very far, and died at Selinus, in Cilicia, August, A.D. 117.

On the retirement of Trajan, the Parthian monarch, quitting Media, returned to Ctesiphon, expelled Parthamaspates without difficulty, and re-established his own rule over the regions which Trajan had overrun, but had not reduced into the form of provinces. Armenia, however, Upper Mesopotamia, and Assyria, or Adiabêné, were still held in force by the Romans, and might probably have been maintained against any attack that Parthia could have made, had the new Emperor, Hadrian, who had succeeded Trajan, regarded their retention as desirable. But Hadrian, who, as prefect of Syria, had been a near witness of Trajan's campaigns, and possessed an intimate acquaintance with the general condition of the East, was deeply convinced that the attempt of Trajan had been a mistake, and that the true policy for Rome was that laid down in principle by Augustus—that the possessions of the empire should not be extended beyond their natural and traditional limits. He resolved, therefore, to withdraw the Roman legions once more within the Euphrates, and to relinquish the newly-conquered provinces, of which so great a boast had been made—Armenia, Mesopotamia, Adiabêné. It is generally allowed by modern historians, that the resolution was a wise one. " There was no soil beyond the Euphrates," says Dean Merivale with excellent judgment, " in which Roman institutions could take root, while the expense of maintaining them would have been utterly exhausting." [1]   As far as the Euphrates Greek colonisation had so leavened the original Asiatic mass as to render it semi-European, and so to prepare it to a large extent for the reception of Roman ideas and Roman principles of government : beyond, the Greek infusion had been too weak to produce much effect—Orientalism pure prevailed—and Western institutions, if introduced, would have found themselves in an alien soil, where they could only have withered and died.   Even apart from this, the Roman Empire was already so large as to be unwieldy, and to endanger its continued cohesion. The chiefs of provinces east of the Euphrates would have been so far removed from the seat of government as to be practically exempt from effectual control and supervision.   They would have had enormous forces in men and money at their command, and have been under a perpetual temptation to revolt and endeavour to secure for themselves an independent position.   The garrisoning, moreover, of such extensive countries would have been a severe drain upon the military resources of the empire, and would have exercised a demoralising influence upon the soldiery, such as was already felt to some extent with regard to the legions quartered in Syria.   Altogether, it is clear that the course pursued by Hadrian in contracting once more the eastern limits of the empire was a prudent one, and entitles the prince who adopted it, not only to the praise of " moderation," but to that of political insight and sagacity.

[1] " Roman Empire," vol. viii. p. 192.

The evacuation of the conquered countries brought about a return to the condition of things in the East which had prevailed ever since the time of Augustus. Rome and Parthia resumed their ancient boundaries. Armenia reverted to its old condition of a kingdom nominally independent, but too weak to stand alone, and necessarily leaning on external support, at one time practically dependent on Rome, at another on Parthia. Its first ruler, after it ceased to be a Roman province, was Parthamaspates, to whom Hadrian seems to have handed it over, and in whose appointment Chosroës must have acquiesced. Chosroës could not but be well disposed towards the ruler who, without being compelled to do so by a defeat, had restored to Parthia the two most important and valuable of her provinces ; and the consolidation of his power in them probably gave him ample occupation, and made him satisfied to have a time of repose from external troubles. He seems to have continued on friendly terms with Hadrian during the remainder of his life. Once only, in A.D. 122, was the good understanding threatened. The exact causes of complaint have not come down to us ; but it appears that in that year rumours of an intended Parthian invasion reached the Emperor, and induced him to make a journey to the far East, in order, by his personal influence and assurances, to avert the danger. An interview was held between the two monarchs upon the frontier, and explanations were given and received, which both parties regarded as satisfactory   The Parthian prince gave up his intention of troubling the peace of Rome, and the two empires continued, not only during the rest of the reign of Chosroës, but till some time after the death of Hadrian, on terms of friendship and amity. Hadrian went so far as to restore to Chosroës (about A.D. 130) a daughter who had been taken prisoner at Susa by the generals of Trajan fourteen years before, and had remained at Rome in captivity ; and he is even said to have promised the restoration of the golden throne

COINS OF VOLOGASES II.

COIN OF MITHRIDATES IV.   COIN OF ARTABANUS IV.

captured at the same time, on which the Parthians set a special value.

Chosroës, during his later years, had to contend with a pretender to his throne, who bore the name, so common at this time, of Vologases. The Parthian empire showed, more and more as time went on, a tendency to disintegration ; and there is reason to believe that, during the space commonly assigned to Chosroës (A.D. 108–130), different monarchs reigned, not infrequently, in different parts of Parthia at the same time. The coins of Vologases II. run parallel for many years with those of Chosroës. A coin of a Mithridates, and another of an Artabanus, fall into the same interval. The classical writers make no mention of these rival kings ; and the native remains are so scanty that it is impossible to draw any continuous narrative from them. We can only say, generally, that Parthia has entered the period of her decadence, and that, even apart from foreign attack, she would, if left to herself, have probably expired within little more than a century.

XIX.

VOLOGASES II. AND ANTONINUS PIUS—VOLOGASES III. AND VERUS.

THE Vologases who had for so many years disputed the crown with Chosroës, appears, on the
decease of the latter, to have been generally acknowledged as king.   He was an aged prince, indisposed to any unnecessary exertion, and quite
content to continue on the friendly terms with Rome
which had been established under his predecessor.
He had not, however, been settled more than three
years upon the throne, when hostilities came upon
him from an unexpected quarter.   Pharasmanes, who
enjoyed the sovereignty of Iberia under Roman protection, but chafed at his dependent position, and had
private grounds of quarrel with Hadrian, in the year
A.D. 133, suddenly threw the whole of the East into
a blaze.   Inviting into Asia a great horde of the
northern barbarians from the tracts beyond the Caucasus, he induced them to precipitate themselves upon
Armenia, Cappadocia, and Media Atropatênê, which
was once more a dependency of Parthia, and to carry
fire and sword into the midst of those fertile regions.
Vologases at once complained to Rome of the injury

done him by her feudatory, and requested assistance ;
but Hadrian regarded troubles in so distant a region as
unimportant, and, satisfied that Cappadocia would be
sufficiently protected by its governor, who was Arrian,
the historian of Alexander, he left Vologases to
struggle with his difficulties as he best might. The
aged monarch, under these circumstances, had recourse
to an expedient at once impolitic and disgraceful—
he bribed the horde of Alans, which had invaded his
province, to quit the country, and turn their arms in
another direction. Such a policy, though occasionally
adopted by the Romans themselves, can never be
other than mistaken and ruinous. Once entered
upon, it is almost certain to be continued, and to bring
about at once the exhaustion and the degradation of
the people that condescends to it.

It is not perhaps surprising that Hadrian, always
studious of peace, abstained from taking any active
part in the Alanic war ; but it certainly seems strange
that, instead of inflicting any punishment on Pharasmanes for his reckless action in introducing the barbarians into Asia, and actually letting them loose
upon the empire, he should have shortly afterwards
loaded him with honours and benefits. He summoned
him indeed to Rome, to answer for his conduct, but,
having done this, accepted his explanations, condoned
his crimes, and not only so, but rewarded him by an
enlargement of his dominion, and by various other
marks of favour. He permitted him to sacrifice in
the Capitol, placed his equestrian statue in the temple
of Bellona, and was present at a sham fight in which
the Iberian monarch, his son, and his chief nobles

exhibited their skill and prowess.   It is not likely
that Vologases can have been much pleased at these
results of his complaints ; but he seems to have submitted to them without a murmur; and, when Hadrian
died (in A.D. 138), and was succeeded by his adopted
son, Titus Aurelius, better known as Antoninus Pius,
he sent to Rome an embassy of congratulation, and
presented his Roman brother with a crown of gold.
The medal, which records this event, was struck in
the first year of Antoninus, and exhibits on the
reverse a female figure holding a bow and quiver in
the left hand, and with the right presenting a crown,
while underneath is the inscription, PARTHIA.

Having thus, as he thought, secured the good-will
of the new monarch by a well-timed compliment,
Vologases ventured on intruding upon him with an
unpleasant demand.   Hadrian, in a moment of weakness, had promised that the golden throne, captured
by Trajan in his great expedition, should be given
back to its proper owners ; but, finding that the act
would be unpalatable to his subjects, had delayed the
performance of his promise, and finally died without
giving effect to it.   Vologases hoped that his successor
might be more accommodating, and instructed his
envoys to bring the matter before Antoninus, to
remind him of Hadrian's pledged word, and make a
formal request for the delivery to them of the much-
prized relic.   But Antonine was as much averse to
relinquishing the trophy as his predecessor had been,
and positively refused to grant the request made of
him.   The envoys had to return *re infecta*, and to
report to their master that, for the present at any

rate, all hope must be laid aside of recovering the emblem of Arsacid sovereignty.

The remainder of the reign of Vologases II. was tranquil and unmarked by any striking incident. No pretensions were put forward by the Parthians with respect to Armenia, to which, probably on the death Parthamaspates, Rome was suffered, without protest, to appoint a new monarch. No further attempt was made to obtain the surrender of the "golden throne." The coolness between the two states, which had followed on Antonine's rejection of the demand preferred by Vologases, merely tended to keep the rival powers apart, and to prevent occasions of collision, while Antonine's truly peaceful policy preserved Parthia even from internal disturbance, and allowed the successor of Chosroës to enjoy his throne, unthreatened by any pretender, for the comparatively long term of nineteen years (A.D. 130 to 149). The aged monarch left his crown to a successor of the same name as himself, who was probably his son, though of this there is no direct evidence.

The third Vologases ascended the Parthian throne either in A.D. 148 or 149. He took the same titles as his predecessor, but added to them, upon his coins, a Semitic legend—either ולגשי מלכא, "Vologases, King," or ולגשי ארשך מלכין מלכא, "Volagases, Arsaces, King of Kings." The dates on his coins extend from A.D. 148–9 to A.D. 190–1, showing that he held the throne for the long space of forty-two years. During the earlier portion of the time (A.D. 148–161) he was contemporary with Antoninus Pius, and, though discontented with the exclusion of Parthia from all influence in Armenia, and meditating a war with Rome on this account, he suffered himself to be persuaded, by letters from the pacific Emperor, to keep the peace as long as *he* occupied the Imperial throne, and to defer his contemplated outbreak until the reign of his successor. On the death of Antoninus, however, he was not further to be restrained, but at once took the field, and marching an army suddenly into Armenia, carried all before him, expelled Soæmus, Rome's vassal and creature, from the kingdom, and placed upon the throne a *protégé* of his own, a certain Tigranes, a scion

COIN OF VOLOGASES III.

of the old royal stock, whose name recalled to the Armenians the period of their greatest glory. The Roman governors of the adjacent provinces learnt with surprise and alarm that Armenia was detached from the empire ; and Severianus, prefect of Cappadocia, the nearest to the scene of action, and a man of an impetuous disposition, being a Gaul by birth, hurried to the scene at the head of a single legion, partly moved by his own hot temper, partly yielding to the persuasions of a pseudo-prophet of those parts named Alexander, who promised him a signal victory. But

the result signally falsified the prophecy. Scarcely
had Severianus crossed the Euphrates into Armenia,
when he found himself in the presence of a superior
force under the command of a Parthian general called
Chosroës, and was under the necessity of throwing
himself into the city of Elegeia, where he was immediately besieged and blockaded. Though he offered a
strenuous resistance, it was unavailing. His troops
were not of good quality, and, unable to break through
the *cordon* which surrounded them, they were in a
short time shot down by the Parthian archers, and
perished almost to a man. Severianus shared their
fate ; and the Parthians obtained a success which was
paralleled with that of Surenas against Crassus, or of
Arminius against Varus. Their mastery over Armenia
was confirmed, and the Roman provinces were laid
wholly open to their attacks. Their squadrons crossed
the Euphrates, and marched into Syria, where they
obtained a second success. L. Attidius Cornelianus,
the proconsul, gathered together the forces of his
province, and gave battle to the invaders, but was
repulsed. The situation became nearly such as had
obtained after the defeat of Crassus, or when Pacorus
and Labienus, in the year B.C. 40, carried ravage
and ruin over the region between the Euphrates and
the Orontes. The Parthians passed from Syria into
Palestine, and the whole of the Roman East seemed
to lie open to them. Intelligence of what had
happened was rapidly carried to Rome, and threw
the Senate into consternation. Aurelius felt that he
could not be spared from Italy, but deputed Verus to
represent him in the East, and bade him hasten to the

scene of action with such forces as could be gathered.
Verus, however, was a lover of pleasure. First he
loitered on his way in Apulia, then proceeded at a
leisurely pace to Syria, finally settled himself in the
luxurious Antioch, and, giving himself up to its
pleasures and amusements, handed over the cares of
war to his lieutenants. Fortunately for Rome, there
were among these several generals of the antique type,
as especially Statius Priscus, Avidius Cassius, and
Martius Verus. Cassius, even before the arrival of
Verus and his army, had begun an effective resistance.
He had, by almost incredible efforts, brought the
Syrian legions into a state of order and discipline, had
with them checked the advance of Vologases, and had
finally found himself in a condition to take the
offensive. In A.D. 163 he fought a great battle with
the Parthians, defeated them, and drove them across
the Euphrates. Meanwhile, Statius Priscus and
Martius Verus had undertaken the recovery of
Armenia. Statius had advanced without a check
from the frontier to the capital, Artaxata, had taken
the city, and burnt it to the ground, after which he
built a new city, which he strongly garrisoned with
Roman troops, and sent intelligence to Rome that
Armenia was now ready to welcome back her expelled
prince, Soæmus. Soæmus upon this returned, and,
though some further disturbances were made by the
anti-Roman party, yet these were successfully dealt
with, chiefly by Martius Verus, and, in a short time,
the Roman nominee was recognised as undisputed
king, and the entire country brought into a state of
tranquillity.

The success which had attended the first rush to arms of Vologases III. was thus completely neutralised. In the space of two years Rome had made good all her losses, and shown that she was fully able to maintain the position in Western Asia which she had acquired by the victories of Trajan. But the ambitious generals, into whose hands the conduct of the war had fallen through the incapacity of Verus, were far from satisfied with the mere recovery of what had been lost. Personal, rather than patriotic, motives actuated them. In the circumstances of the time military distinction was more coveted than any other, and was looked upon as opening a path to the very highest honours. The successful general became, as a matter of course, by virtue of his position, a candidate for the Imperial dignity. If, under the great Napoleon, every conscript felt that he carried a marshal's *bâton* in his knapsack, still more, under the Middle Empire, was every victorious commander persuaded that each step in the path of victory brought him sensibly nearer to the throne. Of all the officers engaged in the Parthian war, nominally under Verus, the most capable and the most ambitious was Avidius Cassius. Sprung from the family of the great "Liberator," who had contended for the supreme power in the state with Augustus and Antony, he had a hereditary bias towards pushing himself to the front, and might be counted upon to let slip no occasion which fortune should put in his way. His position in Syria gave him a splendid opportunity. After his first successes against Vologases, Aurelius had made him a sort of generalissimo ; and, having thus

perfect freedom of action, he resolved to carry the war
into the enemy's country, and see if he could not rival,
or even outdo, the achievements of Trajan half a
century earlier.   No continuous history of his campaign has reached our time, but from the fragmentary
notices of it which are still extant we may gather a
good general idea of its course and character.   Crossing the Euphrates into Mesopotamia at Zeugma, the
most important of the Roman stations upon the river,
he proceeded first to Nicephorium, near the junction
of the Belik with the Euphrates, and thence made his
way down the course of the stream to Sura (probably
Sippara) and Babylon.   At Sura a battle was fought,
in which the Romans were victorious, but it was after
this that the great successes took place which covered
Cassius with glory.   The vast city of Seleucia upon
the Tigris, which had at the time a population of
four hundred thousand souls, was besieged, taken, and
burnt, to punish an alleged treason of the inhabitants.
Ctesiphon, upon the opposite bank of the river,
the summer residence of the Parthian kings, was
occupied, and the royal palace there situated was
pillaged, and levelled with the ground.   The various fanes and temples were stripped of their
treasures; and search was made for buried riches
in all the places which were thought likely to have
been utilised, the result being that an immense
booty was carried off.   The Parthians, worsted in every
encounter, after a time, ceased to resist, and all the
conquests made by Trajan, and relinquished by
Hadrian, were recovered.   Further, an expedition was
made into the Zagros mountain tract, and a portion of

it, considered to lie within the limits of Media, and never yet possessed by Rome, was occupied. Aurelius owed it to the valour and good fortune of his general that he was thus entitled to add to the epithets of " Armeniacus" and " Parthicus," which he had already assumed, the further and wholly novel epithet of " Medicus."

The victories of Avidius Cassius, unlike those of Trajan, were followed by no reverses, and they had further the effect, denied to Trajan's, of making the permanent addition of a large tract to the Roman Empire. When Vologases, after five years of unsuccessful warfare, finally sued for peace to his too powerful antagonist, he was compelled to surrender, as the price of it, the extensive and valuable country of Western Mesopotamia. The entire region between the Euphrates and the Khabour passed under the dominion of Rome at this time, and though not formally made into a province, became wholly lost to Parthia. The coins of the Greek cities within the area bear henceforth on the obverse the head of a Roman Emperor, and on the reverse some local token or legend ; every trace of Parthian influence is removed from them.

But, if Rome thus carried off all the honours of the war with Vologases III., still she did not escape the Nemesis which usually attends upon the over-fortunate. During its stay in the marshy regions of Lower Mesopotamia, the army of Cassius was deeply infected with the germs of a strange and terrible malady, which clung to it on its return, and was widely disseminated along the whole line of the retreat. The superstition of the soldiers assigned to the pestilence a supernatural origin. It had crept forth, they said, from a subterranean cell, or a golden coffer, in the temple of the Comæan Apollo at Seleucia, during the time that a portion of the army was engaged in plundering the temple treasures. Placed there in primeval times by the spells of the Chaldæans, it raged with the more virulence on account of its long confinement, and amply avenged the Parthians for the many woes inflicted on them by Roman hands. Every town that lay upon the route of the returning army was smitten by it ; and from these centres it diverged in every direction, east and west, and north and south, into the adjacent districts. At Rome, the number of victims amounted to tens of thousands. " Not the vulgar herd of the Suburra only, the usual victims of a pestilence, were stricken, but many of the highest rank also suffered." [1] According to Orosius,[2] in Italy generally the whole country was so devastated, that the villas, towns, and fields were everywhere left without inhabitant or cultivation, and fell to ruin, or relapsed into wildernesses. The army suffered especially, and is said to have been almost annihilated. In the provinces more than half the population was carried off, and the pestilence, overleaping the Alps, spread as far as the Rhine and the Atlantic Ocean.

The remainder of the reign of Vologases III. was uneventful. He continued to occupy the Parthian

---

[1] Merivale, " Roman Empire," vol. viii. p. 333.

[2] Paul. Oros., " Hist.," vii. 15.

throne until A.D. 190 or 191, but took no further part, so far as we know, in any military operations. Once only does he seem to have been so far stirred from his inaction as to contemplate resuming the struggle against his powerful enemy. This was in A.D. 174 or 175, when, Aurelius being detained upon the Danube, the inordinate ambition of Avidius Cassius drove him into open rebellion, and the prospect of a Roman civil war seemed to offer a chance of Parthia being able to reassert herself. But the opportunity passed before Vologases could bring himself to make any serious movement. The revolt of Cassius collapsed almost as soon as it had broken out, and the East returned to its normal condition. Vologases repented of his warlike intention; and when (in A.D. 176) Aurelius visited Syria, sent ambassadors to him with friendly assurances, who were received with favour.

Four years later the reign of the philosophic Emperor came to an end; and the Imperial power passed into the hands of his weak and unworthy son, Lucius Aurelius Commodus. A second opportunity for an aggressive movement offered itself; but, again, Vologases resisted the temptation to rush into hostilities, and remained passive within the limits of his own dominions. The reign of Commodus (A.D. 180–192) was, from first to last, untroubled by any Parthian outbreak. Vologases was probably by this time an old man, since he had held the Parthian throne for thirty-two years when Commodus succeeded his father, and may naturally have been disinclined to further warlike exertion. Rome was therefore still allowed to maintain her Mesopotamian conquests unchallenged ; and when Vologases died (in A.D. 190 or 191), the condition of things continued as established by Aurelius in A.D. 165.

XX.

VOLOGASES IV. AND SEVERUS.

THE third Vologases was succeeded by another prince of the same name, who is usually regarded as his son, though there is no distinct evidence of the fact. His coins, which generally present his full face upon their obverse, instead of the customary profile, have dates which run from A.D. 191 to 208. He thus appears to have been contemporary with the Roman

COIN OF VOLOGASES IV.

Emperors—Commodus, Pertinax, Didius Julianus, Pescennius Niger, and Septimius Severus. The great Parthian war of Severus fell entirely within his reign, and it is as the antagonist of this distinguished prince that he is chiefly known to history.

It was very shortly after the accession of Vologases IV. that the officers of the Court of Commodus, unable any longer to endure his excesses and cruelties, conspired against the unworthy son of the good Aurelius and assassinated him in his bed-chamber. This murder was soon followed by another — that of the virtuous, but perhaps over-strict, Pertinax. The Prætorians, after this, put up the office of Roman Emperor to public auction, and knocked it down to Didius Julianus, a rich senator, who is said to have paid for his prize no less than three millions of our money. But this indignity exhausted the patience of the legions, and threw the entire empire into confusion. In three places—in Britain, in Pannonia, and in Syria—revolt broke out, and the soldiers invested their respective leaders, Clodius Albinus, Septimius Severus, and Pescennius Niger, with the purple. Niger, who, as prefect of Syria, held the second dignity in the empire, imagined that his elevation would not be disputed, and, instead of straining every nerve to raise forces, and strengthen himself by alliances, declined at first the offers of assistance made him by various Parthian feudatories, and remained inactive in the East, expecting the Senate's confirmation of his appointment. But the unpleasant intelligence soon reached him that Septimius Severus, proclaimed Emperor in Pannonia and acknowledged at Rome, was on his way to Syria, determined to dispute with him the prize, whereof he had somewhat rashly thought himself assured. Under these changed circumstances, Niger felt compelled to alter his own policy, and to implore the assistance which so shortly before he had rejected. Towards the close of the year A.D. 193 he despatched envoys to the courts of the chief princes beyond the Euphrates, and especially to the kings of Armenia, Parthia, and Hatra, entreating them to send contingents to his aid as soon as possible. The Armenian monarch—Vologases, the son of Sanatrœces—made answer that it was not his intention to ally himself with either side; he should stand aloof from the conflict and simply defend his own kingdom if any attack were made upon it. The reply from the Parthian Vologases was more favourable. He could not send troops at once, he said, as his army was disbanded, but he would issue an order to his satraps for the collection of a strong force as soon as possible. Barsemius, king of Hatra, went further even than his suzerain, and actually despatched to Niger's aid a body of archers, which reached his camp in safety, and took part in the war. Vologases IV. must have given his sanction to this movement on the part of his feudatory, who could certainly not have ventured on such a proceeding against the will of his lord paramount. Still Vologases was not prepared to commit himself unreservedly to either side in the impending conflict, and refrained from taking any active steps in furtherance of his professed design to collect an army, waiting to see to which side the fortune of war would incline.

The struggle between the rival Emperors was soon terminated. Niger passed from Asia into Europe, and took up a position near Byzantium, but, having suffered a defeat at Cyzicus, was soon forced to fall back upon his reserves, and, passing through Asia Minor, gave his adversary battle for the second time near Issus, where his army was completely routed, and he himself captured and put to death. Meanwhile, however, the nations of the East had flown to arms. The newly-subjected Mesopotamians had risen in revolt, had massacred most of the Roman detachments stationed in their country, and had even laid siege to Nisibis, which was the headquarters of the Roman power in the district. Their kindred tribes from the further side of the Euphrates, particularly the people of Adiabênê, had assisted them, and taken part in the attack. The first object of Severus after the defeat and death of Niger was to raise the siege, and to chastise the rebels, with their aiders and abettors. He marched hastily to Nisibis, defeated the combined Osrhoëni and Adiabêni, relieved the distressed garrison, and took up his own quarters in the place. He then proceeded to re-subject Mesopotamia. The inhabitants sought to disarm his resentment by representing that they had taken up arms, not against him, or against the Romans generally, but against Niger, his rival and foe, whom they had endeavoured to distress for his (Severus's) benefit. They professed a readiness to surrender the Romans whom they had taken prisoners, and such portion of the Roman spoil as remained still in their hands ; but it was observed that they said nothing about giving up the strongholds that they had taken, or about resuming the position of Roman tributaries. On the contrary, they put forward a demand that all the Roman troops still in their country should be withdrawn from it, and that their independence should be respected in the future. Severus was not prepared to accept

these terms, or to sanction the retreat of Terminus.
His immediate adversaries—the kings of Osrhoëné,
Adiabêné, and Hatra—were of small account, and he
might expect to defeat them without difficulty. Even
if the Parthian monarch espoused the cause of his
feudatories, he was not indisposed to cross swords
with him. The expeditions of Trajan and Avidius
Cassius had done much to diminish the terror of the
Parthian name; and to ambitious Romans the East
presented itself as the quarter in which, without any
serious danger, the greatest glory was to be won.

Accordingly, the Emperor rejected the Mesopotamian proposals, and applied himself to the task of
reducing their country to complete subjection. From
the central position of Nisibis, where he himself
remained, he sent out his forces under his three best
commanders—Laternus, Candidus, and Lætus—in
three directions, with orders to carry fire and sword
through the entire region, and to re-establish everywhere the Imperial authority. His commands were
executed. Resistance was everywhere crushed; the
old administration was restored; and Nisibis, raised
to the dignity of a Roman colony, once more became
the metropolis of the country. Nor was Severus
contented with the mere restoration of the Roman
power. He caused his troops to cross the Tigris
into Adiabêné, and though the inhabitants offered a
stout resistance, succeeded in overrunning the district
and occupying it. Further aggressions and further
conquests would probably have followed, but the
attitude of Albinus in the West made it imperative
on Severus to quit these distant lands and return to

his capital, which was menaced on the side of Gaul by the commander of the Western legions. The Emperor left Nisibis, and returned to Rome early in the year A.D. 196.

No sooner had he retired than the flames of war burst out more fiercely than before. Vologases, roused from his inaction by the threatened loss of a second province, poured his troops into Adiabênê, drove out the Roman garrisons, and, crossing the Tigris into Mesopotamia, swept the Romans from the whole of the open country. Even the cities submitted themselves, excepting only Nisibis, which was saved from capture by the courage and capacity of Lætus. According to Spartianus, the victorious Parthians, not content with recovering Mesopotamia, even passed the Euphrates, and spread themselves once more over the fertile plains of Northern Syria, as they had done in the times of Pacorus and Labienus. Severus, engaged in his doubtful contest with Albinus on the western side of the empire, could do nothing to relieve the pressure upon the east, and the Syrian prefecture continued open to the Parthian raids for the space of nearly a full year. An enterprising monarch might have done much during this interval ; but Vologases frittered away his opportunity, and at length the victory of Lyons set Severus free, and allowed him again to turn his attention to Oriental affairs. In the summer of A.D. 197 he made a second Eastern expedition for the purpose of recovering his lost laurels, and of justifying the titles, which he had already assumed, of "Arabicus" and "Adiabenicus." It is probable that in his own mind he entertained still loftier aspirations, and, like Trajan, had hopes of reducing the whole Parthian Empire under the Roman yoke.

One of the most important points to be secured by an assailant of Parthia from the west, was the friendship, or at any rate the neutrality, of the two kings of Armenia and Osrhoëné. Armenia had professed itself neutral when the quarrel between Severus and Niger first broke out, but had subsequently, in some way or other, offended the former, and on his arrival in the East, was viewed as hostile to the Roman designs. The first intention of Severus was to fall with his full force on Armenia, and to endeavour to reduce it to subjection ; but, before the fortune of war had been tried, the Armenian monarch, Vologases, son of Sanatrœces, made overtures for peace, sent gifts and hostages, assumed the attitude of a suppliant, and so wrought upon Severus that he not merely consented to conclude a treaty with him, but even granted him a certain extension of his dominions. The Arab king of Osrhoëné, who is called, as usual, Abgarus, made a more complete and unqualified submission. He rode into the Roman camp at the head of a large body of archers, whose services he offered to the Emperor, and accompanied by a number of his sons, whom Severus was requested to look upon as hostages. All being prosperous thus far, Severus had only to determine by which line of route he should advance against the Parthian monarch, who had taken up his position at Ctesiphon, and to make his preparations accordingly. He fixed on the line of the Euphrates, but at the same time masked his intention by sending a strong body of troops under generals across the Tigris to ravage Adiabênê, and create an impression that the main attack would come from that quarter. Meanwhile, following the example of Trajan, he was causing a fleet to be built in Upper Mesopotamia, where timber was plentiful, and was preparing to march his main army down the left bank of the Euphrates, while his transports, laden with stores, descended the stream. In this way he reached the neighbourhood of Seleucia and Ctesiphon without suffering any loss, or even incurring any danger, and took the Parthians by surprise, when, having captured the cities of Babylon and Seleucia, which were deserted by their defenders, he made his appearance before the capital. His fleet, which he could easily transfer from one river to the other by means of the great canals that traversed the alluvium, would give him the complete command of the Tigris, and enable him to attack the city on either side, or indeed entirely to invest it. Vologases appears to have fought a single battle in defence of his capital, but, being defeated, shut himself up within its walls. The defences, however, were not strong; and, after a short siege, Severus took the city, by assault, without much difficulty, the king escaping with a few horsemen in the confusion of the capture. Thus the Parthian capital fell easily—a third time within the space of eighty-two years — into the hands of a foreign invader. On the first occasion it had opened its gates to the conqueror, and had experienced gentle treatment at the hands of a benignant emperor. On the second it had suffered considerably. Now it was to learn what extreme severity meant at the hands of a monarch whose character accorded with his name. The captured city was given up to massacre and pillage. The soldiers were allowed to plunder both the public and the private buildings at their pleasure. The precious metals accumulated in the royal treasury were seized, and the rich ornaments of the royal palace were taken from their places and carried off. All the adult male population was slaughtered; while the women and children, torn from their homes without compunction, were led into captivity by the victorious army, to the number of a hundred thousand.

Thus far the expedition of Severus had been completely successful. He stood where Trajan stood in A.D. 116, master of the whole low region between the Arabian desert and the Zagros mountains, lord of Mesopotamia, of Assyria, of Babylonia, of the entire tract watered by the two great rivers from the Armenian highlands to the shores of the Persian Gulf. What use would he make of his conquests? Would he, like Trajan, endeavour to retain them, or would he, like the wiser Hadrian, relinquish them? He endeavoured to take an intermediate course. Recognising the fact, that to retain the more southern districts was impossible, and that the more eastern portions of the Parthian Empire were beyond his reach, he neither pursued the flying Vologases into the remote tracts in which he had taken refuge nor attempted to organise his southern conquests into provinces, but resolved at once to evacuate them. Notwithstanding the elaborate preparations which he had made for his invasion, and the care which he

had taken to carry supplies with him, he found himself, about the time that he captured Ctesiphon, in
want of provisions. He had exhausted the immense
stores of grain which Lower Mesopotamia commonly
furnished, or else the inhabitants had destroyed or
hidden them, and his troops had, we are told, to
subsist for some days on roots, which produced a
dangerous dysentery. He was obliged to retreat
before famine overtook him. Moreover, as the march
of his army along the course of the Euphrates had
stripped that region of its supplies of corn and fodder,
he could not return as he had come, but was compelled to confront the perils of a new route. The line
of the Tigris was the only route open to him, and
along this he advanced, still supported by his fleet,
which with some difficulty made its way against the
current up the course of the stream. It does not
appear that any opposition was offered to him ; but,
after he had proceeded a moderate distance, he found
himself in the vicinity of Hatra, the capital of a small
state subject to Parthia, which had given him special
offence by lending active support to the cause of his
rival, Niger. His troops had now obtained sufficient
supplies of food in an unexhausted country, and were
ready for a fresh enterprise. Severus regarded his
honour as concerned in the chastisement of a state
which, without provocation, had declared itself his
enemy. He may also have remembered that Trajan
had attacked Hatra unsuccessfully, and have hoped to
place himself above that conqueror by the capture of
a town which had defied the utmost efforts of his
predecessor. At any rate, whatever his motives, it

seems certain that, when in the latitude of Hatra, he diverged from his previous line of march, and, proceeding westward, encamped under the walls of the city which had given him such dire offence, and engaged in its siege. He had brought with him a number of military engines—probably those employed with complete success at Ctesiphon, and, putting them in position, made a fierce attack upon the place. But the inhabitants were not daunted ; the walls of the town were strong, its defenders brave and full of enterprise. They contrived to set on fire and destroy the siege machines brought against them, and repulsed with heavy loss the attacking soldiers. The army, upon this, grew discontented, and threatened mutiny ; Severus was obliged to punish with death some of his leading officers, among them his best general, Lætus. This, however, only increased the exasperation ; and, to smooth matters over, he had to pretend that the execution of this officer had taken place without his knowledge. Even so the soldiers' minds were not calmed down, and at last, in order to bring about a better state of feeling, he had to discontinue the siege and remove his camp to a distance.

He had not, however, abandoned his enterprise. *Reculer pour mieux sauter* was among the principles that guided his actions, and it was in the hope of returning and renewing the attack ere many weeks were past, that he had drawn off his army. In the tranquillity and security of the place whereto he had removed, he constructed fresh engines in increased numbers, collected vast stores of provisions, and made every preparation possible for a repetition of his attack and for bringing it to a successful issue. It was not merely that his honour was concerned in overcoming the resistance offered to him by what had always been regarded as no more than a second-rate town—his cupidity was also excited by reports of the rich treasures that were stored up in the city, and especially of those which the piety of successive generations had accumulated in the Temple of the Sun. He therefore, when his preparations were complete, once more put his troops in motion, and proceeded to renew the siege with a more efficient siege-train, and a better appointed army than before. But the inhabitants met him with a determination equal to his own. They had a powerful cavalry which hung upon the skirts of his army and crippled his movements in every way, often inflicting severe loss upon his foragers ; they were excellent archers, and shot further and with greater force than the Romans ; they possessed military engines of their own, of no contemptible character ; and they had at their disposal a particular kind of fire, which did considerable damage, and created yet greater alarm. Flames believed to be inextinguishable were hurled both against the Roman machines and against their soldiers with an effect that is said to have been remarkable. A great number of the machines were burnt ; and if the soldiers were more frightened than hurt, the advantage to the defenders was still almost as great. Still the Romans persevered. The presence of the Emperor, who watched the combat from a lofty platform, encouraged every man to do his best ; and at length it was announced that a practicable breach had been effected in the outer wall of the place, and the soldiers were ready, and indeed eager, to be led at once to the assault. But now Severus hung back. By Roman usage a town taken by storm must be given up to the soldiery for indiscriminate pillage ; and thus, if the soldiers had their way, he would lose the great treasures on which his heart was set. He therefore refused to give the word, and resolved to wait a day, and see whether the Hatreni would not now, seeing further resistance to be useless, surrender their town. The delay was fatal. In the night the Hatreni rebuilt the wall where it had been battered down, and manning the battlements, stood boldly on their defence. Severus, seeing that they had no intention of surrendering, repented of his resolve of the day before, and commanded the soldiers to attack. But the legionaries declined. They probably suspected the Emperor's motive. At any rate they were unwilling to imperil their lives for an object which but yesterday they might have attained without incurring any peril at all. Severus, not to lose a chance, commanded his Asiatic auxiliaries to see if they could not force an entrance, but with no other result than the slaughter of a vast number. At last he desisted from his attempt. The summer was far advanced ; the heat was intense ; and disease had broken out among his troops, who suffered from drought, from malaria, and from a plague of insects. Above all, his army was thoroughly demoralised, and could not be depended on to carry out the orders given it. Severus himself told one of his officers that he had not six hundred European troops on whom he could place any reliance. The second siege of Hatra by Severus lasted twenty days, and terminated in an ignominious withdrawal. Severus returned to Rome with a slur upon his military reputation which was not regarded as cancelled by all his previous successes.

Still, actual disaster was escaped. Had Vologases been an active and energetic prince, or had the spirit and audacity of the Parthian nation been such as once characterised it, the result might have been widely different. The prolonged resistance of Hatra, the sufferings of the Romans, their increasing difficulties with respect to provisions, the injurious effect of the summer heats upon their unacclimatised constitutions, would have presented irresistible temptations to a prince, or even a general, of any boldness and capacity, inducing him to pursue the retreating enemy, to hang upon their flanks and upon their rear, to fall on their stragglers, to cut off their supplies, to harass and annoy them in ten thousand ways, and render their withdrawal to their own territory a matter of extreme difficulty. A Surena of the temper and calibre of the general opposed to Crassus might not improbably have annihilated the Imperial army, and the disaster of Carrhæ might have repeated itself at the distance of between two and three centuries. But Vologases IV. was a degenerate descendant of the great Arsacids, and remained inert and apathetic when the circumstances of the time called for the most vigorous action.

As it was, the expedition of Severus must be pronounced glorious for Rome and disastrous for Parthia. It exposed for the third time within a century the extreme weakness of the great Asiatic power. It lost her such treasures as had escaped the cupidity of Avidius Cassius. It both exhausted and disgraced her. Moreover, it cost her a second and most valuable province. Severus was not content with fully re-establishing the Roman sway in Mesopotamia. He overstepped the Tigris, and firmly planted Roman authority in the rich and fertile region between that river and the Zagros mountains. Henceforth the title of " Adiabenicus " became no empty boast. Adiabênê, or the tract between the two Zab rivers—the most productive and valuable part of the ancient Assyria—became a Roman dependency under Severus, and continued to be Roman till after the destruction of the Parthian Empire. For the remainder of the time during which Parthia maintained her independence, the Roman standards were planted within less than two degrees of her capital.

Vologases reigned for the space of about eleven years (A.D. 197–208) after his defeat by Severus. Parthian history is for this interval a blank. The decline of national feeling and of the military spirit went on, no doubt, without a pause, and the power of Parthia must continually have grown less and less. No pretenders arose, since there was probably no one who coveted the position of ruler over a state evidently nodding to its fall. Rome abstained from further attack, content, it would seem, with the gains which she had made, and a brief calm heralded the storm in which Parthian nationality was to perish.

XXI.

ARTABANUS IV. AND CARACALLUS—THE LAST WAR WITH ROME—DEFEAT OF MACRINUS.

THE death of Vologases IV. was immediately followed by a dispute between his two sons, Vologases V. and Artabanus IV., for the succession. We do not know which was the elder; but it would seem

COIN OF VOLOGASES VI.   COIN OF ARTABANUS V.

that at first the superiority in the struggle rested with Vologases, who was recognised by the Romans as sole king in A.D. 212, and must have then ruled in the western capital, Ctesiphon. Afterwards Artabanus acquired the preponderance, and from the year A.D. 216 we find no more mention of Vologases by the classical writers. It is Artabanus who negotiates with Caracallus, who is treacherously attacked by him, who contends with Macrinus, and is ultimately defeated and slain by the founder of the New Persian monarchy, Artaxerxes. Similarly, the Persian historians ignore Vologases altogether, and represent the contest for empire, which once more carried Persia to the front, as one between Ardeshir and Ardevan. Still, the Parthian coins show that Vologases, equally with his brother, both claimed and exercised sovereignty in Parthia to the close of the kingdom. The probability would therefore appear to be that about A.D. 216 a partition of the kingdom was amicably made, and that while Artabanus reigned over the western provinces, the eastern were ceded to Vologases.

It was while the struggle between the two brothers continued that the Emperor Severus died, and the period of tranquillity inaugurated by him, on his return from the East in A.D. 198, came to an end. His son and successor, Caracallus, a weak and vain prince, nourished an inordinate ambition, and was scarcely seated on the throne when he let it be known that in his own judgment he was a second Alexander, and that he was bent on imitating the marvellous exploits of that mighty hero. He adopted the Macedonian costume, formed his best troops into a " Macedonian phalanx," made the captains of the phalanx take the names of Alexander's best generals, and caused statues to be made with a double head, presenting the countenance of Alexander on one side and his own upon the other. As Alexander, he was bound to conquer the East ; and, as early as his second year, he began his predetermined aggressions. Summoning Abgarus, the tributary monarch of Osrhoëné, or north-western Mesopotamia, into his presence, he seized upon his person, committed him to prison, declared his territories forfeited, and reduced Osrhoëné into the form of a Roman province. Soon afterwards he attempted to repeat the proceeding with Armenia ; but, although the Armenian king was weak enough to fall into the trap, the nation was on the alert, and frustrated his efforts. No sooner did they learn that their king was arrested and imprisoned than they flew to arms, placed their country in a position of defence, and made themselves ready to resist all aggression. Caracallus hesitated, and when, three years later (A.D. 215), he sent Theocritus, one of his favourites, to effect their subjugation, they met him in arms, and inflicted a severe defeat on the utterly incompetent general. It was perhaps this disaster which suggested to Caracallus a change in his method of proceeding. Professing to put away from him all thoughts of war and conquest, he propounded a grand scheme for the permanent pacification of the East, and the establishment of a reign of universal happiness and tranquillity. Having transferred his residence from Nicomedia to Antioch, the luxurious capital of the Roman Oriental provinces, he sent ambassadors with presents of unusual magnificence to the Parthian monarch, Artabanus, who were to make him a proposal of a novel and unheard-of character. " The Roman Emperor," said the despatch in question, could not fitly wed the daughter of a subject, or accept the position of son-in-law to a private person.

No one could be a suitable wife for him who was not a princess. He therefore asked the Parthian monarch for the hand of his daughter. Rome and Parthia divided between them the sovereignty of the world ; united, as they would be by this marriage, no longer recognising any boundary as separating them, they would constitute a power which could not but be irresistible. It would be easy for them to reduce under their sway all the barbarous races on the skirts of their empires, and to hold them in subjection by a flexible system of administration and government. The Roman infantry was the best in the world, and in steady hand-to-hand fighting must be allowed to be unrivalled. The Parthians surpassed all nations in the number of their cavalry and the excellence of their archers. If these advantages, instead of being separated, were combined, and the various elements on which success in war depends were thus brought into harmonious union, there could be no difficulty in establishing and maintaining a universal monarchy. Were that done, the Parthian spices and rare stuffs, as also the Roman metals and manufactures, would no longer need to be imported secretly and in small quantities by merchants, but, as the two countries would form together but one nation and one state, there would be a free interchange among all the citizens of their various products and commodities." To the Parthian king and his advisers the proposition was as unwelcome as it was strange. The whole project appeared to them monstrous. Artabanus himself misdoubted the Emperor's sincerity, and did not believe that he would persevere in it. But it threw him into a state of extreme perplexity. Bluntly to reject the overture was to offend the master of thirty-two legions, and to provoke a war the results of which might be ruinous. To accept it was to depart from all Parthian traditions, and to plunge into the unknown and the unconjecturable. Artabanus therefore temporised. Without giving a positive refusal, he stated certain objections to the proposal, which made it, he thought, inexpedient, and begged to be excused from complying with it. "Such a union as was suggested could scarcely," he said, "prove a happy one. The wife and husband, differing in language, habits, and modes of thought, could not but become estranged one from another. There was no lack of patricians at Rome, possessing daughters with whom the Emperor might wed as suitably as the Parthian kings did with the females of their own royal house. It was not fit that either family should sully its blood by mixture with a foreign stock."

Upon this answer reaching him, Caracallus, according to the Court historian, Dio Cassius, immediately declared war, and invaded the Parthian territory with a large army. Herodian, however, who seems here to be more trustworthy, gives a different account. Caracallus, he declares, instead of quarrelling with Artabanus for his qualified refusal, followed up his first embassy with a second ; his envoys brought rich gifts to Ctesiphon, and assured the Parthian monarch that the Emperor was serious in his proposals, and had the most friendly intentions possible. Hereupon Artabanus yielded, either satisfied with the assurances given him, or else afraid to give offence ; he addressed Caracallus as his future son-in-law, and invited him to come with all speed, and fetch home his bride. " And then," continues the historian, " when this was noised abroad, the Parthians made ready to give the Roman Emperor a fit reception, being transported with joy at the prospect of an eternal peace. Caracallus thereupon crossed the rivers without hindrance and entered Parthia, just as if it were his own land. Everywhere along his route the people greeted him with sacrifices, and dressing their altars with garlands, offered upon them all manner of spices and incense, whereat he made pretence of being vastly pleased. As his journey now approached its close, and he drew near to the Parthian Court, Artabanus, instead of awaiting his arrival, went out and met him in the spacious plain before the city, with intent to entertain his daughter's bridegroom and his own son-in-law. Meanwhile, the whole multitude of the barbarians, crowned with freshly gathered flowers, and clad in garments embroidered with gold and variously dyed, were keeping holiday, and dancing gracefully to the sound of the flute, the pipe, and the drum— an amusement wherein they take great delight after they have indulged freely in wine. Now, when all the people had come together, they dismounted from their horses, hung up their quivers and their bows, and gave themselves wholly to libations and revels. The concourse of barbarians was very great, and they stood arranged in no sort of order, since they did not apprehend any danger, but were all endeavouring to catch a sight of the bridegroom.

Suddenly the Emperor gives his men the signal to fall on and massacre the barbarians. These, amazed at the attack, and finding themselves struck and wounded, forthwith took to flight. Artabanus was hurried away by his guards, and lifted on a horse, whereby he escaped with a few followers. The rest of the barbarians were cut to pieces, since they could not reach their horses, which, when they dismounted, they had allowed to graze freely over the plain; nor were they able to make use of their legs, since these were entangled in the long flowing garments which descended to their heels. Many, too, had come without quivers or bows, which were not wanted at a wedding. Caracallus, when he had made a vast slaughter, and taken a multitude of prisoners and a rich booty, moved off without meeting with any resistance. In his retreat he allowed his soldiers to burn all the cities and villages, and to carry away as plunder whatever they chose."

The advance of Caracallus had been through Babylonia, probably along the course of the Euphrates; his return was through Adiabênê and Mesopotamia. In Adiabênê he still further outraged and offended the Parthians by violating the sanctity of the royal burial-place at Arbela, where, as a rule, the Parthian kings were interred. Arbela had been regarded from of old as a City of the Dead; and the Arsacidæ had made it their ordinary place of sepulture. Caracallus caused the tombs to be opened, the bodies dragged forth from them, and the remains dispersed to the four winds. No insult could be greater than this, and the act seems rather that of a madman than of a mere ordinary tyrant. We are reminded of Aristotle's observation, that "families of brilliant talents go off after a time into dispositions bordering upon madness," and see that that of the Antonines was no exception. Caracallus can scarcely have been in his senses to have committed an action from which no possible good could arise, and for which, as he might have anticipated, a severe reckoning was afterwards to be exacted.

Meanwhile, however, he was pursuing his gay career, no whit alarmed, and no whit abashed. He wrote to the Senate in the lightest possible tone, to declare, without giving any details, that the whole East was subject to him, and that there was not a kingdom in those parts but had submitted to his authority. The Senate, though not imposed upon, wrote back in flattering terms, and granted him all the honours that would have been suitable to a veritable conqueror. For his own part, he remained in Mesopotamia, passing the winter there, and amusing himself with hunting and chariot-driving. There were still lions in the Mesopotamian region, as in Assyrian times, and the young Antonine, though a poor soldier, seems to have been a bold hunter. He had, apparently, persuaded himself that no external danger threatened him, and was content to idle away his time in the grassy Mesopotamian plains, which now—in early spring—must have been an earthly paradise. April was reached, and it was high time for an active commander to have commenced the marshalling and exercising of his troops, or even the initiatory movements of the designed campaign; but Caracallus continued impassive, occupied in his amusements, his suspicions of his officers, and his consultations of augurs, magicians, and oracles as to what fate was in store for him. He was on his way to visit an oracle in the Temple of the Moon-God, near Carrhæ, when some of his inquiries having leaked out, a conspiracy was formed against him in the camp, and he was murdered by Julius Martialis, one of his guards, on April 8, A.D. 217.

In the place of Caracallus, a new emperor had to be appointed. The choice of the soldiery fell upon Macrinus, one of the Prætorian Prefects, the chief mover in the recent conspiracy. His elevation almost exactly coincided with the advance of Artabanus, who, having reunited and increased his army during the course of the winter months, and brought it into excellent condition, had now conducted it into Roman Mesopotamia, and was anxious to engage the Romans in a pitched battle, in order to exact a heavy retribution for the treacherous massacre of Ctesiphon and the wanton impiety of Arbela. But Macrinus was scarcely prepared to meet him. Though Prætorian Prefect, he had none of the instincts of a soldier, but was far more versed in civil affairs, and adapted to hold office in the civil administration or in the judiciary. Accordingly, no sooner did he find himself menaced by the Parthian monarch than he hastily sent ambassadors to his camp with an offer to surrender all the prisoners carried off in the late campaign as the price of peace. But Artabanus had higher aims. " The Roman Emperor," he said in reply, " must not only restore the prisoners unjustly captured in a time of peace, but must also consent to rebuild all the towns and castles which Caracallus had laid in ruins, must make compensation for the wanton injury done to the tombs of the kings, and must further cede Mesopotamia to the Parthians, and retire behind the line of the Euphrates." It was morally impossible for a Roman Emperor to consent to such demands as these without first trying the fortune of war; and accordingly Macrinus felt himself compelled, much against his will, to risk a battle. He had with him a large army, which, if not exactly flushed with victory, had at any rate not known defeat; and he had, besides, the prestige of the Roman name, always a source of confidence to those who boasted it, and of terror to their adversaries.

Artabanus, on his part, had done his best to make his army formidable. He had collected it from all quarters, had made it strong in cavalry and archers, and had attached to it a novel force of considerable importance, consisting of a corps of picked soldiers, clad in complete armour, and carrying spears or lances of unusual length, who were mounted on camels. The Romans had, besides the ordinary legionaries, in which their strength mainly consisted, a large number of light-armed troops, and a powerful body of Mauretanian cavalry. The battle, which lasted three days, and was fought near Nisibis, in Upper Mesopotamia, began at daybreak on the first day by a rapid advance of the Parthians, who, after saluting the rising sun, rushed with loud shouts to the combat, and, under cover of a sleet of arrows, delivered charge after charge. The Romans, receiving their own light-armed within the ranks of the legionaries, stood firm, but suffered greatly from the bows of the horse-archers and from the lances of the corps mounted on camels ; and though, whenever they could reach their enemy, and engage in close combat, they had always the advantage, yet after a while their losses from the cavalry and the camels forced them to retreat. As they retired they strewed the ground with spiked balls (or caltrops) and other contrivances for injuring the feet of animals, and this stratagem was so far successful that the pursuers soon found themselves in difficulties, and the two armies respectively returned, without any decisive result, to their camps.

On the following day there was again a combat, which is said to have lasted from morning till night, and to have been equally indecisive with the preceding one ; but of this, which is wholly ignored by Dio, we do not possess any description. The third day arrived, and the fight was once more renewed ; but this time the Parthians had recourse to new tactics. Hitherto it had been their aim to rout and disperse their enemies ; now they directed all their efforts towards surrounding them, and so capturing the entire force. Their troops, which were far more numerous than those of the Romans, spread themselves to right and left, threatening to turn the Roman flanks and envelop the whole army. Macrinus, to meet these tactics and baffle them, was forced more and more to extend his own line, and consequently to attenuate it unduly, so that at last it broke up. Confusion once begun was speedily increased by the

cowardice of the Roman Emperor, who was among
the first to take to flight, and hurry back to his camp.
As a matter of course his army followed his example,
and having a refuge so close at hand, suffered no very
severe losses.   The defeat, however, was acknowledged, even by the Romans themselves ; and, in the
negotiations which followed the battle, Macrinus had
to accept terms of peace, which, though less disgraceful than those at first proposed, must be regarded as
sufficiently onerous.   The cession of Mesopotamia
was not, indeed, insisted on ; but, besides restoring
the captives and the booty carried off by Caracallus
in his raid, Macrinus had to pay, as compensation for
the damages inflicted, no less a sum than a million
and a half of our money.   The transactions of Rome
with Parthia were thus brought to an end, after nearly
three centuries of struggle, by the ignominious purchase of a peace.   Macrinus retired within his own
frontier in the summer of A.D. 217, and before Rome
was again called upon to make war in these parts the
sovereignty of the Parthians had terminated.

XXII.

REVOLT OF THE PERSIANS—DOWNFALL OF THE PARTHIAN EMPIRE.

THE tendency of the Parthian Empire to disintegration has been frequently noted in these pages. From the first there was a want of attachment among its parts, and a looseness of organisation which boded ill for the prolonged existence of the body politic. It was not only that the races composing it were so various, the character and conditions of the provinces so unlike, the ideas prevalent in different parts so diverse, but the entire system by which it was sought to give compactness and unity to the *disjecta membra* was so deficient in vigour and efficacy, that a long continuance of cohesion was almost impossible. "Kingdom-Empires," as they have been called, are always unstable; and, unless the dominant power possesses a very marked preponderance, they are sure sooner or later to break up. In the widespread empire built up by the Arsacidæ the Parthians could not really claim any very decided superiority over the other principal component parts, either in physical or in mental characteristics. They were not braver than the Medes, the Hyrcanians, the Armenians, or the

Persians ; they were not more intelligent than the Babylonians, the Bactrians, or the Assyrians. That they had some qualities which brought them to the front, cannot, of course, be denied; but these were not such as to strike the minds of men very strongly, or to obtain universal and unqualified recognition. Their rule was acquiesced in so long, rather because the Oriental appreciates the advantages of settled and quiet government, than because the subject races regarded them as having any special aptitude or capacity for governing. Each of the principal nations probably thought itself quite as fit to hold the first place in the commonwealth as the Parthians ; and under favourable circumstances each secondary monarch was quite ready to assert and maintain his independence.

Revolts of subject kingdoms or tribes were thus of frequent occurrence during the entire period of the Parthian monarchy ; but, as time went on, they became more frequent, more determined, and more difficult to subdue. It has been already related how, as early as the time of Vologases I., Hyrcania broke off from the empire, and was probably not reduced subsequently.[1] Bactria was also from time to time a sort of separate appanage, conceded to a prince of the Royal House, who accepted it in satisfaction of his claims to the chief authority. Armenia was still more loosely attached to the empire, being more often and for longer periods reckoned an independent state than a subjected one. At one time Babylonia is found almost independent under Hymerus.[2] The single tie of a nominal subjection to a distant

[1] Supra, p. 296.　　　　　　　　　　[2] Page 119.

suzerain proved a weak bond when any strain was put upon it, and there was constant danger of this or that province detaching itself from the great mass of the empire, and entering upon a separate existence.

We are thus entitled to say that there was something like a general discontent of the provinces with their condition under the central government, at any rate for the last century and a half of Parthian rule. It is difficult, however, to analyse the grounds of this discontent, or to decide what elements in it had the greater weight, and which were of minor importance. An alien rule must always be more or less irksome to those who have to submit to it, and must more or less chafe and gall them, as they exceed or fall short in pride and sensibility. The friction will be increased or diminished by the character of the rule, its consonance with justice, its regard for promises and engagements, its care for its subjects, its clemency, its power and will to protect, its general fairness and equity. It cannot be said that the Parthians fell flagrantly short in any of these particulars, or deserve to be regarded as either on the one hand weak and careless, or on the other harsh, unjust, and oppressive. They no doubt took the lion's share of pomp, power, and privilege ; but beyond this advantage, which is one taken by all dominant peoples, it does not appear that their subjects had any special grievances of which to complain. The Parthians were tolerant ; they did not interfere with the religious prejudices of their subjects, or attempt to enforce uniformity of creed or worship. Their military system did not press over-heavily on the subject races ; nor is there any reason to believe that the scale of their taxation was excessive. Such tyranny as is charged upon certain Parthian monarchs is not of a kind that would have been sensibly felt by the conquered nations, since it was exercised on none who were not Parthians. If at any time the rulers of the country failed to perform the great duties of civil government, it was rather in the way of laxity that they erred than of tension, rather by loosening the bonds of authority than by over-tightening them.

Some tangible ground for the general discontent, beyond the " ignorant impatience " of a dominant race which is so usual, may perhaps be made out by careful consideration, in two respects, but in two only. In the first place, there were times when the Parthian government very imperfectly accomplished its great duty of preserving internal order and tranquillity. The history of Anilai and Asinai, which has been dwelt upon at some length in a former chapter,[1] brings out very strongly this defect in the Parthian governmental system, and reveals a condition of things which, if it had been permanent, must have been intolerable. We can only suppose that the anarchical times, of which we have so melancholy a picture, were occasional and exceptional, the result of internal disorders, which ere long came to a head, and then passed away ; or we should have to imagine a government, which fulfilled none of the functions of a government, lasting for centuries, and some of the most spirited nations on the earth submitting to it and seeking no better.

[1] Chap. XIV. pp. 246–256.

The other failure of the Parthians belongs to the later period only of their history. It consisted in the general decline of the vigour of the nation, which rendered it less competent, than it had been previously, to afford adequate protection to the conquered states —especially protection against the wholly alien power, which had intruded itself into Asia, and which sought to bring all the nations of Asia under subjection. The suzerainty of Parthia had been accepted by the other Asiatic powers as that of the one out of their number which was most competent to make head against European invaders, and to secure the native races in continued independence of an influence which they recognised as antagonistic, and felt to be hateful. It may well have appeared at this time to the various vassal states that the Parthian vigour had become effete, that the qualities which had advanced the race to the leadership of Western Asia were gone, and that unless some new power could be raised up to act energetically against Rome, the West would obtain complete dominion over the East, and Asia be absorbed into Europe. Vague thoughts would arise as to which nation might be conceived to be the fittest to take the lead, if Parthia had to be deposed ; and the instinct of self-aggrandisement would lead the more eminent to contemplate the possibility of themselves aspiring to the position, if not even to take measures to push their claims. Probably for some considerable time before the movement headed by Artaxerxes, son of Babek, commenced, such thoughts had been familiar to the wiser men among many of the Asiatic nations, and a long preparation had thus been made for the revolution, which seemed to break out so suddenly at last.

If, again, we ask, what peculiar grounds of grievance had the Persians above the other subject races, or why did the burden of raising the standard of revolt fall especially upon them, we have a further difficulty in obtaining an answer. There is no appearance of the Persians having been in any way singled out by the Parthians for oppression, or having had any more grounds of complaint against them than any other of the subject nations. The complaints which are made are negative rather than positive, and amount to little more than the following : — 1. That high offices, whether civil or military, were for the most part confined to those of Parthian blood, and not thrown open in any fair proportion to the Persians. 2. That the priests of the Persian religion were not held in sufficient honour, being even less accounted of in the later than in the earlier times ; and 3. That no advantage in any respect was allowed to the Persians over the rest of the conquered peoples, notwithstanding that they had for so many years exercised supremacy over Western Asia, and given to the list of Asiatic worthies such names as those of Cyrus and Darius Hystaspis. It was thus not because they were worse treated than their brother subjects that the Persians were dissatisfied, but because their pretensions were higher. They thought themselves deserving of exceptional treatment, and, since they did not receive it, they murmured. In fact, the Persians had at no time ever forgotten that they had once been "lords of Asia," and it angered them that their conquerors seemed to have

forgotten it. They had at all times submitted to
Parthian hegemony as it were under protest; now
they were no longer inclined to submit to it. They
believed, and probably with justice, that, under the
changed circumstances of the time, they were better
suited than the Parthians to direct the affairs of
Western Asia, and they resolved at any rate to make
the attempt. Their justification is to be found in
their success. As the Parthians had no right to their
position but such as arose out of the law of the
strongest, so, when the time came that they had lost
this pre-eminence, superiority in strength having
passed to a nation hitherto counted among their
subjects, it was natural and right that the seat of
authority should shift with the shift in the balance of
power, and that the leadership of the Persians should
be once more recognised.

In one respect the Parthian rule must always have
grated upon the feelings of their Persian subjects
more than upon those of the generality, since there
was in the Parthians an ingrained coarseness and
savagery which could not but be especially distasteful
to a people of such comparative refinement as the
Persians. Persian art, Persian manners, Persian
literature had a delicacy and a polish which the rude
Parthians, with their Tâtar breeding, could not
appreciate; and the countrymen of Cyrus and Darius,
of Firdausi and Hafiz, must have had an instinctive
aversion from the nomadic race whose manners were
still deeply tinged with Scythicism.

It may also be suspected, though of this there is
less evidence, that the revolution which transferred the

dominion of Western Asia from the Parthians to the Persians, from the Arsacidæ to the Sassanidæ, was to some extent a religious one. The "Book-Religion" of Zoroaster, with its dualism, its complicated spiritualism, and its elaborate ritual, was unsuited for the rough times through which Western Asia had to pass between the invasion of Alexander and the foundation of the Neo-Persian state, and it appears to have been superseded, except in Persia Proper, by a ruder system, of which the principal elements were devotion to the Sun and Moon and the worship of ancestral images. But the time was now again come when more complicated ideas were in the ascendant. The various forms of Gnosticism show how mysticism once more asserted itself among the Western Asiatics in the first and second centuries of our era, and how speculations were rife which reopened all the deepest problems of spiritual religion. The stir had begun which issued ultimately in Manicheism, and the Persian aspirations after leadership may have been partly caused by a desire to push their religion to the front, and to take advantage of the popular favour with which dualistic tenets were beginning to be regarded. It is certain that among the principal changes consequent upon the success of the Persians was a religious revolution in Western Asia—the substitution for Parthian tolerance of all faiths and worships, of a rigidly enforced uniformity in religion, the establishment of the Magi in power, and the bloody persecution of all such as declined obedience to the precepts of Zoroaster.

The space of about six or seven years seems to have separated the conclusion of peace with Rome from the outbreak of rebellion under Artaxerxes. During this time the division of sovereignty between Artabanus V. and Vologases V. continued without interruption, and the power of Parthia was still further weakened by Arsacid intrigues originating with branches of the royal family which were settled in Bactria. No doubt internal debility showed itself in various ways, and the tributary king of Persia, a young, active, and energetic prince, became daily more convinced of his ability, if not to recover the empire of Cyrus, at any rate to shake off the rude yoke which had galled and chafed his nation for so many centuries. Independence was probably all that he originally looked for ; but, in course of time, as the struggle went on, wider views with respect to the possibilities of the situation opened themselves before him, and the contest became one for life or death between the two kingdoms. After establishing his authority in Persia Proper, he turned his arms eastward against Carmania (Kerman), and in a short space of time easily reduced that sparsely peopled and not very desirable country. He next took in hand a more daring enterprise. The valuable and fertile country of Media adjoined Persia to the north. Artaxerxes proceeded to make war in this quarter, and to annex to his dominions portions of the Median territory. But this was to attack the Parthian kingdom at its heart, since Media, Assyria (Adiabênê), and Babylonia formed the main strength and the central mass of the Empire. Artabanus, who had thought but lightly of a Persian revolt, and had probably regarded incursions into Carmania with absolute indifference, as concern-

ing his brother rather than himself, was now effectually roused. Collecting his forces, he took the field in
person, invaded Persia Proper, and engaged in a
desperate struggle with his rival. Three great battles
are said to have been fought between the contending
powers. In the last, which took place, according to
the Persian authorities, in the plain of Hormuz,
between Bebahan and Shuster, on the course of the
Jerahi river, Artabanus was, after a desperate conflict,
completely defeated by his antagonist (A.D. 226), and
lost his life in the battle.

The struggle, however, was not yet over. Arta-

COIN OF ARTAVASDES.

vasdes, the eldest son of Artabanus, claimed the crown,
and was supported by a large number of adherents.
His uncle, Chosroës, who had received the throne of
Armenia from Artabanus, espoused his cause, gave the
Parthian refugees an asylum in his kingdom, and even
fought a battle with Artaxerxes in their defence. In
this he was so far victorious that the Persian found
it necessary to retreat, and retire to his own dominions
in order to augment his forces. But the struggle was
too unequal for long continuance. Within a very few
years of its commencement the contest was everywhere
ended ; the arms of Artaxerxes prevailed, and the
Parthian Empire was overthrown. All the provinces

submitted ; the last Arsacid prince fell into the hands of the Persian king ; and the founder of the new dynasty sought to give legitimacy to his rule by taking to wife an Arsacid princess.

The duration of the Parthian monarchy was a little short of five centuries. It commenced about B.C. 250, and it terminated in A.D. 227. It was the rule of a vigorous tribe of Tâtar or Turkic extraction over a mixed population, chiefly of Semitic or Arian race, and, for the most part, more advanced in civilisation than their rulers. Though its organisation was loose, it was not ill-adapted for Orientals, who prefer a flexible system to one where everything is " cut and dry," and are opposed to all that is stiff and bureaucratic. Western Asia must be considered to have enjoyed a time of comparative rest under the Parthian sovereignty, and to have been as prosperous as at almost any other period of its history. The savage hordes of Northern Asia and Europe were, in the main, kept off ; and, though the arms of Rome from time to time ravaged the more western provinces, and even occasionally penetrated to the capital, yet this state of things was exceptional ; for the most part European aggression was averted, or quickly repulsed ; very few conquests were made, and when they were made, they were not always retained ; and to the last the limits of the Parthian dominion remained almost the same as they had been under the first Mithridates. Still, there was no doubt a gradual internal decay, which worked itself out especially in two directions. The Arsacid race, with which the idea of the empire was closely bound up, instead of clinging together in

that close " union " which constitutes true " strength,"
allowed itself to be torn to pieces by dissensions, to
waste its force in quarrels, and to be made a handle
of by every foreign invader or domestic rebel who
chose to use its name in order to cloak his own selfish
projects. The race itself does not seem to have become
exhausted. Its chiefs, the successive occupants of the
throne, never sank into mere weaklings or *fainéants*,
never shut themselves up in their seraglios, or ceased
to take an active and leading part, alike in civil broils
and in struggles with foreign princes. Artabanus, the
adversary of Artaxerxes, was as brave and capable a
monarch as had ever sat upon the Parthian throne in
previous ages. But the hold which the race had on
the population, native and foreign, was gradually
weakened by the feuds which raged within it, by the
profusion with which the sacred blood was shed by
those in whose veins it ran, and the difficulty of
knowing which living member of it was its true head,
and so entitled to the allegiance of all those who
wished to be faithful Parthian subjects. Further, the
vigour of the Parthian soldiery must have gradually
declined, and their superiority over the mass of the
nations under their dominion must have diminished.
Marked evidence was given of this when, about A.D.
75, Hyrcania became independent ; and it is possible
that there may have been other cases of successful
rebellions in the remoter eastern regions. Oriental
races, when they are suddenly lifted to power, almost
always decline in strength, and sometimes with
extreme rapidity. The Parthians cannot be said to
have experienced a rapid deterioration ; but they too,

like the dominant races of Western Asia, both before and after them, felt in course of time the softening influence of luxury, and had to yield their place to those who had maintained manlier and hardier habits.

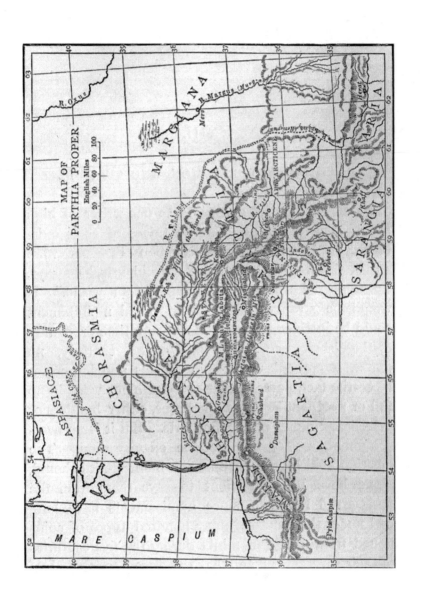

XXIII.

PARTHIAN ART, RELIGION, AND CUSTOMS.

"THE Parthians," according to one writer of high repute, "have left no material traces of their existence."[1] When the Achæmenian Persians were struck down by Alexander, "the old arts," he says, "disappeared from the Mesopotamian world." It would be strange indeed if so broad a statement could be justified, when made of any time or of any distinguished people. Roughly and coarsely, no doubt, it embodies a certain curious and important fact—the fact, namely, that the Parthians were, in no full or pregnant sense of the terms, either builders or proficients in any of the fine arts. But it is an over-statement, a very considerable exaggeration. The position held by the Parthians in numismatics should, alone have been sufficient to save them from the undeserved reproach, since numismatists have long had under their notice many hundred types of coins issued from Parthian mints during the five centuries of their sovereignty, and have assigned to several of them a fair amount of merit. Careful inquiry shows, as might have been expected, that in other branches

[1] See Fergusson, "History of Architecture," vol. ii. p. 422.

of art also, and especially in architecture, Parthia made efforts and produced results not wholly despicable.

The remains at Hatra, or El Hadhr, are the most imposing which can reasonably be assigned to the Parthian period. Hatra first comes into notice in the early part of the first century before Christ, and is then a place of no small importance. It successfully resists Trajan in A.D. 116, and Severus in A.D. 198. It is then described as a large and populous city, defended by strong and extensive walls, and containing within it a famous Temple of the Sun, celebrated for the great value of its accumulated offerings. The people are regarded as of the Arabian stock, and they have their own kings, who are tributary monarchs under Parthia. By the year A.D. 363, Hatra has gone to ruins, and it is then described as "long since deserted."[1] It plays no part at all in Sassanian history, and clearly has for its most flourishing period the last century, or century and a quarter, of the Parthian rule, from A.D. 100 to A.D. 226.

The ruins of El Hadhr have been carefully described by two English travellers, Mr. Ross and Mr. Ainsworth, whose accounts will be found in the ninth and eleventh volumes of the "Geographical Society's Journal." They have also attracted the attention of a professional critic, Mr. James Fergusson, who has given a description of them, with one or two woodcuts, in his "History of Architecture." The following account rests especially on the two former—the only original—authorities.

[1] Ammianus Marcellinus, xxv. 8.

The city of Hatra was circular in shape, and nearly an English mile in diameter. It was enclosed by a wall, ten feet in thickness, built of large square-cut stones, and strengthened at intervals of about a hundred and seventy yards by square towers or bastions. Its circumference considerably exceeded three miles. Outside the bastioned wall was a broad and deep ditch,

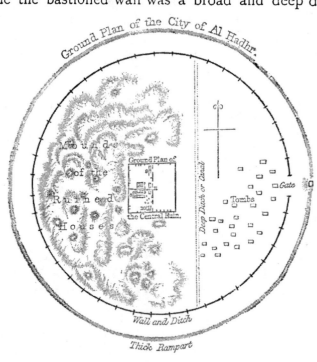

and on the further side of the ditch an earthen rampart of considerable size and thickness. The wall was pierced by four gateways, of which the principal faced the east. Two detached forts, situated on eminences, commanded the approaches to the city, one of them lying towards the east and the other towards the north.

Within the walled enclosure the circular space was divided into two parts by a water-course, which crossed it from north to south, nearly midway in the circle, but somewhat more towards its eastern portion. The city proper lay west of the water-course. Here were the public edifices, and the houses of the more opulent inhabitants. The space towards the east was used chiefly as a necropolis, though a certain number of buildings were interspersed among the graves. Almost in the centre of the circle stood a walled enclosure, nearly square in plan, and fronting the cardinal points, having a length of about eight hundred feet from west to east, with a width of about seven hundred. Strong bastions, similar in character to those of the outer circle, flanked the wall at intervals along its entire course. The space within was again subdivided by a wall running north and south into an outer and an inner court. The outer, which lay towards the east, and was rather the larger of the two, was wholly unencumbered by buildings, while the inner contained two considerable edifices. One of these, and the less important of the two, stretched from north to south across the entire enclosure, and abutted upon the wall which divided the two courts. It was confused in plan, and seems to have consisted only of a number of small apartments, which have been conjectured to have been "guard-rooms." The other building was, however, one of considerable pretension; and it is from this mainly that we must form our conception of Parthian architecture.

The great Palace, or "Palace-Temple" of Hatra, as

it has been called, was an edifice three hundred and
sixty feet long by two hundred and ten feet broad in
the broadest part. It consisted of a series of seven
oblong vaulted halls, placed side by side longi-
tudinally, with a certain number of smaller apartments, and one large building at the back. The
halls were of various dimensions. The smaller ones,

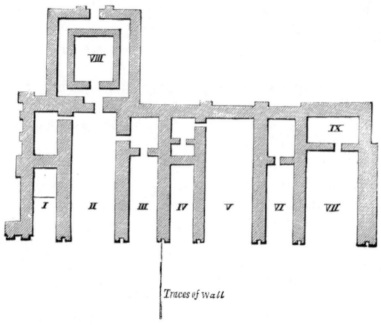

PLAN OF THE PALACE-TEMPLE OF HATRA.

of which there were four (Nos. I., III., IV., and VI.
on the plan), measured about sixty feet long by
twenty wide, and had a height of thirty feet. Two
of the larger ones (Nos. II. and V. on the plan)
measured ninety feet in length, and were from thirty-
five to forty feet broad, with a height of sixty feet.
One (No. VII. on the plan), with a width of forty-

five, had a length of not much above seventy feet.
Variety in the size of the halls was thus carefully
studied, while the shape was almost identical, and
the plan of construction the same throughout. "All
the halls were roofed by semicircular tunnel-vaults,
without ribs or other ornaments ; and they were all
entirely open in front, all the light and air being
admitted from the one end."[1]   The outer and party
walls were alike thick ; the doorways connecting
apartments were awkwardly narrow, and their
position in the walls which they pierced was irregular
and unsymmetrical.   The small apartments behind
the halls received no light, except from these narrow
doorways, and must have been almost absolutely
dark.

The large building attached to the series of halls
at the back lay directly behind the second hall, from
which there was an opening into it.   This building
consisted of a single chamber, square in shape, and
measuring about forty feet each way, surrounded on
all sides by a vaulted passage, into which light
penetrated from two windows, situated at its south-
west and north-west angles, and from a doorway in
the middle of the western wall.   The chamber, however, which the passage surrounded, could only be
entered from the east, where, directly opposite to
the communication with Hall No. II., was a doorway
surmounted by a magnificent frieze.   Above a row
of acanthus leaves, delicately carved, was placed an
ornamentation of inverted gradines, on which followed
a line of oval rings, each containing an oval ball in the

[1] Fergusson, "History of Architecture," vol. ii. p. 424.

centre. Immediately over this was a line of emblematic
figures—griffins, eagles, human and animal heads, and
the like—as will be best understood by the accompanying representation, which is taken from a drawing by
Mr. Ross. Crowning the whole was a cornice projecting
slightly, and covered with a sort of arabesque or scroll-
work. Among the emblematic heads is one, which
so manifestly represents the Sun-God, that the building has been generally recognised as a temple to that
deity. Mr. Fergusson, however, thinks that it " more

FRIEZE IN THE PALACE-TEMPLE OF HATRA.

probably contained a stair or inclined plane, leading
to the roof or upper rooms, which almost certainly
existed over the smaller halls at least." [1]

The chief ornamentation, however, of the Hatra
" Palace-Temple " was on its eastern façade, which
was evidently its main front. Here the seven consecutive arches of the basement storey, which is all
that now exists, formed in themselves no mean adornment, and this was heightened in several ways by
artistic additions. In the first place, the arches

[2] Fergusson's " History of Architecture," vol. ii. p. 424.

sprang from pillars, or rather pilasters, having bases
and capitals of some elegance, the number of such
pilasters along the entire front amounting to sixteen.
Secondly, the stones composing the archivolts of the
arches bore a human head, or mask, under a cornice
of ovals and acanthus leaves, which gave a very
peculiar character to the edifice, and has no exact
parallel elsewhere. "The only thing known at all
similar," says Mr. Fergusson, "is the celebrated arch
at Volterra with three masks; but here these are
infinitely more numerous over all the arches, and
form in fact the principal features of the decora-
tions."[1] Further, in the spaces between the pilasters were, in some
cases, sculptures representing embla-
matic figures, as griffins, and the like.

Internally, the halls had, for the
most part, no ornamentation. The
four smaller ones were absolutely
devoid of it, while even the larger

STONES OF ARCHI-
VOLTS.

ones had only a scanty amount. The longer sides of
the halls II. and V. were broken by three squared
pilasters, rising to the commencement of the vaulting,
and terminated by a quasi-capital of ornamental work,
consisting of a series of alternate ovals and lozenges,
each oval containing in its centre a ball of dark stone·
Underneath these quasi-capitals, at the distance of
between two and three feet, ran a cornice, which
crossed the pilasters, and extended the whole length
of the apartment, sometimes ornamented with flowers
and half-ovals, sometimes with alternate ovals and

[1] Fergusson's "History of Architecture," vol. ii. p. 425.

lozenges. Finally, on the pilasters, immediately below the cornice, were sculptured either two or three human heads, the length of each head being about two feet, and the faces representing various types of humanity, some old and some young, some

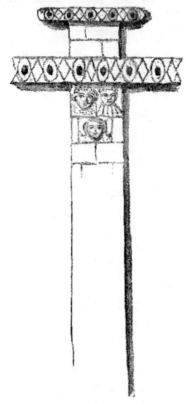

PILASTER AT HATRA, WITH CORNICE AND CAPITAL.

male and some female, some apparently realistic, some idealised and more or less grotesque in their accompaniments. The drawing of the heads is said to be full of spirit and their general effect lifelike and striking.

No. VII. had a peculiar ornamentation. In lieu of

pilasters and cornices, the two side walls appear to have been decorated with two rows of eight human-headed bulls standing out from the wall as far as their shoulders at a distance from the ground of about ten feet.   Similar figures of lions are found occasionally in Phœnicia, but otherwise the ornamentation is very unusual.

It is believed by Mr. Fergusson and others, that

PROPOSED RESTORATION OF THE HATRA BUILDING.

the entire edifice, or at any rate the greater portion of it, had originally an upper story.   At present the ruins nowhere attain a height much exceeding sixty feet ; but it is thought that this height was, originally, at least doubled, either a single story, or two stories, containing apartments, being superimposed upon the existing range of vaulted halls.   One explorer[1] thought that he found some remains of the staircase, which conducted to these upper apartments, at the southern extremity of the building.   If we accept

[1] Mr. Ross.

the view of this traveller, we may suppose, with another explorer,[1] that the entire eastern façade of the edifice presented some such appearance as shown on page 381, and conclude that the type of architecture, which is entirely different from any previously known in the country, either under the Assyrians, the Babylonians, or the Achæmenian Persians, was an invention of the Parthian period, though whether struck out by the Parthians themselves, or by one of the nations subjected to their sway, may be doubted. The type appears to be the germ out of which the Sassanian architecture, well known for its magnificence, grew up, and may be said to have held possession of Mesopotamia and the adjacent countries from about A.D. 150 to A.D. 640, when it was superseded by the architecture of the Arabs.

The general style of the buildings at Hatra has been said to have been " Roman or Byzantine," and the details are declared to be in many cases " almost literal imitations of Roman models." [2] This may well be, since Rome was, at the time of their erection, universally recognised as standing at the head of civilisation and the arts, so that the builders of other nations naturally went to her for instruction. But the plan of the Hatra building is certainly not Roman ; and it is allowed that the execution of the ornaments is too rude to admit of the idea, that the work was done under the superintendence of a Roman artist. Native talent alone can have been employed ; and there is every reason for considering that we may regard the

[1] Mr. Ainsworth.
[2] Fergusson, " History of Architecture," vol. ii. pp. 424-5.

work as a fair specimen of what was achieved by the native builders of the Parthian period during the latter times of the empire. The palace of Vologases III. at Ctesiphon, which Avidius Cassius destroyed in his invasion,[1] was probably of the same general character, a combination of lofty halls, suitable for ceremonies and audiences, with small and dark sleeping or living rooms, opening out of them, the whole placed in the middle of a paved court, with ready access to a chapel or temple, where the devotions of the Court might be performed.

It must be added that the halls and rooms of the Hatra edifice are divided into two groups. Halls I., II., and III., with the apartments in their rear, are inter-connected, and form one group. Halls IV., V., VI., and VII., form the other. A low fence, starting from the wall separating between Halls III. and IV., was carried in a straight line, eastward, across the court in front of the building, to the wall separating the inner court from the outer. Thus there could be no communication between the two groups of apartments excepting by making a long circuit round almost the entire edifice. It is thought that the two groups formed, respectively, the male and the female apartments.

Some architectural fragments, discovered by Mr. Loftus at Warka (the ancient Erech), in combination with a large number of Parthian coins, and therefore possessing a claim to be regarded as Parthian, seem to deserve mention in this place. They consisted of fragments of cornices, capitals, bases of columns,

---

[1] See above, p. 326.

friezes, fragments of open-screen work, with complicated geometric designs of different patterns on the opposite sides, large flakes of painted plaster, and the like. Most of the capitals resembled those of the Greek Ionic order, but presented peculiarities in the proportions of the volutes and other members. Some, however, were of an altogether peculiar type. One in particular, which, though square at the summit, must have crowned a round column, is especially remarkable. "A large and elegant leaf rises from the necking, and bends under each corner of the abacus. Springing

ARCHITECTURAL FRAGMENTS AT WARKA.

from behind a smaller curled leaf in the centre is the bust of a human figure, wearing the same preposterous head-dress which is characteristic of the (Parthian) slipper coffins, and the Parthian coins."[1] Other capitals had crowned square pillars, and were ornamented with ovals, and half-ovals, rosettes, leaves resembling those of the oak, circles containing geometrical tracery, and the like. One large fragment of a cornice bore, among other devices, a spirited crouching griffin, which reminded the discoverer of the

[1] Loftus, "Chaldæa and Susiana," p. 226.

similar figures sculptured on the Temple frieze at Hatra.[1] Some of the friezes had a decoration consisting of alternate vine-leaves and bunches of grapes.

The building, within which these fragments were discovered, was a rectangular chamber forty feet long by twenty-eight feet wide, the mud walls of which, still standing to the height of four feet, had been covered originally with painted plaster of various hues, and further adorned with small Ionic half columns. The columns had half-smooth and half-fluted shafts. The lower portion of each was smooth, and had been striped diagonally with bands of red, green, yellow, and black ; the upper portion was fluted, the flutes being painted black, red, and yellow alternately, while the level ridges between them were painted white. Underneath the floor of the chamber, at the depth of six feet, was discovered a "slipper-coffin" of the type so common at Warka, bearing embossed figures on its upper surface of a type generally regarded as Parthian. The building would thus seem to have been a sepulchral chamber erected over a tomb, such as is found so frequently in Phœnicia and Egypt.

The decorative and fictile art of the Parthians has also received considerable illustration from the remains discovered at Warka. These included several statuettes modelled in terra-cotta ; a vast number of slipper-coffins ; many jars, jugs, vases, and lamps in earthenware ; some small glass bottles ; and various personal ornaments, such as armlets, bangles, beads for necklaces and fillets, finger-rings, ear-rings, and toe-

[1] Compare above, p. 378.

rings.   Of the statuettes the most interesting is one
representing a Parthian warrior, recumbent, and leaning
upon his left arm, wearing a coat-of-mail or padded
tunic reaching to the knees, greaves, and a helmet ornamented in front.   Others represented females: these
had lofty head-dresses, which sometimes rose into
two peaks or horns, recalling the costume of English
ladies in the time of Henry IV.   These figures were
veiled, and carefully draped about the upper part of

PARTHIAN JUGS AND JARS.

the person, but showed the face, and had the legs bare
from the knee downwards.

The jars, jugs, vases, and lamps in earthenware
greatly resembled those of the Assyrian and Babylonian periods, but were on the whole more elegant and
artistic.   The influence of Greek models is apparent
in them.   One jug, the central one of the engraving,
is of "extremely artistic form,"[1] and was placed in
a recess, within arm's length of a coffin, probably for

[1] Loftus, "Chaldæa and Susiana," p. 213.

PARTHIAN SLIPPER-COFFIN.

the refreshment of the deceased. The lamps reproduce well-known Greek types.

The "slipper-coffins" found at Warka possess a peculiar interest. They are of a very beautiful green glazed ware, and vary in length from three feet to six. Great skill in pottery must have been required for their construction. The upper surface presents at one end a large oval aperture, by means of which the body was passed into the interior—an aperture which is furnished with a depressed ledge for the reception of a lid, which exactly fitted it, and was firmly fixed in its place by a layer of lime cement. At the lower extremity was a semicircular hole, to prevent the bursting of the coffin by the gases disengaged during decomposition. Both the lid which closed the large aperture, and the remainder of the upper surface of the coffin, were ordinarily divided by elevated ridges into small rectangular compartments, each containing an embossed figure of a man, standing with his arms akimbo and his legs astride, with a short sword hanging from his belt, and on his head an enormous coiffure of a very curious appearance.

The personal ornaments were in many cases of tasteful and elegant design. Tall pointed head-dresses in thin gold are said to have been not uncommon, and one or two broad ribbons of thin gold not unfrequently occurred in the tombs, depending on either side of the head. Gold and silver finger-rings abounded, and some had stones set in them. Bead-necklaces were found, together with armlets, bangles, and toe-rings of silver, brass, and copper. Many of the ear-rings were exceedingly elegant, and small gold plates, which seem to have been strung together for necklaces or fillets, were very delicately modelled.

The glass bottles were perhaps lachrymatories. They closely resemble glass-work of the Assyrian and Babylonian periods, and exhibit the same iridescent hues which are the result of slow decomposition. The commonest shape is a rounded belly, surmounted by a short, round neck, having a small handle on either side of it, but flattened so that the smaller diameter of the bottle is less than one-third of the greater one.

In purely æsthetic art—art, that is, into which the idea of the useful does not enter at all—the Parthians

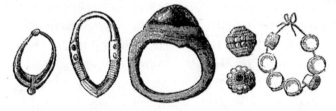

PARTHIAN PERSONAL ORNAMENTS.

appear to have been very deficient. Beyond the statuettes, in clay and terra-cotta, which have been already described,[1] no figures " in the round " can be ascribed to them. Nor are there more than three or four reliefs which have much claim to be pronounced Parthian. One alone is undisputable. At the foot of the great rock of Behistun, which exhibits at the height of many feet above the plain the long inscription, and remarkable sculpture, of Darius, the son of Hystaspes, is a much-worn sculpture in *alto relievo*, which is proved by the inscription accompanying it to belong to

[1] See above, p. 386.

the second reign of Gotarzes (A.D. 46–51), and which was almost certainly set up by that monarch after his defeat of the pretender, Meherdates.[1]   It seems to have contained a series of tall figures, looking towards the right, and apparently engaged in a march or procession, while above and between them were smaller figures of men on horseback, armed with lances, and galloping in the same direction.   One of these was attended by a Niké, or figure of Victory, floating in the air, and about to place a diadem around the rider's brow.   The present condition of the sculpture is exceedingly bad.   Time and atmospheric influences have almost completely worn away the larger figures, which the latest travellers appear not even to have perceived ; and a recent governor of Kirmanshah has barbarously inserted into the middle of the relief an arched niche, in which he has placed a wholly worthless Arabic inscription.   Under these circumstances, there is a difficulty in forming any opinion on the original artistic merit of the work ; but the best judges are agreed in pronouncing that, even at its best, it must have been a work of inferior quality, falling considerably below the level attained by the Assyrian and even the Achæmenian artists.   The resemblance is rather to the productions of the Sassanian, or New-Persian, period. The human figures have a heaviness and clumsiness about them which it is painful to contemplate ; the horses are rudely outlined, and are too small for the men who ride them ; the figure of Victory is out of all proportion to that of the hero whom she crowns, and the diadem which she places upon his head is

[1] Supra, p. 267.

ridiculously large, being almost as big as herself! On the other hand, there is spirit in the attitude both of men and horses; the Victory floats well in mid-air; and the relief is free from the coarse grotesqueness which is so offensive in the greater part of the Sassanian sculptures.

Another relief, belonging probably to a later period, after the Parthians had adopted a Semitic instead of the Greek character, has the Sassanian defects still more accentuated. It represents a king mounted on horseback, and receiving a chaplet at the hands of a subject. The king wears a low cap bound round with the diadem, the two long ends of which depend over his shoulder. He is dressed in a closely fitting tunic and loose trousers, and wears also a short cloak, fastened under his chin, and reaching nearly to the knee. On his right arm he seems to carry a bracelet; and his feet are encased in boots. The horse which he bestrides is small but strongly made; the tail is long; the ears seem to be cropped, and the mane plaited. The whole representation is rude and clumsy, the forepart of the horse, and the Parthian who offers the chaplet, being particularly ill drawn. The relief is accompanied by an inscription in the Parthian (Semitic) character.

A series of reliefs, discovered by the Baron de Bode in the Bakhtyari mountains in the year 1841, is also generally regarded by those best acquainted with the subject as Parthian. In one of these a hunter, mounted on horseback, and armed with a bow and arrows and a sword, or short spear, is engaged in combat with a bear. The bear raises itself on its hind legs to a level with the horse's head, and advances boldly to the attack. The hunter, who is clothed simply in a long flowing robe, like a dressing-gown, and a rounded cap, leans forward on his horse to meet the angry animal, and thrusts his sword, or spear, whichever it may be, into its neck. The horse shows no alarm, but ambles gently to the encounter. The execution is somewhat rude, but the figures are fairly well drawn, if we except the head of the house.

Another relief on the same rock shows a female figure reclining on a couch, and guarded by three male attendants, one at the head of the couch, unarmed, and the remaining two at its foot, seated, and armed with spears. The female has puffed-out hair, and carries in her right hand, which is out-stretched, a chaplet or wreath. One of the spearmen has a curious rayed head-dress; the other has a short streamer attached to the head of his spear. Below the main group are three rudely carved standing figures, which represent probably other attendants. The third relief of the series is the largest and most elaborate. It shows us a personage of importance, perhaps a Magus, engaged in what seems to be a religious ceremonial, standing with his right arm elevated by the side of a cippus, adorned with wreaths or chaplets, and mounted upon a threefold pedestal. Fifteen spectators are present, arranged in two rows, one above the other, and all of them, except the first in each row, standing. The first in each row sits upon a rudely designed chair or stool. A religious function is probably represented. We can scarcely fail to recognise in the principal figure, who

wears a conical cap, has his hair puffed out in
enormous masses on either side of the head, like the
kings upon the later coins, and is altogether richly
costumed, a priest of the Parthian religion, probably
a great hierarch, engaged in one of the duties of his
office. Perhaps we may best regard the set of reliefs
as forming a connected series, No. I. representing the
Parthian monarch occupied in the chase of the bear ;
No. II. the queen awaiting his return on her couch in
the midst of her attendants ; and No. III. exhibiting
the chief Magus attached to the Court making prayer
for the monarch's safety.

Altogether, the Parthians cannot be said to have
shown more than a very moderate degree of artistic
or æsthetic talent. Their architecture is their best
point ; and even that falls far below the architecture
of the other dominant races of Western Asia, whether
before or after them, whether Assyrians, Babylonians,
Achæmenian Persians, Sassanian Persians, Mongols,
or Arabs. Their glyptic art is even worse, and, considering that they had access, not only to Assyrian
and Achæmenian, but also, in some degree, to Greek
models, must be regarded as possessing a very low
amount of merit. A certain number of their coins are
fairly good, and one or two of their reliefs, though rude
and clumsy, have spirit. But, speaking generally, we
must admit that the vocation of the people was not
towards the artistic, and that they were probably well-
advised to employ their energies in other directions.
The scant remains of their art are an indication that
they recognised their own deficiencies, and, conscious
that it was not in their power to excel in the æsthetic

field, preferred to occupy themselves in pursuits for which they were better fitted, as war, hunting, and government.

Not much can be said on the subject of the Parthian religion. It seems probable that, under the Achæmenian Persians, they submitted to the Zoroastrian system, as maintained by the princes of the house of Cyrus from Xerxes downwards ; but, as this was certainly not their own ancestral religion, they cannot be supposed to have been at any time very zealous followers of the Bactrian prophet. As age succeeded age, they naturally became more luke-warm in their feelings, and more lax in their religious observance. The main characteristic—the essence, if we may so call it—of the Zoroastrian belief, was Dualism—recognition of Two Great Principles of good and evil, called respectively Ormazd and Ahri-man. We need not doubt that, with their lips, the Parthians from first to last admitted this antagonism, and professed a belief in Ormazd as the supreme god, and a dread of Ahriman and his ministers. But, prac-tically, their religious aspirations rested, not on these dim abstractions, but on beings whose existence they could better realise, and whom they could feel to be less remote from themselves. The actual devotions of the Parthians were rendered to the Sun and Moon, to deities which were supposed to preside over the Royal House, and to ancestral idols, which each family possessed, and conveyed with it from place to place with every change of habitation. The Sun was saluted at his rising, was worshipped in temples, probably under the Arian name of Mithra, with sacrifices and offerings ; had statues erected in his honour, and was usually associated with the lesser luminary.[1] The deities of the Royal House were probably either genii, ministers of Ormazd, like the *bagâha vithiya* of the Persians, or else the ancestors of the reigning monarch, to whom a qualified divinity seems to have been assigned in the later times of the empire. The Parthian kings usually swore by these deities on solemn occasions, and other members of the royal family made use of the same oath. The main worship, however, of the great mass of the people, even when they were of the royal stock, was concentrated upon ancestral images, which had a place sacred to them in each house, and received the constant adoration of the household. ·

In the early times of the empire the Magi were held in high repute, and most of the peculiar tenets and rites of the Magian religion were professed and followed by the Parthians. Elemental worship was practised. Fire was held sacred, and there was an especial reverence for rivers. Dead bodies were not burned, but were exposed to be devoured by birds and beasts of prey, after which the dry bones were collected and placed in tombs. The Magi formed a large portion of the great national council,[2] which elected, and, if need were, deposed the kings. But, in course of time, much laxity was introduced. The Arsacid monarchs of Armenia allowed the Sacred Fire of Ormazd, which ought to have been kept continually burning, to go out ; and we can scarcely

---

[1] See the " Armenian History " of Moses of Chorené, ii. 74.

[2] Compare above, Chap. V. p. 78.

suppose but that the Parthian Arsacidæ were equally negligent. Religious respect for the element of fire so entirely passed away, that we hear of the later Parthians burning their dead.[1] The Magi fell into disrepute, and, if not expelled from their place in the national council, at any rate found themselves despised and deprived of influence.[2] The later Parthian religion can have been little more than a worship of the Sun and Moon, together with a cult of the *teraphim*, or sacred images, which were the most precious possessions of each household.

The manners and customs of the Parthians may be most conveniently considered under the two heads of their customs in war and in peace. As they were essentially a warlike people, the chief interest must attach to their military customs, and to these will therefore be assigned the foremost place. It appears that, like the European monarchs of the feudal times, they did not regard it as necessary to maintain any standing army. When hostilities threatened, and war seemed likely to break out, the king made his immediate vassals acquainted with the fact, and demanded from each of them a contingent. A certain rendezvous was named, and all were required to meet together on a certain day. The troops thus summoned were of two kinds, native and foreign. The governors of the provinces, whether tributary kings or satraps, called out the military strength of their respective districts, saw to their arming and provisioning, and, marching each at the head of his contingent, brought a foreign auxiliary force to the assistance of their

---

[1] Herodian, iv. 30.   [2] Agathias, ii. 26.

suzerain. But the backbone of the army, the portion on which alone much reliance was placed, consisted of Parthians. Each Parthian noble was bound to call out his slaves and his retainers, to arm and equip them at his own expense, and bring them to the general rendezvous by the time fixed upon. The number of troops brought into the field by each noble varied according to his position and his means; we hear in one instance of their amounting to ten thousand,[1] while in another recorded case [2] the average number which each of them provided did not exceed 125. The various contingents had their own baggage trains, consisting ordinarily of camels, in the proportion (as it would seem) of one to every ten fighting men.

The Parthian armies, like most others, consisted usually of both horse and foot, but in proportions which were not common elsewhere. The foot soldiers were comparatively few in number, and were but very little esteemed. Every effort, on the contrary, was made to increase the number and improve the equipment of the horsemen who bore the brunt of every conflict, and from whose exertions alone victory was expected. Sometimes armies consisted of horsemen only, or rather of horsemen followed by a baggage train composed of camels and chariots; but this only happened under special circumstances.

The horse was of two kinds, heavy and light. The heavy horsemen (κατάφρακτοι) wore coats of mail reaching to the knee, composed of raw hide covered

---

[1] Plutarch, "Vit. Crass.," i. § 21.   [2] Justin, xli. 2.

PARTHIAN HELMET.

with plates or scales of iron or steel, very bright, and capable of resisting a strong blow. They had their heads protected by burnished helmets of Margian steel, whose glitter dazzled the spectator. A specimen in the British Museum, figured by Professor Gardner, will best convey the shape. They do not seem to have ordinarily worn greaves, but had their legs encased in a loose trouser, which hung about the ankles and embarrassed the feet, if by any chance the horseman was induced or forced to dismount. They carried no targe or shield, being sufficiently defended by their coats of mail. Their chief offensive arms were a spear (κόντος), which was of great strength and thickness, and a bow and arrows of unusual dimensions. They likewise carried in their girdle a short sword or knife (μάχαιρα), which was intended to be used in close combat. Their horses were, like themselves, protected by a defence of scale-armour, which was either of steel or of bronze, polished like the armour of the men.

The light horse appears to have been armed with the same sort of bows and arrows as the heavy cavalry, but carried no spear, and was not encumbered with armour. It was carefully trained to the deft management of the horse and bow, and was unequalled in the rapidity and dexterity of its movements. The archer delivered his arrows with as much precision and force in retreat as in advance, and was almost more feared when he retired than when he charged his foe. Besides his bow and arrows, the light horseman seems to have carried a sword, and he no doubt wore also the customary knife in his belt; but it was as an archer that he was chiefly formidable.

During the later period of the monarchy, the Parthians, who had always employed camels largely in the conveyance of stores and baggage, are said to have introduced a camel corps into the army itself, and to have derived considerable advantage from the new arm. The camels could bear the weight of the mailed riders and of their own armour better than horses ; and their riders were at once less accessible in their elevated position, and more capable of dealing effective blows upon the enemy. As a set-off, however, against these advantages, the spongy feet of the camel were found to be more readily injured by the *tribulus* or caltrop than the harder feet of the horse, and the corps was thus more easily disabled than an equal force of cavalry, if it could be tempted or forced to pass over ground on which these obstacles had previously been scattered.

We do not hear of any use of chariots by the Parthians, except for the conveyance of the females who commonly accompanied the nobles on their warlike expeditions. The wives and concubines of the chiefs followed the camp in great numbers, and women of a less reputable class—singers, dancers, and musicians—swelled the ranks of the supernumeraries. Many of these were Greeks from Seleucia, Nice-phorium, and other Macedonian settlements. The commissariat and baggage departments are said to have been badly organised,[1] but some thousands of baggage camels always accompanied an army for the conveyance of stores and provisions. Of these a considerable portion were laden with arrows, of which

---

[1] Dio Cassius, xl. 15.

the supply was in this way rendered practically inexhaustible. The employment of the elephant in war was even m re rare in Parthia than that of the chariot. Parthian coins occasionally exhibit the creature[1] ; so that it was certainly known to the pe ple, but its actual employment in warfare is mentioned on one occasion only,[2] and then we hear of only a single animal, which is ridden by the monarch. As both the Seleucid princes and the Sassanidæ made large use of the elephant in their campaigns, its entire neglect by the Parthians is somewhat remarkable. Probably the unwieldy creature was regarded by them as too heavy and clumsy to suit the light and rapid movements of their armies, and was therefore almost wh lly disused during the period of their supremacy.

The Parthian tactics appear to have been of a simple kind, and to have differed but little from those of other nati ns in the same region which have depended mainly on their cavalry. To surround their foe, to entangle him and involve him in difficulties, to cut of his supplies and his stragglers, and ultimately to bring him into a po iti n where he might be overwhelmed by missiles, was the aim of all Parthian commanders of any military ability. Their warfare was suited for defence rather than for attack, unless against contemptible enemies. They were particularly inefficient in sieges, and avoided engaging in them as far as possible ; but when cir-

---

[1] Lindsay, " History and Coinage f the Parthians," pl. vii., No. 11 ; pl. viii., No. 30: Markoff, " Arsac. Monet. ' Tab. iii., N . 2.

[2] Tacit., " Ann.," xv. 15.

27

cumstances made it necessary, they did not shrink from undertaking the uncongenial operation. Long wars were very distasteful to them ; and, if they did not find victory tolerably easy they were apt to retire and allow their foe to escape, or to baffle him by withdrawing their forces into a distant and inaccessible region. After their early victories over Crassus and Antony, they never succeeded in preventing the steady advance of a Roman force into their territory, or in repulsing a determined attack upon their principal capital. Still they generally had their revenge after a little time. It was easy for the Romans to overrun Mesopotamia, but it was not so easy for them to hold it ; and it was scarcely possible for them to retire from it after an occupation without incurring disaster. The clouds of Parthian horse hung upon their retreating columns, straitened them for provisions, galled them with missiles, and destroyed those who could not keep up with the main body. The towns, upon the line of their retreat, revolted and shut their gates, defying even such commanders as Severus and Trajan. Of the six great expeditions of Rome against Parthia, one only, that of Avidius Cassius, was altogether successful. In every other case either the failure of the expedition was complete, or the glory of the advance was tarnished by suffering and calamity during the retreat. Other enemies they usually repulsed with but little difficulty.

When the Parthians entered into battle it was with much noise and shouting. They made no use of trumpets or horns, but employed in their place the kettledrum, which resounded from all parts of the field when they made their onset. Their attack was— for the most part—furious. The mailed horsemen charged at speed, and (we are told) often drove their spears through the bodies of two enemies at a blow. The light horse, and the foot (when any were present), delivered their arrows with precision, and with extraordinary force. But if the assailants were met with a stout and firm resistance, the first vigour of the attack was rarely long maintained. The Parthian warriors very quickly grew weary of an equal contest, and, if they could not force their enemy to give way, soon changed their tactics. Pretending panic, beating a hasty retreat, and scattering in their flight, they endeavoured to induce their foe to pursue hurriedly and in disorder, being themselves ready at any moment to turn and take advantage of the least appearance of confusion. If these tactics failed, as they generally did after they came to be known, then the simulated flight was commonly converted into a real one ; further conflict was for the time avoided, and the army withdrew itself into a distant region.

If the Parthians wanted to parley with an enemy, they unstrung their bows and, advancing with the right arm outstretched, asked for a conference. They are accused by the Romans of sometimes using treachery on such occasions; but, except in the single instance of Crassus, the charge of bad faith breaks down when it is examined into. On solemn occasions, when the intention was seriously to discuss grounds of complaint likely to lead to war, or to bring an actual war to an end by the arrangement of terms of peace, a formal meeting was ordinarily held by appointment between the representatives of either side, generally on neutral ground, as on an island in the Euphrates, or on a bridge newly constructed across it. Here the chiefs or envoys of the respective nations met, accompanied by an equal number of guards, while the remainder of their forces occupied the two opposite banks of the river. Matters were discussed in friendly fashion, some language known to both parties being employed as a means of communication ; after which festivities usually took place, the two chiefs mutually entertaining each other, or accepting in common the hospitalities of a third party. The terms of peace agreed upon were reduced to writing ; hands were grasped as a sign that faith was pledged ; and oaths having been interchanged the conference broke up, and the chiefs with their armies set out on their return to their respective countries.

The wonderful splendour of the Parthian Court is celebrated in general terms by several writers, but not many particulars have come down to us respecting it. We are told that it was migratory, moving from one of the chief cities of the empire to another at different seasons of the year; and that, owing to the vast numbers of the persons composing it, there was sometimes a difficulty in providing for their subsistence while they were upon the road. The Court comprised, of course, the usual extensive harem of an Oriental sovereign, consisting of a single recognised queen, and a multitude of secondary wives or concubines. The legitimate wife of the prince was with rare exceptions a native, and in most cases was a member of the royal race of the Arsacidæ ; but sometimes she was the daughter of a dependant monarch, and she might even be a slave, whom the royal favour had elevated from that position. Both wives and concubines remained ordinarily in the closest seclusion, and we have but little mention of them in the Parthian annals. In one instance however, at any rate, a queen, educated in the notions of the West, succeeded in setting Oriental etiquette at defiance ; she boldly asserted herself, took the direction of affairs out of the hands of her husband and subsequently ruled the empire in conjunction with her son.[1] Her name and image were even placed upon the coins.[2] Generally, however, the Parthian kings were remarkably free from the weakness of subservience to women and managed their kingdom with a firm hand, without allowing either wives or ministers to exercise any undue ascendency over them. In particular, we may note that they never, so far as appears, fell under the baleful influence of eunuchs, who, from first to last, play a very subordinate part in the Parthian history. Here the contrast is striking between the Parthian and the early Persian monarchy.

The ordinary dress of the monarch was the long loose " Median robe " which had been adopted from the Medes by the Achæmenian Persians. This robe flowed down to the feet in numerous folds, enveloping and concealing almost the entire figure. Trousers and a tunic were ordinarily, it is probable, worn beneath

[1] See above, p. 226.

[2] Gardner, " Parthian Coinage," pl. iv., Nos. 27, 28 ; Lindsay, " History and Coinage of the Parthians," pl. iii., Nos. 62, 63.

it, the latter of linen, the former made of silk or wool.

As head-dress, the king wore either the simple diadem, which was a band or ribbon passed once or oftener round the head and terminating in two long ends which fell down behind, or else a more pretentious cap, which in the earlier times was a sort of Scythian pointed helmet and in the later a rounded tiara, sometimes adorned with pearls or gems. His neck appears to have been generally encircled with two or more collars or necklaces, and he frequently wore ear-rings in his ears. The beard was almost always cultivated, and, with the hair, was worn variously. Generally, both hair and beard were carefully curled, but sometimes they hung down in long straight locks. Mostly the beard was pointed, but occasionally it was worn square. In later times a fashion grew up of puffing out the hair extravagantly on either side of the head—a practice continued by the Sassanians.

When he went out to war, the monarch seems to

have exchanged his " Median robe " for a short cloak, reaching halfway down the thigh. His head was protected by a pointed helmet, without crest or plume, and he carried the national arm of offence, the bow. Under his cloak he wore a coat of mail. He usually took the field on horseback, but was occasionally mounted on an elephant trained to encounter the shock of battle. Gold and silver were lavishly employed in the trappings of his charger and on his arms. For the most part he took the command, and freely exposed his person in the fight, though it was regarded as no disgrace if he preferred to avoid the perils of the actual encounter. A bodyguard protected his person, surrounding him on ordinary occasions, and interposing themselves between him and his assailants : he had also attendants, whose duty it was to assist him in mounting on horseback, and in dismounting, which the armour that he wore made no easy business.

It has been already observed that the queen lived, ordinarily, in seclusion. When, however, under peculiar circumstances, she emerged from privacy, her status and dignity were not much below those of the monarch. She wore a tiara far more elaborate than his, and one which, like his, was encircled with the diadem. Her neck was adorned with a necklace or necklaces. In the typical instance of Musa or Thermusa, we find her allowed the title of "Heavenly Goddess" (ΘΕΑ ΟΥΡΑΝΙΑ). Separate apartments were of course assigned to the queen and to the royal concubines in the various palaces, which were buildings on a magnificent scale and decorated with the utmost richness. Philostratus, who wrote in Parthian times (A.D. 172–244), and had a good knowledge of the East, thus describes the royal palace at Babylon : "The palace is roofed with brass, and a bright light flashes from it. It has chambers for the women and chambers for the men, and porticoes, partly glittering with silver, partly with cloth-of-gold embroideries, partly with solid slabs of gold, let into the walls like pictures. The subjects of the embroideries are taken from the Greek mythology, and include representations of Andromeda, of Amymoné, and of Orpheus, who is frequently repeated. Datis is, moreover, represented, destroying Naxos with his fleet, and Artaphemes besieging Eretria, and Xerxes gaining his famous victories. You behold the occupation of Athens and the battle of Thermopylæ, and other things still more characteristic of the great Persian War, rivers drunk up and disappearing from the face of the earth, and a bridge stretched across the sea, and a canal cut through Athos, and the like. One chamber for the men has a ceiling fashioned into a vault like the heaven, composed entirely of sapphires, which are the bluest of stones, and resemble the sky in colour. Golden images of the gods whom they worship are set up about the vault, and show like stars in the firmament. This is the chamber in which the king delivers his judgments. Four golden magic wheels hang from the roof, and threaten the monarch with the Divine Nemesis, if he exalts himself above the condition of man. These wheels are called 'the tongues of the gods,' and are set in their places by the Magi who frequent the palace."[1] This description must not be taken as altogether exact. The tapestries may have represented other scenes than those which Philostratus imagined; the ceiling was certainly not "composed entirely of sapphires," but either of enamelled bricks or plaster painted blue; and the "magic wheels" are questionable; but the general effect was probably very much that which the philosopher of Tyana

[1] See Philostratus, "Vit. Apoll. Tyan.," i. 25.

portrays, and presented an *ensemble* that was curious, striking, and magnificent.

It is probable that the state and pomp which surrounded the monarch fell little short of the Achæmenian standard. Considered as in some sort divine during his life, and always an object of national worship after his death, the "Brother of the Sun and Moon"[1] occupied a position far above that of the most exalted of his subjects. Tributary monarchs were shocked, when, in times of calamity, the "Great King" stooped to solicit their aid, and appeared before them in the guise of a suppliant, shorn of his customary splendour. Nobles coveted the dignity of "King's Friend," and were content to submit to blows and buffets at the caprice of their royal master, before whom they prostrated themselves in humble adoration after each such castigation. The Parthian monarch dined in solitary grandeur, extended on his own special couch, and eating from his own special table, which was placed at a higher elevation than those prepared for his guests and retinue. His "friend" sat on the ground at his feet, and was fed by scraps from his master's board. Guards, ministers, and attendants of various kinds surrounded him, and were ready at a word, or at a sign, to do his bidding. Throughout the empire he had numerous "Eyes" and "Ears"—officers who watched his interests, and sent him timely notice of whatever touched his safety. The bed on which the monarch slept was of gold, and subjects were forbidden to take their repose on couches of the same material. No stranger could

---

[1] Ammian. Marcellin., xxiii. 6,

obtain access to him unless introduced by the proper officer : and it was expected that whoever asked an audience should be prepared with a present of considerable value. For the gifts which he received the monarch made a suitable return, allowing such persons as he especially favoured to choose the presents that they most desired.

The Parthian nobles enjoyed a power and dignity greater than that which is usually possessed by any subjects of an Oriental king. Rank in Parthia being hereditary and not simply official, the Megistanes were no mere creatures of the monarch, but a class which stood on its own indefeasible rights. As they had the privilege of electing to the throne upon a vacancy, and even the further privilege of deposing a duly elected monarch, the king could not but stand in wholesome awe of them, and feel compelled to treat them with considerable respect and deference. It is to be remembered, moreover, that they were not without a material force calculated to give powerful support to their constitutional rights and privileges. Each stood at the head of a body of retainers accustomed to bear arms, and to serve in the wars of the empire. Together these bodies constituted the strength of the army; and though the royal body-guard might perhaps have been capable of dealing successfully with each group of retainers separately, yet such an *esprit de corps* was sure to animate the nobles generally, that in almost every case they would make common cause with any one of their number who was attacked, and would support him against the Crown with the zeal inspired by self-interest. Thus the Parthian nobility were far more powerful and independent than any similar class under the Achæmenian, Sassanian, Modern Persian, or Turkish sovereignties. They exercised a real control over the monarch, and had a voice in the direction of the empire. Like the great feudal vassals of the Middle Ages, they from time to time quarrelled with their liege lord, and disturbed the tranquillity of the kingdom by prolonged and dangerous civil wars ; but these contentions served to keep alive a vigour, a life, and a spirit of sturdy independence very unusual in the East, and gave a stubborn strength to the Parthian Monarchy, in which Oriental states and governments have for the most part been remarkably deficient.

There appear to have been several grades of rank among the Parthian nobles. The highest dignity in the kingdom, next to the Crown, was that of the Surena, or " Field-Marshal " ; and this position was hereditary in a particular family, which can have stood but a little below the royal house in wealth and consequence. The head of this noble house is said to have at one time brought into the field as many as ten thousand retainers and slaves, of whom a thousand were heavy-armed.[1] It was his right to place the diadem on the king's brow at his coronation. The other nobles lived for the most part on their domains, but took the field at the head of their retainers in case of war, and in peace might sometimes serve the offices of satrap, vizier, or royal councillor. The wealth of the class was great ;[2] its

---

[1] Plutarch, " Vit. Crass.," § 21.   [2] See above, pp. 80 and 397.

members were inclined to be turbulent, and, like the barons of the European kingdoms, acted as a constant check and counterpoise to the royal authority, which they often resisted, and occasionally even overthrew.

After war, the employment in which the king and the nobles took most delight, was hunting. The lion continued in the wild state an occupant of the Mesopotamian river banks and marshes; and in other parts of the empire bears, leopards, and even tigers abounded. Thus the higher kinds of sport were constantly and readily obtainable. But the ordinary practice of the monarch and his courtiers seems to have fallen short of the true sportsman's ideal. Instead of seeking the more dangerous kinds of beasts in their native haunts, and engaging with them under the conditions designed by Nature, the Parthians were generally content with a poorer and tamer method. They kept lions, leopards, and bears in enclosed parks, or "paradises," and found pleasure in the pursuit and slaughter of these denaturalised and half-domesticated animals. The employment may still, even under these circumstances, have contained an element of danger which rendered it exciting; but it was a poor substitute for the true sport which the "mighty hunter before the Lord" had been the first to practise in these regions (Gen. x. 9).

The ordinary dress of the Parthian noble was, like that of the monarch, a long loose robe reaching to the feet, under which he wore a vest and trousers. Bright and varied colours were commonly affected, and sometimes dresses were interwoven or embroidered with threads of gold. In seasons of festivity it was usual for garlands of fresh flowers to be worn upon the head. A long knife or dagger was carried at all times, and by all classes, suited for use either as an implement or as a weapon.

In the earlier and simpler period of the empire— when the nation was just emerging from barbarism— the Parthian was noted as a spare liver ; but, as time went on, he aped the vices of more civilized people, and became an indiscriminate eater and a hard drinker. Game formed a main portion of his diet ; but he indulged also in pork, and probably in other sorts of butcher's meat. He ate leavened bread with his meat, and various kinds of vegetables. The bread, which was particularly light and porous, seems to have been sometimes imported by the Romans, who knew it as *panis aquaticus* or *panis Parthicus.* Dates were also consumed largely by the Parthians, and the fruit grew in some parts of the country to an extraordinary size. A kind of wine was made from it ; and this seems to have been the intoxicating drink in which the nation generally indulged overmuch. The liquor made from the dates of Babylon was the most highly esteemed, and was reserved for the use of the king, and the higher order of satraps. The vulgar herd had to content themselves with drink of an inferior quality. Of the Parthian entertainments music was commonly an accompaniment. The flute, the pipe, the drum, and the instrument called the *sambuca,* appear to have been known to them ; and they understood how to combine these instruments in concerted harmony. They are said to have concluded all their feasts with dancing,[1] an amusement of which they were inordinately fond ; but this was probably the case only with the lower orders of the people. Dancing in the East, unless associated with religion, is viewed as degrading, and is not indulged in by those who wish to be considered respectable.

The Parthians were jealous of their women, and the separation of the sexes was very decided among them. The women took their meals, and passed the greater portion of their lives, apart from the men. Veils were commonly worn, as in modern Mohammedan countries ; and it was regarded as essential to female delicacy that women, whether married or single, should converse freely with no males who were not either their near relations or else eunuchs. Adultery was punished with extreme severity ; but divorce was obtained without much difficulty, and women of rank released themselves from the nuptial tie on light grounds of complaint, and with little loss of reputation. Polygamy was the established rule ; and every Parthian was entitled, besides his chief wife, to maintain as many concubines as he pleased. Some of the nobles supported an excessive number ; but the expenses of the seraglio prevented the generality from taking very much advantage of the indulgence which the law permitted. It is probable that the bulk of the population, as is the case now in Mohammedan countries, was monogamous.

As to the degree of refinement and civilisation whereto the Parthians attained, it is difficult to judge

---

[1] Philostratus, " Vit. Apoll. Tyan.," i. 21.

and determine with accuracy. In mimetic art their remains (as we have already seen) do not show much taste or sense of beauty. There is perhaps sufficient ground to believe that their architecture possessed a certain amount of merit ; but the existing monuments can scarcely be taken as representations of pure Parthian work, since they may have owed their excellence —in some measure—to foreign artists, or at any rate to foreign influence. Still the following particulars, for which there is good evidence, seem to imply that the nation had risen in reality far above that "barbarism," which it was the fashion for the Greek and Roman writers to impute to it. In the first place, the Parthians had a considerable knowledge of foreign languages. Plutarch tells us,[1] that Orodes, the opponent of Crassus, was so far conversant with the Greek language and literature, that he could enjoy the representation of a play of Euripides. The general possession of some knowledge of Greek—at any rate by the kings and upper classes—seems to be implied by the use of the Greek letters and language in the legends upon coins, and in inscriptions. Other languages were also to a certain extent studied and understood. The later kings almost invariably placed a Semitic legend upon their coins ; and there is at least one instance of a Parthian prince adopting an Arian legend of the type known as Bactrian.[2] Josephus, moreover, regarded the Parthians as familiar with Hebrew, or Syro-Chaldee, since he wrote his history of the Jewish War in his own native tongue,

[1] Plutarch, " Vit. Crassi." § 32.
[2] " Numismatic Chronicle," No. vi. p. 104.

before he put out his Greek version, for the benefit especially of the Parthians, among whom he declares that he had a large number of readers.[1]

It does not appear that the Parthians had any native literature; writing, however, was familiar to them, and was widely employed by them in matters of business. Not only were negotiations carried on with foreign powers by means of written despatches, but the affairs of the empire generally were transacted by means of writing. A custom-house system was, we are told, established along the frontier, and all commodities liable to duty that entered the country were registered in a book at the time of entry by the custom-house officer. In the great cities where the Court passed a portion of the year, account was kept of the arrival of strangers, whose names and descriptions were placed upon record by the keepers of the gates. The orders of the Crown were signified in writing to the satraps; and they doubtless corresponded with the Court in the same way. In the earlier times the writing material commonly used was linen; but, shortly before the date of Pliny, the Parthians began to make paper from papyrus, which grew in the neighbourhood of Babylon, though they still continued also to employ, and gave the preference to, the material to which use had accustomed them.

The Parthians had many usages which seem to imply a fairly advanced civilisation. There was a considerable trade between Rome and Parthia, carried on by means of travelling merchants. Parthia imported from Rome various metals, and a multitude of

---

[1] Joseph., "Bell. Jud.," Proem, § 1 and § 2.

manufactured articles of a high class. Her principal exports were textile fabrics and spices. The textile fabrics seem to have been produced chiefly in Babylonia, and to have consisted principally of silks, carpets, and coverlets. The silks were largely used by the Roman fashionable ladies. The coverlets, which were patterned with a variety of colours, fetched enormous prices, and were regarded as fit adornments of the Imperial palace. Among the spices exported, the most celebrated were bdellium, and the *juncus odoratus*, or sweet-scented bulrush. Advanced civilisation· is also implied in the Parthian tolerance of varieties in religion, which has been already mentioned.[1] Even in political matters they appear to have been free from the narrowness which generally characterises barbarous nations. They behaved · mercifully to prisoners, admitted foreigners freely to offices of high trust, gave an asylum to refugees, and treated them with respect and kindness, were scrupulous observers of their pledged word, and eminently faithful to their treaty obligations. On the other hand, it must be admitted that they had some customs which imply that they retained a tinge of barbarism. They used torture for the extraction of replies from accused persons, employed the scourge to punish trifling offences, and, in certain cases, condescended to mutilate and insult the bodies of their dead enemies. Their addiction to intemperance is also a barbaric trait. They were no doubt, on the whole, considerably less civilised than the contemporary Greeks and Romans ; but the difference does not appear to have been so

[1] Supra, p. 360.

great as the classical writers would have us imagine it.

We cannot, however, deny, and we do not wish to conceal the fact, that the Parthians exhibited, especially during the later period of the empire, a strong tendency to degenerate. They lost their primitive virtues of simplicity and abstemiousness. They became luxurious, and to a certain extent effeminate. The dash or *élan*, which characterised their warfare in the earlier times, is " conspicuous by its absence " in the campaigns of the later monarchs. A decline in art and letters is also observable in the Parthian remains that have come down to us, especially in the coins, which, after the reign of Gotarzes, proceed from bad to worse, and end with presenting to us effigies that have neither force nor character, and legends that are absolutely illegible. A knowledge of Greek is still possessed, the Greek letters being employed, and the words, when they can be deciphered, being clearly intended to be Greek. But they are often misspelt ; the forms used are ungrammatical ; while, at the last, the letters merely straggle over the field of the coin, and are not really formed into words. Further, the anomaly is introduced of a second legend, which is Semitic both in language and character, and reads from right to left.

Still, to judge fairly of the Parthians, we must view them, not in their decline, but rather in the earlier stages of their career, before decline had set in. Speaking broadly, the position which they occupied among the nations of the old world was not very dissimilar to that which is held by the Turks in the system of Modern Europe. They possessed a military strength which caused them to be both respected and feared, while they were further noted for a vigour of administration rarely seen among Orientals. It is true that a certain coarseness and rudeness attached to them which they found it impossible to shake off, and this gave their enemies a plausible ground for representing them as absolute barbarians. But we must not be led away by the exaggerations of prejudiced writers, who sought to elevate the fame and reputation of their own countrymen by blackening the character of their chief rivals. Except in respect of their military prowess, it is doubtful if justice is done to the Parthians by any classical author. They occupied the position of the second nation in the world from about B.C. 150 to A.D. 226. They were a check and a counterpoise to Rome, preserving a " balance of power," and preventing the absorption of all other nations into the Tyrant Empire. They afforded a refuge to those whom Rome would fain have hunted down, allowed a freedom to their subjects which no Roman Emperor ever permitted, excelled the Romans in toleration and in a liberal treatment of foreigners, and gave the East a protection from foreign foes, and a government well suited to its needs, for a period of nearly four centuries.

THE END.

APPENDIX.

(See p. 132.)

THE king alluded to has been called Mnascires or Mnasciras, and was formerly admitted into his list of Parthian monarchs by the author, who followed Lindsay and others. But Professor Gardner has shown that the name, which occurs in no author but Lucian, should probably be read as Kamnascires, and not Mnascires (καὶ Μνασκίρης δέ being a manifest corruption from Καμνασκίρης δέ), and that the king intended is probably a tributary monarch of the Parthian period, well known to numismatologists, whose coins bear the legend of ΒΑΣΙΛΕΩΣ ΚΑΜΝΑΣΚΙΡΟΥ.

COIN OF KAMNASCIRAS.

The probable date of the monarch is about that of Mithridates I. of Parthia. (See Professor Gardner's "Parthian Coinage," pp. 8 and 61.)

INDEX.

UNWIN BROTHERS, THE GRESHAM PRESS, CHILWORTH AND LONDON.